Hatless JACK

The President, the Fedora, and the History of an American Style

NEIL STEINBERG

A PLUME BOOK

—For Ross and Kent—

PLUME
Published by the Penguin Group
Penguin Group (USA) Inc., 375 Hudson Street, New York, New York 10014, U.S.A.
Penguin Group (Canada), 10 Alcorn Avenue, Toronto, Ontario, Canada M4V 3B2
(a division of Pearson Penguin Canada Inc.)
Penguin Books Ltd, 80 Strand, London WC2R 0RL, England
Penguin Ireland, 25 St Stephen's Green, Dublin 2, Ireland (a division of Penguin Books Ltd)
Penguin Group (Australia), 250 Camberwell Road, Camberwell, Victoria 3124, Australia
(a division of Pearson Australia Group Pty Ltd)
Penguin Books India Pvt Ltd, 11 Community Centre, Panchsheel Park,
New Delhi – 110 017, India
Penguin Books (NZ), Cnr Airborne and Rosedale Roads, Albany, Auckland, New
Zealand (a division of Pearson New Zealand Ltd)
Penguin Books (South Africa) (Pty) Ltd, 24 Sturdee Avenue, Rosebank, Johannesburg
2196, South Africa

Penguin Books Ltd, Registered Offices: 80 Strand, London WC2R 0RL, England

First published by Plume, a member of Penguin Group (USA) Inc.

First Printing, December 2004
10   9   8   7   6   5   4   3   2   1

LIBRARY OF CONGRESS CATALOGING-IN-PUBLICATION DATA

Steinberg, Neil.
    Hatless Jack : the president, the fedora, and the history of an American style / by
Neil Steinberg.
    p. cm.
    Includes bibliographical references and index.
    ISBN 0-452-28523-2 (trade pbk.)
    1. Hats—United States—History. 2. Presidents—United States—History. 3. Presi-
dents—United States—Clothing. 4. Kennedy, John F. (John Fitzgerald), 1917–1963—
Inauguration, 1961, 5. Kennedy, John F. (John Fitzgerald), 1917–1963—Clothing.
I. Title.

GT2110.S84 2004
391.4'3—dc22   2004016952

Printed in the United States of America
Set in Sabon, Designed by Leonard Telesca

"I wear my hat as I please."
—*Walt Whitman*
"Leaves of Grass"

Contents

Introduction

"Can't you *do* something
about this?"

William R. Agnew, a shareholder in the Hat Corporation of America, the nation's largest hat company, rose to his feet at the 1962 annual stockholder meeting in New York City and held up a page torn from a newspaper. The page featured a large photograph of the popular young president, John F. Kennedy, sitting at the tiller of a sailboat. Kennedy was squinting into the sun, confident and relaxed, wearing a light sweater and khaki pants, his reddish brown hair blowing freely in the sea breeze. The headline read "The American Look."

"Can't you *do* something about this?" Agnew demanded.

At the podium, Hat Corporation chairman Bernard Salesky, the industry's dapper, oft-quoted spokesman, stood silent and stricken.

"And *this*," Agnew continued, holding up another photo, this one of Soviet Union premier Nikita Khrushchev sporting his ever-present, conspicuously large, homburg hat, with its high crown and rolled brim, "is an even sadder commentary."

Salesky found his voice.

"This is one of the heartbreaks of my business career," began the man sometimes referred to as "Mr. Hat," going on to describe just a few of the efforts the hat industry had taken trying to nudge Kennedy toward his duty. A full dozen gift hats in a range of popular styles had been dispatched to the White House, delivered by Abraham Ribicoff, secretary of the Department of Health, Education and Welfare and former governor of Connecticut, where the city of Danbury was home to the struggling remnant of the nation's once-mighty hat industry. Alex Rose, the powerful head of the United Hatters, Cap and Millinery Workers International Union and president of New York's Liberal Party was also lobbying the president and presenting him with hats at every opportunity.

Salesky didn't mention it, but countless big hat companies and small local haberdashers were pressing their goods upon the president, either by mail or in person. Kennedy's former Navy buddies had even been recruited for the task. Fashion magazines at home and abroad were applying pressure. The great Leo Burnett himself had challenged his famous advertising agency to get young men such as the president thinking about hats again. All, so far, for naught. As for the Russians. . . .

"If you can figure out a way to get Khrushchev to stop wearing hats and Kennedy to start wearing hats, Hat Corporation will supply you with hats for life," Salesky promised.

* * *

Climb on a bus on a cold winter's day. Get on a subway car. Or just stand on the corner of a busy city street. Watch the men go by. At least half will be hatless, no matter the weather.

The rest will be sporting a motley assortment of headgear of all descriptions, from baseball caps to enormous, sprawling fur edifices. There will be colorful ski bands, gray sweatshirt hoods, braided Greek fisherman's caps, wide-brimmed Indiana Jones fedoras, ornate cowboy hats, cocked Australian sheepherder's hats, plain green fleece hats, rolled stocking caps, maybe even a solitary derby.

Hats are as varied as socks and as little considered. Yet the determined hatlessness of most American men, and the casual attitude with which the rest wear a variety of hats at the beginning of the twenty-first century, represents a break with hundreds of years of tradition. Those who know only one thing about hats know that men once wore them when in public, uniformly and always. An essayist in 1918 wrote that the average man "has become so accustomed to the habit of wearing his hat that he does not feel that he is himself out of doors without it."

Everyone has seen those old photographs of crowds—at baseball games, typically, or parades, or pouring out of subway stations—an unbroken sea of straw boaters, black, beetle-backed derbies, or snap-brim fedoras, depending on the mandatory fashion of the year. Wearing a hat while on business was a given, like wearing shoes. Hats were, in the words of a late-nineteenth-century author, "as essential and integral a portion of human attire as the human hair is of the human head."

The unquestioned need to wear a hat in public motivates the entirety of Irish writer Lord Dunsany's brief, almost absurdist 1914 play, *The Lost Silk Hat.*

"But I must have my hat," exclaims the frantic "Caller,"

lingering by the door of a house he has just exited, unable to go back and fetch the hat he accidentally left inside because of an argument with a lady, but unable to depart bareheaded. "I can't be seen in the streets like this."

Can't be seen "in the streets like this" by *whom*? The caller's concern with passersby, hardwired into hat wearers for centuries, has almost vanished today. Of course in the past a man could, physically, go into the street hatless, and some did. But those all-important passersby would certainly notice such a man and wonder about him. Maybe he was deranged, or penniless, or drunk. Maybe he had been robbed, or been in an accident. Maybe he had lost his hat and was on the way to buy a new one. Hat loss was a particularly disturbing condition that had to be remedied immediately.

Maybe he had pawned his hat: for centuries there was a brisk trade in secondhand hats. Maybe he was one of the eccentrics who believed that wearing a hat caused baldness by constricting the flow of blood to the scalp.

At best, he was an aging errand boy, or someone who had dashed outside for a moment.

At worst, he was a fiend. The arrival of a man without a hat was cause for alarm: it is one of the first things that a terrified Pip notices about Magwitch, the convict who accosts him in a graveyard at the beginning of Charles Dickens's *Great Expectations:* "A fearful man, all in coarse grey, with a great iron on his leg. A man with no hat, and with broken shoes, and with an old rag tied round his head."

When the word *hatless* was first generally used, around the Civil War, it typically appeared in a series of adjectives describing wretchedness—hatless, coatless, trouserless, hopeless.

In 1864, the *New York Times* described Union soldiers received in a prisoner exchange as "men looking like living skeletons, almost naked, shoeless, hatless, and spiritless." Society would have to go through a transformation before being hatless could be considered a good thing.

"Not one man in 10,000," declared a 1929 book on the psychology of dress, noting hats' ubiquity with only slight exaggeration, "would risk being the butt of ridicule by failing to conform."

And ridicule you they would. A man without a hat risked being hissed at by strangers and insulted by hatcheck girls. Even wearing a hat was no guarantee of safety: bosses, friends, fellow pedestrians—none would be reluctant to tell you if your hat was old, shabby, out-of-fashion, or worn wrong. "Where did you get that hat?" was not a flattering question, but an insinuation, and it became a mocking comic song popular for half a century.

If you wore a straw hat during the felt hat time of year, a stranger might feel free to lift it off your head and crumple it into a ball in front of you. Or worse. Men have been killed in the United States in living memory for wearing a straw hat out of season.

The social pressure was strong enough to make almost every man go through the bother and cost of wearing hats— the purchase, the maintenance, and the daily ransom from the hat checks in every hotel, club, and restaurant lobby. You needed not just one hat, but many hats, to coordinate with the hour of the day, the day of the week, and the fashion dictate of the year. At its Philadelphia convention in 1929, the National Association of Merchant Tailors announced that in order to be prepared to go outdoors, the well-dressed man must own a dozen hats, to go with his twenty suits and twenty-four pairs of shoes. A decade later, the Hat Style Council, another industry group, agreed that a dozen hats were necessary to be "exactly right" for "every occasion."[1]

Other experts disagreed, arguing that fashion demanded a man own not twelve hats, but fifteen.[2]

And that was just among the business classes. In high society, you might as well go without a shirt as go without a hat. When flamboyant Gay Nineties socialite E. Berry Wall became so taken with the Easter liturgy at New York's St. Patrick's Cathedral that he carelessly sat on his silk hat, he felt compelled to sneak out through a side door in the middle of the service, hurry home and get another.

What was going on under those hats that would make men not only all wear one, but often the exact same style as everybody else? What made these men—our fathers and grandfathers and great-grandfathers—act so differently than we do? And why did they stop? It is a puzzle for which possible solutions are inevitably shrugged off as unknowable, even by the most observant wits.

"Until the last years of the Eisenhower era, WASPs wore

---

[1] The council listed those hats as "the high silk, the folding opera, the black or midnight blue soft hat, the derby, the homburg, the snap brim, the off-the-face, the lightweight felt, the sports, the straw sailor, the panama and the semi-sport type."

[2] To be fair, there were more moderate opinions. The Hat Institute of America issued a counterdirective, declaring the tailors' decree "harmful and entirely misleading" and reassuring men that a man could adequately face the world with only five hats, six if he went for "sports and country pastimes." Still, that is five or six more dress hats than most men own today.

wonderful haberdashery," wrote humorist P. J. O'Rourke. "They went about in perfectly blocked and creased homburgs, jaunty straw boaters, majestic opera hats and substantial bowlers. A gentleman would sooner wear two-tone shoes to a diplomatic reception than appear in public without a proper hat. And then something happened."

Yes, but what? O'Rourke doesn't say. Nobody does, leaving the subject open to rumor, hearsay, and speculation. There are three popular theories as to why the fashion of men's hats died out in the United States.

One is that men grew tired of being compelled to wear hats in the military during World War II, and abandoned the fashion when they returned to civilian life. The second is that the growing popularity of automobiles, with their isolation, heaters, and low roofs, killed off men's hats. And the third and most popular theory is that President John F. Kennedy hated hats, didn't wear one at his inauguration, and his adoring public followed his example.

Two of these explanations are simply wrong; the third offers only a suggestion of the complex range of social forces that doomed the hat. As we will see, men had an unexpected inspiration to abandon their hats, one that is entirely forgotten today.

It might be tempting to dismiss the matter as a whim of fashion. Men carried watches in their vest pockets and now strap them to their wrists. They wore eyeglasses clipped to their noses, and now they don't. All manner of men's apparel—knee breeches, spats, suspenders, detachable collars, sock garters, vests, capes—had periods of universality then disappeared, or their popularity greatly dwindled. Hats were here, but now they're gone. There doesn't have to be a reason. Their disappearance doesn't have to *mean* anything.

But it does. It has to. Hats were not minor accessories, like canes or gloves. They were not hidden, like sock garters and pocket watches. They were the most prominent article of clothing on a man's body,[3] worn, religiously, between the end of the War of the Roses and the start of the Vietnam War, and during that time carried enormous symbolism and perceived importance. Sometimes fashion dictated men wear two hats. Or three, one under the other. During the century and a half when men wore wigs, and wearing a hat became at times impossible, men would still carry their hats—the *chapeau bras*—though they never put them on. Hats were once seen as essential even when they couldn't be worn.

The development of the hat, like that of the wheel, vanishes into prehistory. The basic hat—a piece of felt or fur or straw molded to the shape of the skull and usually surrounded by a brim of some kind—runs unchanged back to ancient Greece. When we see a statue of the Roman god Mercury, we are struck today by the impression that he is wearing a winged helmet; but it is actually a hat, the Greek *petasus,* worn because not only is Mercury the god of messengers, but he is also the god of roads and travel, and travelers always wore hats. Even Kennedy wore a hat—or at least carried one—when he went abroad. At the time, this was not seen as a break with his famous hatlessness—the president was traveling; he had to have a hat.

---

[3] As women's hats represent another matter entirely, and are far better documented, I will generally not address them, except where they become relevant to men's hats.

Mercury's round hat might seem a little odd on a downtown street today. But the knit Peruvian *chollos*—those close-fitting brimless hats with long ear flaps worn by young people nowadays in cities—are exactly the same style, right down to the slight peak on top, worn by the two-thousand-year-old Tollund man discovered in a bog in Denmark. And why not? A hat is inherently practical, a perfect piece of technology, like a spoon. Hats keep you warm in the winter, cool in the summer, and protect your eyes from glare and your head from wind and water year-round.

There were a thousand other practical uses for a hat besides being worn—people stored papers in them, bailed water, held apples. John Adams used his hat to hold corn to feed his horse and, as a result, could lure the animal to him by holding out his empty hat as if it contained something.

In addition to their utilitarian uses, hats were wonderfully expressive. Hats were touched, tipped, raised, handed, tossed, snapped, tilted, cocked, passed, checked, waved, and eaten, at least metaphorically. When James Thurber described certain Columbus politicians as being the sort of men who "fanned their soup with their hats," he needn't say anything more. Our language is filled with echoes of hat-wearing—"at the drop of a hat," "hat in hand," "hat in the ring," "hats off," "talking through his hat"—too many to even begin to list completely. The usage of such phrases has far outlasted the practices that inspired them.

And those are just the common expressions. The blunt English diarist Samuel Pepys, while dining with a benefactor in London in 1660, gossiped about the hasty marriage of the Duke of York to his pregnant mistress. Later he wrote, "My

Lord told me that among his father's many old sayings that he had writ in a book of his, this is one: 'That he that doth get a wench with child and marries her afterwards is as if a man should shit in his hat and then clap it upon his head.' "

Beyond their practical and expressive uses, hats had a third vital function. A hat revealed the wearer's status. If you were walking down a street in ancient Egypt, you'd know a lot about the person walking toward you by his head—whether it was the shaved skull of a slave, the bulbous crown of a pharaoh, or one of the variously helmeted and becapped soldiers and administrators. For a thousand years, a king wore his crown of gold and a fool wore his motley of bells, and everybody else in between used their hats to establish their spot in the pecking order.

Scanning the entirety of hat-wearing around the globe and throughout history, it is easy to see that this third, symbolic function was the most important of all. Hats protect from the rain and the sun, true, but human beings don't really need that—tribesmen in sub-Saharan Africa do not wear hats, nor do Indians in South American rain forests, or primitive peoples in general. But their chiefs do, if only a string and a nonutilitarian clump of feathers to set them apart as Head Men. No matter what society you examine, in any era anywhere in the world, ninety-nine times out of a hundred the guy with the biggest, most expensive hat is the boss.

Except, of course, today, when a bum and a banker can walk down the street wearing the same kind of baseball cap without either seeming out of place. What happened?

Hats were a mark of manhood. Boys wore knickers and went bareheaded or wore caps. When they became men, they wore pants and hats (a cap has no brim or only a partial brim; a hat has a brim that goes all the way around).

The association of hats with fully being a man goes back to the ancient world. After Brutus murdered Julius Caesar, he celebrated what he considered the overthrow of tyranny by having a coin struck: on one side, the goddess of liberty; on the other, a hat, flanked by two daggers. The Latin idiom for freeing a slave, *capere pileum,* means, literally, "to take the hat." Seneca, urging slaves to revolt, encouraged them to *vocare ad pileum*—"to take up the hat." This meaning continued for millennia; Booker T. Washington noted that when an American slave was freed he traditionally received his owner's last name and old hat. In Switzerland, coats of arms of free citizens sometimes prominently displayed a hat. In China, a boy reaching manhood was given a hat. During the French Revolution, the revolutionaries seized on the Phrygian cap to represent liberty herself, and the practice spread to the United States, whose early-nineteenth-century coinage shows Lady Liberty holding the cap of freedom on a stick.

A hat not only established you as a man, a free man, but told of your tastes and your successes. The proverbial "feather in your cap" was once real, proof you could pay for expensive, exotic plumage. If feathers weren't costly enough, hats were also adorned with bands of gold or silver and jeweled broaches. Those were a mixed blessing in battle—the flash of the diamond broach on Lord Nelson's hat drew the attention of the French sniper who killed him at Trafalgar; on the other hand, Oliver Cromwell's life, it is said, was saved twice when the buckle on his hat deflected the bullets of assassins.

Hats also broadcast a man's decline. Those expensive hat-bands and buckles were easily pawned. The Baltimore police-man who found Edgar Allan Poe lying unconscious in a gutter in 1849 noted in his report that Poe's hat lacked a band though he was "obviously a gentleman." A century later, in *Death of a Salesman,* Arthur Miller wrote, "You get yourself a couple of spots on your hat and you're finished."

The type of hat you wore carried a significance that rolled right along, more or less unchanged, until midway through the twentieth century. In Billy Wilder's 1960 movie, *The Apartment,* Jack Lemmon's hapless C. C. Baxter celebrates his ill-gotten promotion to an actual office by running out and buying a bowler. He's an executive now, and executives wear bowlers, though Baxter gives his a jaunty tilt, to show he is a young executive.[4] Quitting, he claps his new bowler on the janitor on his way out.

The buying, wearing, and storing of hats, their complex symbolism and myriad practical uses, and the way men moni-tored each other and reinforced the convention of hat-wearing—historically, men were beaten and imprisoned for not tipping their hats at the proper moment, and in the twenti-eth century, men were hung by their government for wearing the wrong hat—made hat-wearing a central element in the lives of the male population. Watch an old movie and focus on the hats. It can seem, at times, that the film consists mostly of men handing hats back and forth, putting them on, taking them off.

[4] The bowler, which had fallen from fashion in the United States, enjoyed a brief spurt of popularity among sharp young men in the late 1950s.

Then, in the span of a decade, it all stopped. Many believe it actually stopped in the span of a day. Of the three theories about the death of hat-wearing—World War II, automobiles, and Kennedy—the last is unquestionably the most popular. "John F. Kennedy was the first president to go bareheaded, and he ruined the hat business," Andy Rooney said in a segment on hats in 2001 on CBS television's *60 Minutes*. It is a notion repeated again and again in uncritical news accounts: "Dress-hat sales tanked after John F. Kennedy appeared hatless at his inauguration in 1960," claimed an article that ran in the *Detroit Free Press* in 2000, managing to cram three major factual errors in a fifteen-word sentence.

First, dress-hat sales did not tank after Kennedy's inauguration. They had tanked long before—decades before. The peak year for men's hat manufacture in the United States was 1903, a year that also saw a widespread hatless fad. By the mid-1920s, hatlessness was a major problem for the industry, which was in free fall by the late 1940s and early 1950s. Men's dress-hat sales in the United States in 1960 were half of what they had been a decade earlier.

Second, Kennedy *did* wear a hat at his inauguration—a fine black silk top hat. As did the outgoing president and vice president, not to mention dozens of guests, senators, incoming cabinet members, and other dignitaries. This fact was not concealed. Kennedy's decision to wear a top hat was front-page news. *Newsweek*'s inauguration issue featured a close-up, full-face painting of Kennedy in his top hat, and many newspapers splashed photographs of Kennedy wearing his silk topper throughout their special inaugural sections. He also carried hats on other occasions—not only while visiting Europe, but to church and certain formal occasions. His inauguration was not even the first time Kennedy ventured out in public in a tall silk hat; he had appeared with a top hat just the summer before, while attending graduation at Harvard. True, he seldom put these hats on this head, but he would sometimes allow himself to be photographed wearing them. Newspapers invariably published these photos—Kennedy in a hat was considered news—particularly during the campaign of 1960, and the captions typically drew attention to the hat. Kennedy was seen wearing a fedora, a cowboy hat, an Indian headdress, a safety helmet, a VFW cap, even a comic Saint Patrick's Day hat.

Given these facts, the general public notion that Kennedy didn't wear a hat at his inauguration is a true puzzlement. How can perception veer so far from reality?

(The third *Free Press* error was the common gaffe of placing an inauguration in the same year as the election, in this case 1960, when of course it occurred twenty days into 1961.)

But beyond the specifics of the inauguration, the idea that hats, a useful, intimate aspect of life for every male for hundreds of years, could simply be eradicated by an individual's fashion whim, even an individual as influential as John F. Kennedy, is far-fetched on its face. To give an idea of how far-fetched, consider this: Kennedy's glamorous, beautiful wife, Jacqueline, wore hats all the time. She felt wearing a hat was her duty as First Lady. Told she would have to make concessions when living in the White House, she replied, "I will; I'll wear hats." She grew famous for her pillbox hats, which were widely imitated. Yet ladies' hats as a social necessity died out anyway, at exactly the same time men's hats did. Obviously, something else was afoot.

People blame Kennedy because of our tendency to assign responsibility for shifts in culture and fashion to leaders, even though, almost invariably, a closer examination shows the leaders are actually following trends that have already begun. They blame him because the passing decades have wiped away the details of what happened, and replaced them with broad, often incorrect cultural memories. Even more curious, however, is that Kennedy not only receives blame now, aided by the fog of years, but he was blamed at the time. "I am in the hat business," began Jerry Rolnick, head of the Byer-Rolnick Hat Corporation, in a letter to Kennedy in June 1963. He continued that while he was "both an admirer and a follower" of the president's, he was finding it increasingly difficult to defend that position against people wondering how he can back the man responsible for destroying his industry. "The question I cannot answer is usually: 'What's the matter with you? How can you support a man who is going to put you out of business?'"

Rolnick was one of a variety of interests pressuring Kennedy to wear a hat. Publications around the world lectured him. Union officials and private citizens pressed hats upon him. Top executives from giant hat companies were reduced to begging. "Please, Mr. President," wrote William J. McKenna, executive vice president of the Hat Corporation of America, "wear a hat, anybody's hat." They sent emissaries with hats, or dragooned their congressmen, their governors, or local judges to deliver hats to the White House. They seemed convinced that, if only Kennedy would wear a hat, the fifty-year decline of their industry would somehow abate.

They saw what Kennedy did for other industries. When he was photographed in a straight-back rocking chair, which he used to ease the pain of his bad back, sale of such rockers soared. He wore two button suits; sales of two-button suits took off. As did cigars, though Kennedy took pains to hide his habit of smoking them.

Kennedy seemed like natural prey for the hatters. Getting famous men to endorse their products was a long tradition. The rare individual who balked at wearing a hat could be won over. There is an assumption buried within shareholder Agnew's question at the Hat Corporation meeting, an assumption almost poignant to consider today. "Can't you do something about this?" implies there was something the hat makers *could* do to reinvigorate hat-wearing among men. If only they approached Kennedy in the right way, or, barring that, if only they could reach over Kennedy's bare head and somehow get through to the young men of America directly with the perfect promotion or the right slogan. If only.

Their efforts didn't begin with Kennedy. The industry had been trying for decades, at least since the late 1920s, to reverse the hatless trend. By the 1940s, the Hat Style Council, which earlier had satisfied itself with flooding newspapers with photos of the style of the moment, was reformed under a more scientific guise as the Hat Research Foundation, an aggressive PR firm devoted to reminding men of the social and business doom that awaited all those who avoided hats. A series of promotions—National Hat Weeks, Hat Clubs, stylistic experiments, gimmicks like hat insurance, and pointed, almost desperate advertisements ("Somebodies wear hats; Nobodies don't")—flowed from the weakening might of the hat industry, which under Kennedy flared for a last, swan-song moment in the public eye before flickering out to a dull, largely ignored ember, unable to even get employees in their own factories to wear the product they were manufacturing, defeated by a trend toward the casual and the individual that had ground relentlessly in one direction for centuries.

Hats were an issue in the Kennedy administration from the day of his inauguration, when reporters made careful note of every time he placed his top hat on his head or took it off, until quite literally the day he died, when he was presented with a cowboy hat at a November 22, 1963, breakfast with the Fort Worth Chamber of Commerce and brushed aside the pleas of two thousand Texans to put it on.

An issue, yes—though, it should be acknowledged, a minor one. It would be ludicrous to argue that hats were an important part of the Kennedy saga. Most Kennedy biographies deal with hats in a single sentence, if that. Kennedy, however, was an important part of the hat story, in perception if not in reality. The decline of hats is a result of the shift of American society from a network of men so concerned with acceptability and conformity that they'd all wear the identical object on their heads, to an atomized world where individuals revel in their uniqueness and fiercely protect their right to do whatever they please, using the courts when necessary. The seeds of this change can be plainly seen sprouting in the drama that swirled around Kennedy and headgear.

"The American male is both the busiest and most carefree

of species," began the newspaper advertisement promoting
the March 1962 issue of *Gentleman's Quarterly* that Agnew
held aloft at his stockholder meeting. "He works hard. He
plays hard. . . . His clothes express his taste, his personality,
his individualism."

"Individualism" was John F. Kennedy's defining trait. He
was not beholden to political parties or staid social conventions, and the public embraced him for it. The brief Kennedy
administration marked a turning point in the self-perception
of the United States, between consensus and conflict, between
a nation concerned that it was unified to the point of stultifi-
cation and a nation genuinely worrying that it would fly apart
through social discord and unchecked personal freedom.
Between the trust-the-government-or-else decade of the 1950s
and the counterculture revolution accompanying the Vietnam
War that Kennedy escalated. The Kennedy era is a barrier
beyond which lies an unexplored, often-forgotten world—a
world that can be known by how and why men wore hats.
That is not as silly as it sounds. If it had been another tradition
spanning the breadth of recorded history that was thought to
have died out within a few years—say the keeping of dogs as
pets—a cottage industry would have sprung up in academia to
understand why something so established, so general, providing so much practical and emotional value to so many, could
simply disappear. Yet hats have been allowed to swirl into
oblivion without any factual study, critical thought, or
attempt at understanding. This is unfortunate. The small tem-
pest over whether John F. Kennedy wore a hat on his head at
his inauguration and during his administration deserves to be

remembered completely, for the insights it provides both about Kennedy and about his nation. Centuries of habit and tradition—habits and traditions that were about to vanish and be forgotten—can be seen reflected in the single day of his inauguration. And how Kennedy handled this tiny aspect of his public persona says much about him. Hats might at first seem a narrow lens through which to view Kennedy, but then so is his assassination, and five hundred books have been published about that tragedy. Why shouldn't an aspect that he embraced—his choice to be hatless—reveal as much if not more about his life and his nation as the violent death imposed upon him? Kennedy and hats are a historical blip, yes, but also a moment in time, not when society changed, but when the public thought it had changed.

Hats are the focus of nostalgia now, of recollections of fathers and grandfathers. Every few years it is reported, mistakenly, that hats are "back." But hats are not back—perhaps are never coming back—and their story should be told without succumbing to either nostalgia or celebration. Hatters fought to save their dying livelihood with ingenuity and courage, and painted the loss of hats as a disaster, which to them it was. But while we can appreciate their struggles and admire their determination, there is no reason for us to be so partisan about the outcome. Like most shifts in culture, the loss of hat-wearing as a custom is ultimately both a good and a bad thing. We gain something in not bothering with hats—time, money, convenience. But we also lose something. We lose the traditions and gestures of a hat, not to mention their warmth and coolness, in both the literal and metaphorical senses of those words.

Hats were a joy—the joy of ownership, of display, of being part of a uniform crowd, of being physically protected. They were also a bother—often uncomfortable to wear, easy to lose, expensive to maintain. Lost joys and forgotten bothers we will now attempt to recapture.

Chapter 1

"This is for you, Alex."

The snow they predicted began falling at midday. Big, wet flakes that would accumulate to seven inches by the next morning, paralyzing Washington, D.C., and delaying the inauguration of the thirty-fifth president of the United States, John Fitzgerald Kennedy, by nearly an hour. This despite the efforts of three thousand soldiers working all night to clear the parade route, shoveling and, it is said, using flame-throwers to melt the ice. They were assisted by seventeen hundred Boy Scouts armed with brooms, sweeping the reviewing stands.

By the time the first flakes fell on January 19, 1961, Kennedy already had put in a full morning. Harry Truman had stopped by Kennedy's Georgetown home to dispense his wisdom on the presidency. Allowing the visit was a courtesy on Kennedy's part—or at least a show of political fence-mending, tempered perhaps with kindness for an old man. Over the summer, the peppery Truman had publicly blasted Kennedy, doubting whether he had the maturity to be president and calling on him to drop out of the race. But Truman had not been the only prominent Democrat to do that, so Kennedy couldn't afford to hold grudges, at least not against party icons beloved by large segments of the country. He gave Truman thirty minutes.

After Truman left, Kennedy went to the White House to see Dwight D. Eisenhower in his last hours in power. They sat in a bare Oval Office, already stripped of Ike's possessions, and talked, the youngest and, at the time, oldest man ever elected president.

It was their second real conversation. The first had been a get-to-know-you session the previous December, arranged to add a little presidential luster to a man many still found inconceivably boyish to hold the most powerful job in the world. Eisenhower had gone out of his way to be cordial to Kennedy; he was determined to avoid the frosty transition he himself had endured eight years earlier. Eisenhower greeted Kennedy for their first formal meeting[1] with pomp, a brass band, and an apology for his remaining standing on the White House steps as Kennedy arrived. "I would have come down the stairs to meet your car," Eisenhower told him, shaking hands, "but the photographers wouldn't let me."

That politeness carried into their January 19 meeting. While both had privately expressed contempt for each other during the tough campaign—Eisenhower referred to Kennedy as "that young whippersnapper," and Kennedy referred to

---

[1]Eisenhower didn't recall it, but they had met in Germany at the end of World War II when Kennedy, then an aspiring newsman, interviewed him for the Hearst newspapers. And during the 1958 campaign, they bumped into each other at the Cedar Rapids airport and had a friendly encounter.

Eisenhower as "that old asshole"—now each was trying to impress the other. Kennedy displayed his firm grasp of world events. Eisenhower talked about the threat from the Soviets and showed Kennedy the "football," the valise carrying the nuclear codes that followed the president at all times. Ike also gave Kennedy a taste of presidential power; picking up a telephone, he uttered a code phrase, "Opal Drill Three," and a few minutes later a Marine helicopter was hovering over the South Lawn. A born admirer of savoir faire and power, not to mention quick transportation, Kennedy liked that, and marveled at Ike's casual attitude toward subjects as grave as the end of the world. The two men issued a prepared joint statement lauding the orderly transfer of authority from one party to another in a free democracy.

After an hour and a half, Kennedy and Eisenhower were joined by their top advisers: the incoming and outgoing secretaries of defense, state, and treasury, plus each man's special assistant. They talked about Cuba, Laos, and what was then known as the "gold crisis"—the imbalance of trade that had money flowing from America to countries abroad.

Kennedy left the White House—the skies were leaden, but no snow quite yet—and then went to the home of his friend, the artist William Wharton. There he met with General Lyman L. Lemnitzer, the chairman of the Joint Chiefs of Staff, who afterward would only say to the press that their conversation involved "procedural matters and his duties as commander in chief" and "nothing of an emergency nature."

The president-elect ate lunch, and at 1:30 PM was driven to the Sheraton-Carlton Hotel with Arthur J. Goldberg, a Chicago labor lawyer and the secretary of labor designate.

There Kennedy had coffee with twenty-nine union leaders, members of the executive board of the American Federation of Labor and the Congress of Industrial Organizations, or, as it is commonly known, the AFL-CIO.

The session with the rough-and-tumble union bosses might seem incongruous, coming as it did immediately after meetings with two presidents, the chairman of the Joint Chiefs of Staff, and a half-dozen incoming and outgoing cabinet members. But labor made Kennedy. Despite his famous roots in Boston wealth, organized labor had been the ladder Kennedy climbed to national attention, first as a congressman and then as a senator. It had helped him squeak by in the tight election and now, just before his triumphant inauguration, a key relationship threatened to go sour. Two days earlier, Kennedy's secretary of defense designate, Robert S. McNamara, had "blown up" Kennedy's budding friendship with AFL-CIO president George Meany by vetoing the appointment of Joseph D. Keenan, a popular union official whom Kennedy had promised a job as assistant secretary of defense for manpower. Worse, McNamara neglected to go on bended knee to break the news personally to Meany, and this "gratuitous insult" threatened to taint the inauguration festivities. But not if Kennedy could help it, which was why he was there—to smooth matters over. When Kennedy entered the room, he strode over to Keenan first and shook his hand.

Kennedy and the unions were bound closer than the usual ties of Democrat and big labor. He had served on the Labor Committee of both House and Senate, and the Kennedy–Ervin Labor-Management Reform Bill was the only major legislation he produced as a senator. His brother Robert was chief counsel of the Senate's labor rackets committee hearings. While these efforts against union crime caused Kennedy to be loathed by corrupt bosses like Jimmy Hoffa, they earned him the grudging, tentative respect of many union officials. And of course Kennedy had the same effect on the officials that he had on so many ordinary Americans.

"They liked him," said labor leader Albert J. Hackman. "They felt at home with him, and they don't always feel at home with a lot of politicians. I can't ever remember anybody saying, 'There's a rich kid. What's he doing on our side of the tracks?' "

That said, labor hadn't initially come out for Kennedy during the scramble for the presidential nomination. The unions were interested in results, not ideology, and their traditional method was to sit back and wait until a Democratic winner arose from the pack, and then pile on their numbers. That way they got the most return for the least risk. One man in the room at the Sheraton-Carlton, however, had stood up early and backed Kennedy. Alex Rose, president of the United Hatters, Cap and Millinery Workers International Union, had known Kennedy since 1946, and introduced him to powerful New York politicians like New York mayor Robert F. Wagner.

Months before Kennedy convened the first Hyannis Port meeting among his insiders to map out a presidential strategy, Rose singled out Kennedy as the front-runner. The union chief had been burned in the election before by supporting the stillborn presidential hopes of diplomat W. Averell Harriman in 1956. Rose had become so disillusioned with the Democratic Party, which he didn't feel rewarded the labor movement sufficiently for its efforts on the party's behalf, that he urged his fellow labor bosses to break away and form their own third party, a labor party, modeled on his own tiny Labor Party, which exerted influence in New York State. But Rose's pleas were ignored. If labor couldn't form a party of its own, he thought, the next best thing was to back a winner and back him early. In June 1959, he invited Kennedy to be the keynote speaker at the hatters' tenth triannual union convention.

"He now represents the state of Massachusetts in the United States Senate," Rose told the convention, introducing Kennedy. "He may some day extend that jurisdiction."

Rose's meaning did not go unnoticed.

"He virtually nominated Jack Kennedy from the platform of the Hatters Union convention for president of the United States," Victor Riesel, the powerful syndicated labor columnist, wrote in his column the next week.

Kennedy's speech before the hatters was straightforward: he wanted to increase the minimum wage, modernize unemployment insurance, boost social security, and ease immigration from Eastern and Southern European countries, the origin of many United Hatters members. His opening joke was half humor, half a grab for solidarity, suggesting that, as a senator, he "may be considered a fugitive from the most restrictive closed shop in the country."

"We have a guaranteed wage for six years," he deadpanned. "But we have no job security, no pay for overtime, no unemployment compensation, and no assurance that our contract will be renewed. The strange part about our closed shop is that there are plenty of people who want to take our place— but none of our current members ever want to go out on strike."

Kennedy detailed his labor racketeering bill "as it was reported out by the Senate Labor Committee," his way of skirting the fact that it was later gutted by his colleagues. Kennedy stressed its provisions for the "elimination of hoodlums in high union office."

"The Kennedy–Ervin bill," he said, was "a bill which Alex Rose could live with—but Jimmy Hoffa couldn't."

* * *

Told it was "a social visit," the press was barred at the door of the meeting between Kennedy and the union bosses at the Sheraton-Carlton. But a photographer for *The Hat Worker,* the hatters union newspaper, was inside, and he captured Kennedy spending a few moments alone with Rose, chatting and posing for pictures.

They made an odd pair, Kennedy and Rose. Kennedy was slim and handsome, with a head of hair that could be described without exaggeration as "famous." Rose was heavier, with liverish lips, a big nose, and huge ears. He wore thick glasses and was balding. One was a Catholic, the other, a Jew. One avoided hats, and the other lived by them.

Where Kennedy was born in 1917 to a politically connected family, the son of a soon-to-be rich stock speculator who would become an intimate of Franklin D. Roosevelt, Alex Rose was born Olesh Royz in Warsaw in 1898, the son of a Polish dealer in raw hides. Rose came to the United States as a teenager, intent on becoming a doctor, but the First World War kept his father from supporting him. The youth—now going by the English version of his name—ended up as a sewing machine operator in a millinery shop for six dollars a week.

Kennedy's father had been, if not quite a criminal, then an

associate of criminals, financing bootlegging operations and Hollywood movies; as a young man, Rose was beaten by mobsters trying to muscle in on the hatters union. But just like Kennedy, Rose was an astute politician, straight-arming the Communist and Socialist surges of the 1930s and avoiding the organized crime that so riddled the AFL and CIO in the 1940s and 1950s.

Rose was not given to the loud, John L. Lewis oratorical bluster of many labor leaders. He liked the squeezed shoulder and the quietly negotiated deal. This was another quality he shared with Kennedy, who hated that arms-extended-overhead, V-for-Victory gesture that Nixon took from Eisenhower. Kennedy vowed he'd quit politics before he ever copied it. The same day he met with the labor leaders, the day before his inauguration, Kennedy was asked by a reporter if he was excited about the festivities that lay just ahead. Kennedy paused, grinned, and answered, "Interested."

Kennedy was cool and understated. He shied away from the wild-eyed, exaggerated side of politics he had witnessed so closely—sometimes as practiced by his grandfather, John Francis Fitzgerald, or "Honey Fitz." The former mayor of Boston had been known to break into choruses of "Sweet Adeline" on request, a fact that perhaps contributed to his grandson's avoidance of displays of any kind. John F. Kennedy never kissed his wife in public—not once during his entire political career. He only belatedly used her as a campaign tool, in the face of overwhelming public demand. He hated the ritual presentation of the spouse, hated the trite routines of politics—the corny, the fake, and the comic. He especially hated the odd costumes that found their way into campaigns.

"He also thought that candidates for public office did not look dignified putting on all kinds of funny hats," said his brother, Senator Edward Kennedy. "So he tried to avoid putting them on."

Other politicians would have been wise to imitate him. Democratic presidential candidate Adlai Stevenson embarrassed himself by riding a horse in a parade in the California primary while dressed in full cowboy regalia, complete with boots, ten-gallon hat, and a bolo necktie. Tennessee senator Estes Kefauver, who had just barely beaten Kennedy for the vice presidential nomination in 1956—fortuitously for Kennedy, as it turned out—had his photo taken while grinning foolishly under a coonskin cap at the height of the Davy Crockett craze. Kennedy would never do that.

"He would make his little pushing gesture at the crowds, he would not wave his arms exuberantly above his head like Eisenhower, or thump his chest like Theodore Roosevelt," noted Tom Wicker, who called Kennedy "the man of detachment."

Without speaking a word of his presidential intentions in public, Kennedy had become the darling of the "Stop Nixon in '60" movement. His appearance at the hatters convention was part of a methodical campaign of showing his face around the country, making friends, polishing his speaking style, learning how to smile and kiss babies—another old campaign tradition he never grew to like.

Kennedy formally announced his candidacy in January 1960. While he was well known, and popular, particularly in Massachusetts, he was not necessarily the front-runner. The Democrats had several attractive candidates. Leading the pack was a trio of senators: Hubert Humphrey, the former mayor of

Minneapolis; Stuart Symington, Truman's protégé, a power-house from Missouri; and the master of the Senate, Lyndon B. Johnson. There was also Stevenson, yet again, a complex, aloof intellectual whose star had been tarnished by twin defeats at the hands of Eisenhower in 1952 and 1956, but was nevertheless considered a contender, at least by his fervent supporters. Stevenson remained coy in 1960; like Kennedy, he disdained the rough and tumble of politics, but unlike Kennedy he wanted to play the reluctant hero and be courted. His apparent hesitation only inflamed the desires of his fiercely loyal fans to see him run again.

Whoever emerged would have to face Nixon. The vice president was Eisenhower's political heir and quite popular, despite a reputation permanently soiled by his zealous red-baiting on the House Un-American Activities Committee during the McCarthy years (a famous cartoon by the *Washington Post*'s Herbert Block shows Nixon arriving at a rally by emerging from a sewer—a suitcase in one hand, a hat in the other; "Here he comes now!" cries an enthusiastic follower). Still, Nixon was seen as a foreign policy expert. He was an accomplished, sought-after speaker and considered very smart. Support for Nixon was widespread. A Gallup poll of Republican and Democratic party chairmen at the time showed that 61 percent thought Nixon would beat Kennedy in a head-to-head match.

They had been paired up early, as natural presidential opponents. In a July 1958 article weighing Nixon versus Kennedy, Cabell Phillips found Nixon "relatively aloof and enigmatic" compared to "the young Eastern millionaire with the Harvard accent, the Brooks Brothers couture and the egghead ideas." Nixon "has been sedulously working to dispel the popular and unflattering image of himself as a free-swinging political hatchet man and to create in its place the image of a young statesmen who has achieved 'maturity.'"

A quality that Phillips believed Kennedy was grievously lacking.

"Maturity, incidentally, that vague hallmark of virtue which a prospective President is required to exhibit is not today conspicuous among Kennedy's gifts," he wrote, in the *New York Times Magazine.* "His youthful look and a certain glibness of speech and manner are against him on this count."

As the "maturity" criticisms reflected, Kennedy was young—forty-two years old during his presidential campaign, running in an era before youth grabbed the reins of culture and gave them a snap. His age was seen as a conundrum: appealing to voters while at the same time, perhaps, barring him from election.

"Kennedy's personal appearance of youth is at once his thorn and his triumph," wrote journalist Roger Greene, after interviewing Kennedy at his "grubby, old-fashioned apartment with dog-eared furniture and faded green drapes" in Boston at the end of 1957.

It was a problem to many voters, and it was a problem with Democratic leaders. They sensed Nixon's vulnerability. Eisenhower had almost tossed Nixon off the ticket in 1952 due to a scandal involving a slush fund Nixon's backers had set up for his use. Nixon had saved himself at the last moment with his infamous, heart-tugging speech diverting attention from the money to a non-cash token of generosity: his daughters' little dog, Checkers. Top Democrats were jockeying for the chance to defeat Nixon and didn't envision an upstart sweeping in to eat their lunch. Voters wanted a president "with a touch of gray in his hair," said Johnson, who, though reluctant to officially announce his intentions, intended to work the levers offstage and become that gray-haired president. Dues and pecking orders were very important in politics, particularly in the Senate. Kennedy was cutting in line.

The strength of the forces allied against him in the party, and the certainty that he would lose in any backroom maneuverings formed Kennedy's campaign strategy: win the nomination in the primaries by going straight to the voters and proving his popularity, first, thus forcing support from party leaders.

But if that might solve his problem with the party, any attempt to reach the general public exposed his second, even greater political liability: he was Catholic, wooing a Protestant nation whose bigotry felt almost no need to conceal itself. Kennedy addressed the hatters convention, but so did a speaker who claimed that opposition to a nurses' strike at Catholic hospitals in New York City was being orchestrated by Rome. A slice of America seemed, at least initially, all too happy to toss Kennedy onto the ash heap of history based solely on his religion, along with the only previous major Catholic presidential contender, New York governor Alfred E. Smith, who lost in 1928 to a man who was not precisely a political dynamo: Herbert Hoover.

"Our people built this country," an old lady in Sutton, West Virginia, told a reporter covering the primary battle there. "If they had wanted a Catholic to be president, they would have said so in the Constitution."

Kennedy had a lot on his résumé that would help him overcome his handicaps. He was a war hero; his exploits saving his crew after a Japanese destroyer rammed his torpedo boat, PT-109, had been widely publicized, in part through his father's efforts. He was the Pulitzer Prize–winning author of the best-seller *Profiles in Courage*. He was rich and handsome, with a pretty wife and an attractive, growing family. He had the money and contacts to swarm states where he was running with advertising and volunteers. His campaign organization was extraordinary. Voters were flooded with letters, phone calls, visits from eager, young Harvard classmates. When the support behind his victory against a flailing, underfunded Humphrey in the Wisconsin primary broke down along religious lines, with largely Catholic districts swinging the balance, he regrouped and went after Humphrey again in 95 percent Protestant West Virginia, whose primary in May 1960 became the key battle for Kennedy, the place where he shunted aside charges of inexperience with a cool mastery of facts that wowed his audiences. He turned the Catholic question to his benefit in a particularly clever way. Rather than let qualms about his religion be whispered and become a nagging undercurrent, he dragged the issue into the open by raising the subject himself. At first, people were shocked that he would talk about it: one did not discuss one's religion. But by emphasizing the matter, Kennedy turned the vote into a referendum on West Virginia's tolerance. With the poor, rural, coal-mining state finding itself in the unaccustomed glare of national attention—to its pride and discomfort—a vote for Humphrey practically became a vote for bigotry, while a vote for Kennedy proved that West Virginia was not a backwater of barefooted Hillbillies and haters.

* * *

Prior to his buildup to the 1960 presidential campaign, Kennedy had appeared in the national press as a war hero, as Ambassador Joe Kennedy's son, as a carefree, young Washington man-about-town. Those early descriptions often picked up on something distinctive about the young senator: he didn't wear a hat. As early as a June 1953 *Saturday Evening Post* article titled "The Senate's Gay Young Bachelor," Kennedy was portrayed as a good-looking millionaire roaring around town in "his long convertible, hatless, with the car's top down."

Kennedy's entrance into the presidential race only intensified the spotlight, and that one detail continued to catch the attention of reporters. Press veteran T. H. White, in his first glimpse of Kennedy in the chill of the March primary, described him as "a bareheaded, coatless man, lithe as an athlete, his face still unlined, his eyes unpuffed with fatigue, wandering solitary as a stick through the empty streets of the villages of Wisconsin's far-northern Tenth Congressional District."

"Bareheaded" or "hatless" became a common way for reporters to describe Kennedy—almost a trope, like Homer's "wine-dark" sea. Unlike the nineteenth-century descriptions of the disheveled, here it was meant as praise, pointed out by journalists because it was different and thus noteworthy. "Sen. John F. Kennedy, hatless in the blazing sun," begins an article by the *Boston Globe* political editor, "stood on the court-house steps of this Raleigh County seat—in the heart of a deeply depressed coal-mining area—and looked out upon

1500 men, women and children who gave him a whistling, applauding, enthusiastic reception."

This attention to headgear was not something unique to descriptions of Kennedy. Men wore hats. They noticed hats. Hats were interesting. Hats were news. The surest way to get its picture in the paper was for a group—firemen, Indian tribes, Western delegations—to give a leader a special hat. This ritual acceptance was good for the leader and for the group because it got publicity for both, and good for the papers because it gave them something light and colorful to break up the solemnity of more serious news.

Conversely, any man who didn't wear a hat received attention for that, too. And it wasn't limited to Kennedy. When Eisenhower visited South America in February 1960, he took his hat off and waved it to the crowd during a rainy parade in Rio de Janeiro, and that fact became part of the lead in stories of the event: Eisenhower hatless in the rain.

But Eisenhower eventually put his hat back on. Kennedy didn't: in some campaign photographs, Kennedy is the only man not wearing a hat, surrounded by a dozen hat-wearing newsmen, aides, and voters. This caused simple notice in the press, but consternation in the hat industry, which otherwise supported him as a Democrat and a friend to labor. If the world consisted only of Kennedy, the media, and the general public, Kennedy's hatlessness would never have caused a fuss. It would have just been another characteristic, like Nixon's ski-slope nose or Johnson's hill country drawl, which deepened when he spoke in Texas and waned on the Senate floor.

But what struck journalists and the public as a mere blip in the Kennedy saga, another detail that showed his youthful energy, no more important than touch football or a *Hahvahd* accent, instead sounded an alarm with hatters, who were used to pestering public men who went without hats. As far back as the 1930s, hatless young members of the Roosevelt administration's Brain Trust were sent rebuking letters and reprimanded in industry magazines for setting a bad example. Now, with a popular hatless man running for president, hatters began to act, even in the primaries. They mailed him hats. They accosted him in the street as he campaigned.

"Hat salesmen also dogged our route," wrote Kennedy photographer Jacques Lowe, during a description of the "pressure groups" that would gather to confront Kennedy during the primaries, espousing their narrow concerns. "They were irritated by the Senator's bareheaded rides through blustery weather. Every now and then he obliged them by donning a hat—briefly."

To Kennedy's staff, the hatters' concerns were something of a joke. "A humorous footnote to history," press secretary Pierre Salinger, in his memoirs, called the attention to whether Kennedy wore a hat or not. Pausing from the campaign to visit her dying father, Kennedy's private secretary, Evelyn Lincoln, cheered the bedridden man with the latest news of the mad hatters nagging her boss.

"He smiled when I told him how the hatters were still after Senator Kennedy because he wasn't wearing a hat," she wrote.

Kennedy avoided the salesmen and their hats with such consistency that the rare times a hat found its way onto his head were treated as news. Like one of those optical illusions that keep flashing back and forth, as the eye takes in one area, and then the other, so Kennedy's bareheadedness was first noted and then, as observers became aware of his general hatlessness, his occasional wearing of a hat was also emphasized.

The day before voters went to the polls in West Virginia, Kennedy was shaking hands on Main Street in Spencer, the twenty-six-hundred-person seat of Roane County, when the sky opened up with rain. While passersby took refuge under awnings and umbrellas, Kennedy continued to press the flesh in the downpour. Finally, his suit soaked under his raincoat and water trickling down his hair, he collared *Boston Globe* reporter John Harris.

"Can the *Globe* afford to buy me a hat?" Kennedy whispered, grinning. The pair ducked into a department store opposite the Roane County courthouse. Kennedy selected a Rainchamp, size 7½. Harris paid the $2.04.[2]

"What am I going to wear on good days?" said Kennedy, clamping the hat on his head and going back on the sidewalk to mingle with the crowd. Later, on the bus, the candidate jokingly professed affection for the rubberized canvas hat, popular in the West Virginia countryside.

"I love this hat," he said. "I'm even going to wear it on good days."

He didn't. But the purchase made newspapers across the country.

"Jack Buys Hat," read a large headline in the next day's

---

[2] This was inexpensive, considering that a light straw hat was going for $5.95 over at Frankenburger's Department Store in Charlotte, but more than Kennedy—notorious for not carrying money and sticking friends, flunkies, and reporters with the tab for minor purchases—kept in his pockets.

Charlotte Gazette-Mail. The *Boston Globe* ran the story on its front page, next to the latest on the growing crisis over the American U-2 spy plane the Soviets had shot down.

Kennedy, who like any politician was not adverse to building upon his own myths, told the *Globe* man that the new hat was the only one he owned. "It's the first I bought in fourteen years," he said.

That wasn't exactly true, and not just because it was the *Globe* that bought the hat. During his initial plunge into politics, a congressional run that pitted the twenty-eight-year-old Kennedy against a field of nine seasoned opponents in Boston's gritty Eleventh District, his family, which served as a campaign staff and rump cabinet, had urged him to wear a hat to make him seem older. (An H. T. Webster panel cartoon of the 1940s shows a gangly teen opening a birthday present. "A *hat!*" exclaims the astonished youth. "For cryin' out loud! What in time would I do with a *hat?*" The joke is only funny if the reader, as opposed to the green youth, knows precisely what a hat is good for, and in case there is any question, Webster's cartoon shows, through a window, a portly man wearing a hat, struggling against the rain.)

Joe Kane, Joseph Kennedy's cousin, a "bald, crusty, cynical, wise politico" who spearheaded the 1946 campaign, and who himself wore an "ever present fedora pulled down over one eye in the manner of Edward G. Robinson," begged the young man to wear a hat. It was the obvious solution to his maturity problem. There is a story—usually told to illustrate the habitually late Kennedy's indifference to time—about the day that Kane finally convinced Kennedy to wear a hat and dragged him to a hat shop, where he tried on every hat in the store before selecting one. He then arrived at one of the rallies his mother held across Boston, promoting his candidacy. Rose Kennedy was at the lectern, gamely holding down the fort until the guest of honor arrived. "Well, Mother, how do you like my hat?" Kennedy asked, striding into the hall, happily oblivious. She gave him a withering stare. "Dear," she said, "it would have looked a lot better two hours ago."

Kennedy was elected to Congress in 1946. In his early years in the House of Representatives, he sometimes wore a hat, the same wide-brimmed gray fedora all the other men were wearing. Or at least he carried one. In most pictures, the hat is in Kennedy's hand, as he walks out of the White House after meeting with Truman, or in the 1949 Evacuation Day march in Boston, where a news photographer caught Kennedy marching, one of four men abreast, and the only one holding instead of wearing his hat.

The younger, thinner Kennedy—he weighed 140 pounds when first elected—actually looked fine in a hat. But by the time he was in his forties, his face had filled out from age, the cortisone and steroids he took for his painful back, and a campaign trail diet of cheeseburgers and malteds ("If I don't lose five pounds," he told Evelyn Lincoln, as he pulled at his cheeks the week before the inaugural, "I'm going to call the inauguration off."). In a hat, he looked far older and almost unrecognizably ugly. And he knew it.

"Jack just never found hats comfortable and probably didn't think they looked particularly good on him," said Senator Edward Kennedy.

"You put a hat on Kennedy, you lose three-quarters of the head and all the charisma," said his close friend and aide Dave Powers.

The importance of Kennedy's head of hair should not be overlooked. It was his most noticeable feature. William Manchester's first impression on meeting Kennedy at Harvard was "of a thick shock of chestnut hair and oddly opaque blue eyes, hooded, friendly but impenetrable." His hair was what editorial cartoonists latched onto in their caricatures, like Teddy Roosevelt's teeth or Ike's forehead. "Kennedy's hair is almost a trademark," the *Charlotte Gazette-Mail* noted, in its analysis of the Spencer hat purchase. Like all trademarks, it allowed easy identification. A bareheaded Kennedy stood out in a crowd. In an Associated Press photograph of Kennedy in the rain at Spencer, wearing his cheap beige hat as he shakes hands among the throng, umbrellas up, it takes a second to pick him out, even though he is clear and in the center of the picture.

And as with any trademark, the Kennedy hair went through subtle modifications over time to keep it current. Prior to January 1960, Kennedy affected a more tousled look. "Senator John F. Kennedy with his unruly shock of hair, left," read a caption of one wire service photo. Though some doubted just how "unruly" his hair was, and how much it was a careful construction. "A masterpiece of contrived casualness" is what *New York Times* columnist James Reston called Kennedy's "hair-do" in the fall of 1958.

There was certainly nothing accidental about it. "Barbers get minute instructions on how much to trim it," the Associated Press wrote in a January 1, 1958, profile. And for good reason: "His aides admit that without the wistful forelock dangling over his right eyebrow . . . his appeal to women voters might suffer."

When asked about it, Kennedy answered candidly, "Two million more women than men are eligible to vote in this country."

By the time he officially entered the presidential race, however, he had his hair styled into the more orderly "work of art on the part of his barber." The forelock was trimmed considerably and combed back from his brow.

This caused a momentary stir.

"The boyish looking forelock and the more sedate appearing head of hair have their adherents," wrote the AP. "Some think that the tame hair will aid his battle for the Democratic presidential nomination. Others think the forelock is a good trademark."

"It must have been a tough decision," the *Mansfield News Journal* editorialized. "That forelock has served Kennedy well as a political trademark. Still, as any advertiser knows, if a trademark becomes a liability the thing to do is to drop it. Kennedy does look a shade older now—though not quite as old as Vice President Nixon."

The Kennedy campaign refused to discuss the change, sensitive to an issue that smacked of vanity and thus something that could be seized upon by opponents. "I can't help the feeling that now it's perhaps just a little overdone," murmured Stevenson, assessing the Kennedy persona and the candidate's chances in 1960. "That the mop of hair and the pretty wife may turn out to be liabilities more than assets. He does lack a sense of maturity that people feel."

Stevenson, the archetypical egghead for both his lofty intellect and his bald pate, failed to grasp the enormous political asset of qualities like a handsome head of hair or a pretty wife. The public was another matter entirely. On the campaign trail, growing crowds roared their approval for Kennedy. Women wept, fainted, crawled onto the hood of his car, or hopped up and down, trying to see Kennedy above the heads of crowds. "Jumpers, shriekers, huggers, lopers and touchers," summarized Illinois senator Paul Douglas. Kennedy combined "the best qualities of Elvis Presley and Franklin D. Roosevelt," another senator quipped.

In the early summer of 1960, leading up to the July convention in Los Angeles, Kennedy quietly lined up the delegates he needed to win the nomination on the first ballot, convinced that if he didn't, his support would be horse-traded away in back-room deals. He succeeded, with enough certainty that he overcame the tendency of labor to withhold its support until it was time to uniformly back the Democratic winner. Alex Rose considered himself key in pushing labor's early leap to Kennedy.

"I convinced George Meany that in my judgment Kennedy is the man who can win," Rose told a meeting of the executive board of the United Hatters in June. "I have maintained very close relations with Kennedy, and I can reveal to you that he will be nominated because he already has the required votes needed to win. He will be chosen on the first ballot. The reason it is being kept secret is to maintain the suspense and drama of the campaign."

Rose saw a Kennedy win as a victory for "clean unionism," and a chance to have an attorney general who would go after corrupt bosses such as Hoffa. For his part, Hoffa was so concerned about Kennedy as president that for a time he actually followed Kennedy around on the campaign trail, trying to undercut him. Rose also saw Kennedy as being vital to shift Congress away from the South, where right-to-work states threatened to sap the power of the unions.

The convention unfolded as Alex Rose had foreseen. Kennedy hit Los Angeles with the same massive, organized effort he had brought to the primaries. His campaign put out a daily convention newspaper—circulation twelve thousand, larger than many small-town dailies—that was delivered to all the delegates. His team, trying to coordinate over the sprawling city, kept in touch using a then-unknown device that Salinger called "the 'locator' system." He wrote:

"Key Kennedy aides carried a small telephone company gadget in their pockets. When they were needed at headquarters a prearranged telephone number would be dialed and the gadget in the pocket would emit a sound. The recipient would then know that he was to call in the 'locator's' office to find out who was looking for him."

In other words, the staff of the 1960 Kennedy campaign in Los Angeles became among the first people outside phone company employees to use beepers.

Kennedy won the nomination on the first ballot, though in victory he made a decision that almost shook loose the union support Rose had worked so hard to line up. Seeking to balance his Massachusetts liberal base with a Southern conservative, Kennedy picked a man many Democrats considered practically a Republican: Lyndon Johnson.

It was a daring political choice. With Johnson, true, came

Texas and a portion of the South. But Johnson had been a devious, determined foe. Late to the campaign and failing to grasp the forces at play, he had lashed out at Kennedy, and lured him into a brief televised "debate" in front of the Texas delegation where he bitterly criticized Kennedy as an absentee senator. Kennedy bested him with a dismissive, humorous reply. In desperation, on the day the convention began, Texas governor John B. Connelly, acting on Johnson's behalf, held a press conference announcing that Kennedy suffered from Addison's disease and was unfit to hold the presidency. The accusation was universally seen as a low blow, and Kennedy's camp vehemently denied the charges.[3] After that, no one expected Kennedy to turn around and offer Johnson the number two spot on his ticket, and his doing so is something of an enigma. There is a possibility that Kennedy was offering an olive branch to the powerful Johnson, whom he assumed would refuse, and then was trapped when Johnson eagerly accepted.

Labor leaders, meeting with Kennedy to discuss the vice presidency, were "dumbstruck" by his choice. Hardened union bosses wept. "Tears were literally rolling down his cheeks," Leonard Woodcock said of United Auto Workers counsel Joseph Rauh. As Texas was the most notorious of open-shop, pro-management states, labor leaders meeting with Kennedy "seemed ready to jump from a hotel window." Johnson was also seen—ironically, in light of later events—as being

---

[3] The accusation turned out to be true: Kennedy did have Addison's disease, an ailment of the adrenal glands.

weak on civil rights, as the previous year he had helped fellow Southern senators block a change in the rules that would have eased civil rights legislation.

To make it worse, members of Kennedy's staff had been reassuring the union leaders that "it'll never be Johnson." So the news came as both a shock and a betrayal. The fear was that the Michigan delegation, in the thrall of the auto unions, would bolt and challenge Johnson's nomination, leading to a messy and embarrassing floor fight. Meany gathered all the union officials he could find in Walter Reuther's hotel suite. The turning point, as recollected by every leader there, came when Rose phoned David Dubinsky, the most respected union man in America.

"The liberals were still muttering about the 'sellout,' until Alex Rose called David Dubinsky, labor's elder statesman," Manchester wrote. "After phoning, he turned to [Walter] Reuther and reported, 'He said Kennedy is making a smart move! He said picking Johnson is a political masterstroke!' Johnson's nomination went through smoothly."

With Johnson at his side and labor firmly, if reluctantly, on board, Kennedy used his energy and his organization, his wealth and his smarts, his looks and his cool to go after the Republican presidential candidate, Vice President Richard M. Nixon.

To compare Nixon to Kennedy today is to realize the power of image. Nixon seems so much older than Kennedy though he was forty-seven, just four years Kennedy's senior. Both were World War II Navy veterans, both had entered Congress in the same year, 1946. Their offices in the Senate were across the hall from each other. Nixon, too, was also thought of as handsome; his wife, Pat, praised as pretty, poised, and stylish. We think of them as worlds apart now, but in 1960 they were equally matched rivals, though even then there was something in Nixon's demeanor, the way he spoke and carried himself, that made him seem, if not quite old, then, to use Richard Reeves's tart phrase, "an old man's idea of what a young man should be."

Nixon thought that an advantage. He harped constantly on Kennedy's inexperience, particularly in foreign affairs, where Nixon shined, having gone nose-to-nose with Soviet premier Khrushchev during their famous "kitchen debate" at a trade fair in Moscow the year before. If anything, Nixon was the wunderkind, not Kennedy. Nixon was the one with the distinguished congressional record. Nixon was the one who had been elected vice president at the age of thirty-nine while Kennedy was still being challenged by Senate elevator operators and Washington, D.C., cops who mistook him for a page or a senator's son trying to scoot by on his dad's credentials.

Yet somehow during the campaign, when Nixon and Kennedy faced each other, it was Kennedy who came out ahead, for the very reasons Nixon disdained him. In their famed first television debate, Nixon—who displayed his confidence by agreeing to the contest, which required suspension of FCC fairness rules so they could exclude the lesser fringe candidates—won based on the arguments. Nixon marshaled his facts with a debater's skill. But Kennedy looked better; he was tanned, calm, and poised, while Nixon, just recovering from an infected knee that required hospitalization, appeared so sweaty and pallid that his own mother phoned after the program to ask if he was ill. Kennedy's looking better was enough to persuade the American people—by a hair, so to speak—that he was the man for the job.

Kennedy's aura of confidence was such that it was assumed that, like royalty, whatever he did was the right thing to do. This was neatly illustrated a few weeks before the election, at the Alfred E. Smith Memorial Dinner, the only other time outside the televised debates that he and Nixon appeared in public together. The annual late October dinner, a tribute to the late Happy Warrior, was traditionally a white-tie affair, held at New York's Waldorf-Astoria. Richard Nixon dutifully wore his white tie and tails. Kennedy, however, surprised him by showing up in a tuxedo—still formal, but decidedly more relaxed than the boiled and starched white shirtfront, white tie, and swallowtail coat.

Nixon was not yet as stiff and distant as he would become. Though doomed to play the struggling Daffy Duck, whose frantic efforts to please were greeted by a chorus of crickets, to Kennedy's smooth Bugs Bunny, arching an eyebrow while patting down the wild applause, Nixon yearned to present himself as a regular, easygoing guy, particularly in front of his suave opponent. Standing at the microphone, he quipped, "Well Jack, I'll make a deal with you. Whoever is elected president will abolish white ties. And these shirts ought to have zippers. They're agony."

That line went over well in the hall. But in modern politics, there are audiences beyond the audience in front of you. Having the basis of their livelihoods described as "agony" by the vice president of the United States and possible future president was not something likely to be ignored by the formal-wear trade.

"For shame," began a telegram Sam Rudofker, of After Six Formals, sent to Nixon and, of course, the newspapers. "Please say it isn't so." Nor was his the lone complaint.

Nixon no doubt appreciated the bitter irony of the dinner. Kennedy showed up underdressed, but Nixon took the heat for trying to laugh it off. Kennedy's way was the right way. His suits had already made an impact. Before the election, the three-button suit was the standard business uniform de rigueur for any ambitious young man. ("How to commute in a three-button suit / with that weary, executive smile . . . ," sings former window washer J. Pierrepont Finch, pausing from his decidedly Kennedyesque climb to the top of World Wide Wickets in 1961's hit musical *How to Succeed in Business*.) But Kennedy wore two-button suits—the more relaxed style was supposedly easier on Kennedy's problematic back— and the difference was noticed, praised, and imitated. Three-button suits went out of fashion and didn't come back for thirty years.

Hatters, seeing this enormous potential influence, continued to press their wares on Kennedy. But his avoidance of their product was not seen as a reason to withhold support.

During the campaign, Rose spoke to Kennedy every week. He mobilized his 300,000-member Liberal Party in New York State, pushed for voter registration among hatters, and dispatched top union executives to stump for Kennedy. The meeting minutes of many locals include references to addresses from board members, reminding the rank and file of the need to come out strong for Kennedy.

"Brother Mendelowitz spoke briefly on the national elections," wrote Catherine Pignanelli, recording secretary of the Baby Bonnet Workers Local 110, of the monthly meeting held October 18, 1960, at the Woodstock Hotel. The meeting included employees from companies such as Kute Kiddie, Dear Child, Tiny Tots, and Dainty Kiddie Cap. "He urged the members not to forget that on November 8, we have a date, with our way of life at stake. It is an opportunity to eliminate the many inequalities, and a chance to adjust the injustices. As members of an affiliated union, we should vote on the Liberal Party line, as we endorse only men of integrity."

Letters were also being sent to all current and former union members, such as the one that went out November 1, 1960, to retired millinery workers, stressing a point calculated to touch an emotional chord.

"Your vote will help to return to government an administration in the spirit of Roosevelt and the New Deal," wrote Mendelowitz.

Hatters were not alone in wanting to get a hat on Kennedy's head. Among the many symbolic uses of a hat is that it shows membership in a group, and groups of all sorts tried to get Kennedy to wear their hats, so as to wed him to their causes, just as he was trying to wed them to his. Plunking a hat on the candidate, that traditional bit of cheap electioneering—everyone had laughed at those photos of a grim Calvin Coolidge wearing his Indian headdress—was given the spice of drama by Kennedy's growing fame for being averse to hats. It became something of a game: pin the hat on Kennedy. During the campaign, a representative of Viva Kennedy, a group of his Hispanic supporters, lay in wait for him in at the airport in San Francisco and, as Kennedy spoke, threw a serape over his shoulder and tried to plant an enormous sombrero on his head. But Kennedy twisted out from under it.

Every so often, however, Kennedy did put on one of these honorary hats. On a hot Texas day, September 13, 1960, Kennedy and Johnson campaigned together at the enormous Chance Vought Aircraft plant in Dallas. Some six thousand workers were gathered in the parking lot when the two arrived in an open car, Kennedy seated, Johnson standing up, enthusiastically waving his distinctive Western hat, a scaled-back version of the classic cowboy hat. When the car stopped, Kennedy climbed onto the car's trunk and was handed a microphone and a new cowboy hat of his own, perched atop a hatbox.

"I've just been presented this hat, but I don't have the guts to wear it quite yet," Kennedy told the crowd, tossing down the hat. "I got to stay in Texas about two more days before I put that on."

After a brief, well-delivered speech about the need for America to be first, Kennedy picked the hat back up, and somebody in the crowd shouted, "Put your hat on, Jack!" Kennedy did, smiling, adjusting it at the front, at the sides, then at the front again, and wearing the hat for a single moment.

"I'm going to wear this in the Saint Patrick's Day parade in Boston," he quipped, deftly removing the hat to wave it and never putting it back on again.

* * *

Kennedy beat Nixon. The two men came to be viewed with such wildly differing degrees of affection that it is always worthwhile to remember how thin the vote margin was: two-tenths of a percent. The shift of one vote in a thousand from the Kennedy to the Nixon camp could have changed the outcome. The recount dragged on through December. Even now the final tally is open to question. It is a tribute to the revisionist quality of human nature, and to the fallibility of polls, that while 49.7 percent of the voters actually cast a ballot for Kennedy in November 1960, by June 1963, 59 percent of the respondents to a national survey reported that they had voted for Kennedy. A year later it was 65 percent.

As popular as Kennedy was before the election, interest in him only intensified afterward—his candor and his wit, the glamour of his family, his model-beautiful young wife, Jackie, who, two weeks after the election, at age thirty-two, gave birth to their first son, John Fitzgerald Kennedy Jr., the only child ever born to a president-elect in the history of the United States. Every coo and gurgle was reported to a breathless nation.

This did not make Kennedy immune to criticism, however. As the inauguration approached, Kennedy's London tailor began issuing confident pronouncements to the British press.

"Five weeks ago we sent a dark gray pinstripe suit to Mr. Kennedy," said King Wilson, of the firm of John Morgan and Company. "When he moves into the White House, I expect he'll be wearing it. It's a formal suit—just right for his new job."

That was too much in a nation where the "gold drain" was nearly an obsession. "Stacks of gleaming gold bars were moving fast out of U.S. ownership and into the possession of foreign nations," intoned a story appearing in *Life* magazine the same month Kennedy's London tailor started talking to the press. The reaction was to be expected.

"I don't know why Mr. Kennedy has to go to England to have his clothes made," Robert E. Stein, custom tailor, wrote in the letters section of the *Washington Post* on November 26. "Certainly the finest clothes in the world, and that includes England, are made in the good old U.S.A. It seems to me that people that make their money here and represent the American people certainly should spend it here. . . . It ill behooves a public servant to do otherwise."

Stein's complaint was seized upon by embittered Republicans, who, Nixon-like, saw a chance to lash out at the sophisticates who had just barely beaten them. Republican congressman Thomas M. Pelly said Kennedy should "relieve the pressure on the dollar" by buying American. Pierre Salinger was quick to claim that most of Kennedy's clothing came from New York's H. Harris & Co. To Kennedy's eventual embarrassment, jowly tailor Sam Harris was trotted to meet the media. Kennedy stopped wearing British suits entirely; John Morgan and Company ended up dressing, not John F. Kennedy on his inauguration day, but the waxwork Kennedy at Madame Tussaud's museum in London.

Even Lyndon Johnson, recently portrayed by the Republicans as a hill country yokel with "cow flop on his boots," was suddenly a dandy siphoning dollars to foreigners because he had bought five suits from Carr, Son and Woor on Savile Row during a visit to England.

"At a time when it's important to the stability of the dollar to hold down purchases from abroad," said Pelly, "Senator Johnson sets a bad example for the American people by buying his suits from a London tailor."

Johnson was torn between imitating the fashionable Harvard grad he now worked for—hence the London suits—and reveling in his Texas roots, of which he was immensely proud. He had an enormous ranch in Texas, and a week after the election a reluctant Kennedy went there on a brief visit, taking along his old Harvard roommate, Congressman Torbert Macdonald, "for moral support."

Johnson obviously hoped to inculcate Kennedy with Texas style, but he was disappointed. Johnson greeted Kennedy and his party wearing boots, work pants, a leather jacket, and his trademark cowboy hat. Kennedy wore a suit and tie and was, of course, bareheaded. Photographers urged the pair to pose together.

"They could see you if you'd take that hat off," said Kennedy, referring to the phalanx of photographers who, a *Dallas Morning News* columnist recalled, "were shooting as madly as if they had never seen either man before—and never expected to see either again."

Johnson took off his hat in deference to Kennedy, but his gesture was not reciprocated. When Kennedy was later given a cowboy hat, he refused to be photographed wearing it, to Johnson's distress.

"Did you notice," Kennedy later said to Macdonald, "how upset he got when I didn't want my picture taken with that hat on my head? It took a little time for him to understand why I would rather not do it." (Johnson did get him to go deer hunting the next day, for seven hours, and Kennedy bagged a pair.)

It was during the imported suit imbroglio that Kennedy touched off a period of intense anxiety for America's hatters. Asked at the end of November by a probing reporter whether he planned to wear the traditional silk top hat at his inauguration, Kennedy responded, "I don't know."

"I don't know" was not the ringing endorsement the hatters were looking for. Inaugurations were important: the eyes of the nation were upon them. For businessmen, inaugurations were the Super Bowl before there was a Super Bowl. The United States has no coronations, no royal weddings. The quadrennial swearing in of a president is the closest the nation gets to official pomp. As the most formal state event, the inauguration served as a barometer of the fashion of the day, and a chance for an industry to show off. George Washington had considered wearing a suit of gold thread, as befitting the splendor of a nation's birth, but what he ended up wearing was a suit of brown linen—cloth woven by proud Hartford weavers and donated to the president for his benefit and their own. Washington's vice president, John Adams, wore a nearly identical suit, cut from the same brown cloth, donated by the same Hartford weavers, a reminder to those concerned about commercialization in this country that it was present, albeit subtly, even as George Washington first stood with his hand on a Bible.

Kennedy ducked the hat issue. The press didn't let go of the matter, although it was definitely seen as comic relief, the sort of facetious question that tells everybody the press conference has come to an end. After his get-acquainted meeting with Eisenhower in early December, Kennedy held a news conference outside the West Wing lobby. He was quizzed about NATO, about nuclear talks in Geneva, about the transition, and then one reporter asked, "Did you discuss what hat you would wear on Inauguration Day?" The room erupted into laughter.

"No," Kennedy said. "I'll take your advice on that." And the press conference was over.

The press certainly seemed to be bracing the public for a hatless inauguration.

"When playing touch football and attending other rituals of his generation," the *Philadelphia Inquirer* mused, "he is accustomed to wearing no headgear of any sort. To the horror of the hatters, he just might find this a wholesome innovation for inaugurals, too."

The Hat Institute, following Hartford's lead but perhaps betraying a certain inexperience at dealing with a politician of Kennedy's vast wealth, offered to buy Kennedy an inaugural hat of his choosing, as if expense were the issue.

Alex Rose did not resort to anything so crude. He didn't have to; Kennedy's secretary of labor designate, Arthur J. Goldberg, was a longtime hatters union lawyer. He not only had been special council to the United Hatters, but also was the Cap & Cloth Hat Institute's Washington representative. Goldberg always ordered vests with his suits, even when vests weren't fashionable, because doing so, he said, meant work for members of the Amalgamated Clothing Workers of America. Whether prompted by Rose or of his own accord, Goldberg reported delivering the following inauguration advice to Kennedy: "The least you could do for Alex Rose is to wear a hat."[4]

---

[4] Goldberg was not alone among Kennedy's incoming cabinet members in using his person to promote trades close to him. Secretary of Commerce Luther Hodges, the former governor of North Carolina, posed for a photo standing in a tub in a suit and a tie while being drenched by the shower, "to demonstrate the quick-drying fabrics made in North Carolina mills."

That was not the extent of political input regarding the inauguration hat. The first man Kennedy named to his cabinet was Abraham Ribicoff, who he picked for the Department of Health, Education and Welfare. Ribicoff at the time was governor of Connecticut, where Danbury was still a hub of hat manufacture, though weakened by a century of imports, a devastating strike in 1954, and loss of jobs to right-to-work states. The hatters lobbied Ribicoff, and Ribicoff passed along the message to Kennedy: It would be deeply appreciated in Connecticut if he wore a hat at his inauguration.

The matter must have been on Kennedy's mind, too. In December, he took a break from the chores of the transition—the press was hanging around his front door, waiting for each new cabinet appointment—to take a quick vacation to New York. He attended the opening of Gore Vidal's play *The Best Man,* a political drama with a character patterned, in part, on Kennedy. Backstage after the performance, Kennedy explained the hat he brought with him to actor Lee Tracy: "A friend told me I had better wear a hat. It might help the people of Danbury."

Carrying a hat to the theater wasn't the same as wearing a hat at his inauguration, however. While it would be an exaggeration to say the world hung on Kennedy's decision, the press did focus even more attention to his habitual reluctance to wear hats.

"President-elect Kennedy wearing a hat . . . ," begins a caption of a large, full-face newspaper photograph of Kennedy leaving his Georgetown home the day after his meeting with Ribicoff, quite obviously doing just that.

During this time, the nation's premier advertising agency

produced a newspaper ad intended to reach over the president's bare head and appeal directly to American men.

The ad is a curious artifact. It promotes the Hat Corporation of American but didn't come from any of the agencies representing the Hat Corporation. It came instead from Leo Burnett—not Leo Burnett the advertising company, but Leo Burnett the man. The head of a $100 million agency whose work was widely admired (Burnett ads "stood out like blood-red slabs of raw meat tossed on a table crowded with delicate soufflés," an advertising executive of the time recalled), Burnett also hated delegating authority, was constantly on the prowl for new business, and was willing to spend a great deal of company time and money developing speculative campaigns trying to woo it. The company had already done work for the Tea Bureau and for the American Meat Institute, and Burnett saw the hatters' agony as a chance to pick up a new client. When Bernard Salesky, who admired the masculinity of Burnett's Marlboro man, told him of the Hat Corporation's dilemma—it was grabbing a growing share of a rapidly shrinking market—Burnett offered to develop a pro-hat ad as a business pitch.

The full-page advertisement, which ran only once, in the January 12, 1961, edition of the *New York Times*, is a classic piece of Leo Burnett lapel-grabbing. It shows an enormous close-up photo of a scowling, bearded, bespectacled, greasy-haired "Greenwich Village beatnik," chin resting languorously on his cupped hand, a cigarette dangling from his petulant lips. "There are some people," the headline reads, "that even a hat won't help."

On its face, the ad is a pitch to young men. "No miracles

happen when you put on a hat," the copy begins, "but it can make the rough, competitive road between you and the top a little easier to travel. You look more of a man with a hat on, and the men who run things have a deeply ingrained executive habit of reserving responsible jobs for those young men who look mature enough to handle them."

While nothing in the advertisement specifically mentions Kennedy, considering the timing, and the emphasis on maturity, the implications for a certain young man about to be sworn in as chief executive of the most powerful nation on earth were obvious, at least to *Time* magazine. In a brief article noting the ad, *Time* asked the man responsible what the Hat Corporation was trying to do.

"We want to get Mr. Kennedy to wear hats," Salesky said. "He'll feel better in a hat, and he won't get head colds. A president shouldn't get head colds."

You had to know Bernard Salesky—the son and grandson of hatters—to appreciate the level of desperation reflected in that comment. For years, he had been stressing the importance of style over utility and ridiculing the idea of selling hats by appealing to concerns for health. "Other manufacturers sell hats for protection against colds," Salesky told *The New Yorker* in 1956. "I say, 'Tommyrot.' I say, 'Sell the hat as a matter of fashion. Sell it not as a separate entity but to complete the ensemble.' Hats have to complement the wardrobe and complement the man."

But when the man was John F. Kennedy and he was entering the White House, Salesky's scruples as to the ideal way to sell hats vanished, and suddenly he was pointing fearfully at the bogeyman of colds.

Burnett's ad ended up being moot, at least when it came to Kennedy. By the time it ran, Kennedy had already announced he would not only wear a hat at his inauguration, but he would wear the traditional silk top hat, which hadn't been worn at a presidential inauguration in twelve years, since the inauguration of Harry Truman.

If Kennedy thought this would mollify the hat industry, he was mistaken. As he worked the room at the Sheraton-Carlton the afternoon before his inauguration, Alex Rose presented him with a gift. The newsmen huddled at the door could hear laughter and applause among the "prominent labor men" gathered in the room. Afterward, George Meany came out and told them that Kennedy had won over the union men by modeling the gift—a fedora that Rose had brought. Kennedy "looked so good" in the hat, Meany reported, that the president-elect placed a hat order with Rose.

That's one interpretation. Kennedy certainly did put the hat on, and gamely posed for a photographer. But the man in the photographs that ended up in *The Hat Worker* looks old, tired, and almost unrecognizably ugly.

"This is for you, Alex," the president-elect said.

Kennedy took the hat with him, wearing it past the news photographers and out into the growing snowstorm, whose ferocity inspired the organizers of that evening's inaugural gala to go on the radio and urge suburbanites not to bother going home to change into their tuxedos and fancy dresses, because they'd never make it back. Even some of the entertainers were forced to perform in their street clothes.

The next morning's *New York Daily News* ran a picture of

Kennedy in his fedora over the entire top half of its front page, under the headline, "KENNEDY INAUGURAL TODAY."

The caption sounds like a line from an ad touting the protective qualities of headgear: "Making a rare appearance in a hat," it reads, "President-elect John F. Kennedy is virtually oblivious of snow."

Chapter 2

"Melancholy Doom of the Silk Hat."

Inauguration morning at 8:55, John F. Kennedy walked out of his brick Georgetown home on his way to attend mass at Holy Trinity Church, two and a half blocks down N Street. He was wearing a light gray suit with a dark blue overcoat. Kennedy spied a cluster of waiting newsmen, attired in their Sunday best, some wearing homburgs. He couldn't resist tweaking them as he passed.

"Didn't you get the word?" Kennedy teased, as if he were back at Harvard. "It's top hat time."

It would never be again, at least not for the next half century. Kennedy was the last president to wear a tall hat to his inauguration, ending a 132-year arc that began with Andrew Jackson traveling to his inauguration in a top hat trailing a train of black crepe, a "weeper" in memory of his wife, Rachel, who had just died.[1]

[1]Jackson wore his top hat on the way to his inauguration, but not to the ceremony itself. Most historians trace the top hat at inaugurals only as far back as Franklin Pierce.

The fall of the top hat predicts and parallels the death of hats in general. It was worn without self-consciousness for a century—from around 1805 to about 1905—by ordinary men: police officers and cabdrivers and shop clerks hoping someday to be owners. Then men gradually drew away from it, first damning the hat as hideous and uncomfortable, then as somehow morally suspect. The top hat accumulated its own symbolic baggage, becoming a totem of extravagant wealth or the extreme of elegance. The tall silk hat became an image, one so strong that it drove the hat right out of fashion and into costume, worn with sincerity only by the two segments of society whose magnified joy makes them impervious to how they actually appear: teenagers attending proms and grooms on their wedding day.

The top hat arrived in Europe along with the dawn of the nineteenth century, replacing the cocked hat, or what is thought of as the tricornered hat of the Revolutionary War. The tricornered hat had emerged a century and a half earlier when the enormous brims of the cavalier-style hats exhibited a tendency to flop down into the wearer's face. To remedy this, men would pin up their hat brims—or "cock" them. Cocking a hat in two places formed the bicorne hats we associate with Napoleon and various admirals; in three places, it created the hat of George Washington. Men would give their names to their own distinctive style of cocking a hat, and books were even written on the subject.

The French Revolution helped sweep away cocked hats as hated symbols of the aristocracy. They were replaced by a hat not too different from the hat the pilgrims wore before the cocked hat took hold, still a cylinder with a brim, but the brim was much narrower, and the crown, instead of sloping toward the top, like a truncated cone, flared out away from the brim. Men were sketched wearing a classic top hat in Paris as early as 1792, and the style soon spread everywhere, supplanting the cocked hat for good.

As with all changes, the transition was eagerly embraced by the young and resisted by the old, while those in between cast a melancholy eye on the process. To English essayist Leigh Hunt, writing in the 1840s, the cocked hat inspired "a certain retrospective reverence," evoking images of seventeenth-century drawing rooms, while the new top hats seemed like "chimney-tops with a border," redolent of factories and modern efficiency. "In proportion as society has been put into a bustle, our hats seem to have narrowed their dimensions," he wrote. "The flaps were clipped off more and more till they became a rim; and now the rim has contracted to a mere nothing; so that what with our close heads and our tight succinct mode of dress, we look as if we were intended for nothing but to dart backwards and forwards on matters of business, with as little hindrance to each other as possible."

Modern and efficient though they seemed, top hats had their drawbacks. The hat presented a wide profile to the wind and tended to blow away; the early history of railroad travel is filled with stories of open trains being stopped so that their daring passengers could retrieve their lost hats from trackside. Those hats had to be recovered because they cost a lot. Made of beaver, in short supply due to two hundred years of diligent trapping to make headwear, the hats were hugely expensive.

In the 1660s, Pepys records, "This day Mr. Halden sent me a beaver which cost me £4 5s"—roughly the equivalent of seven hundred dollars today.

Their cost, coupled with the increasing number of events that demanded a top hat—weddings, funerals, christenings, civic ceremonies—led to the creation of rental hats, or "subscription hats," which could be had by the week, the day, or even the hour. There was a brisk market in secondhand hats. Rich patrons might give an old hat to a favored flunky, and hats were passed from one generation to the next.

"A hat would descend from father to son, and for 50 years make its regular appearance at meeting," a descendant of John Adams's wrote.

Because of the great cost and the transience of fashion, historians believe that top hats would not have continued in popularity into the second half of the nineteenth century had not two key technological developments given them a boost. First, in the 1830s, English hatters figured out how to make the hats out of hardened silk instead of beaver pelt. "Silk plush not only saved the tall hat, but gave it a new lease of life," wrote R. S. Loveday. "For if beaver excelled in lightness and in pliability, silk plush excels in splendour, and it is hardly necessary to say that there is no comparison in its price."

The cost of the new silk top hats in London—four shillings and ninepence, or about one-twentieth the cost of Pepys's hat—was so radically low that it entered nursery rhymes, such as this ballad about Queen Victoria's marriage to Prince Albert in 1839:

> *When Albert comes to Britain's isle*
> *We'll dress him out in the first of style.*
> *With a shirt and a four-and-ninepenny tile,*
> *To marry the Queen of England.*

Albert returned the favor by wearing, and helping to popularize, the silk topper, which, beginning in about 1850, relegated the beaver top hat to the stage and quaint memory.

One group far less happy about the new technology were American fur trappers, who saw prices for pelts tumble. "Hell is paved with silk hats," grumbled Kit Carson. He gave up trapping to become a guide in 1842, the year raw beaver pelts were selling for a dollar, one-sixth of the price they had fetched a decade earlier.

The other development addressed the problem of the top hat's shape. Because the crown did not taper—if anything, it widened at the top—the hats could not be stacked, leading to storage problems, since their crowns could be up to eight inches tall. That might not seem tall, but then top hats are deceiving[2]—in some years the crown of a top hat was no taller than other hats, though it seemed taller because of its cylindrical shape. The crown of Kennedy's top hat was just five inches tall; Lincoln's stovepipe was seven inches, a "kite-high dandy" was seven and three-eighths. This surprised people even during the top hats' heyday. A nineteenth-century parlor game was to

---

[2] This is probably because of their proximity to the face, whose social importance makes features seem bigger than they actually are. A large nose, for instance, is about two inches long.

mark on a wall the point players thought a top hat would come up to and then place the hat down, to the wonder of those whose marks were two feet off the floor.

The storage problem was cleverly solved in 1837 by Frenchman Antoine Gibus, who invented the collapsible opera hat, a hat whose stiffness was provided by an ingenious spring that could be squashed flat and then snapped open with "a delicious plopping sound." The process called for a certain flair. An opera hat aficionado described how to do it right: "To open, you grab the front brim and with a flick of the wrist—it must be subtle not ostentatious—hit the back rim against the palm of the left hand. Punching out the crown is vulgar and causes the Gibus spring to open badly. To close the hat, you grasp both sides of the brim, place the crown against the chest, and exert even inward pressure."

While the distinction is lost today, for a century society differentiated between the collapsible and the hard silk hat. The collapsible top hat was definitely a concession to the crowds and commotion of the theater—somewhat the way plastic wineglasses are welcome at an outdoor symphony picnic but might be considered gauche if offered to dinner guests at home.

"If I meet a man with a 'gibus' in broad daylight, I generally murmur to myself, 'Fiddler,' "[3] George Augustus Sala wrote in his 1880 critique of hats. "Sometimes I perpend,[4] and whisper, 'out all night;' but I never set him down as a gentleman."

---

[3] By "fiddler," he means a dabbler, a fraud.

[4] "Perpend" is an archaic way to say "contemplate."

As late as 1922, Emily Post gave this advice on opera wear: "The 'collapsible' hat is for us in the seats rather than in the boxes," she wrote, but "it can be worn perfectly well by a guest in the latter if he hasn't a 'silk' one."

Eventually, the ease of storing the opera hats made them the hat of preference, and enough men absentmindedly tried to crush their rigid silk hats that at least one manufacturer felt the need to put warning labels—"Not Collapsible . . . Do Not Attempt to Fold"—inside their hard silk hats.

As the nineteenth century progressed, the brims of top hats widened and narrowed, curled and arched, the crown grew and shrank, sometimes straightening—begetting its extreme: the straight-sided "stovepipe" hat of Abraham Lincoln.

Lincoln was so closely identified with his stovepipe that when threats on his life forced him to sneak into Washington, D.C., for his first inauguration in 1861, he was considered sufficiently disguised when he replaced his tall hat with a cloth cap (though not a "Scotch-plaid cap," as anti-Lincoln newspapers would claim in order to give his camouflage a hint of the ridiculous).

As they would a hundred years later with Kennedy, hatters in Lincoln's time sent the president samples of their wares, for his benefit and their own. Professional hatters gave Lincoln top hats. So did average citizens. Louisa Livingston Siemon sent the president-elect a pair of hats in 1860. "As a slight testimonial of my admiration of you as a man, a patriot and a statesman," she wrote, "allow me, an entire stranger, to present for your acceptance the accompanying two hats, which I have caused to be manufactured expressly for this purpose."

The phrase "expressly for this purpose" is a reminder that

secondhand hats were a brisk business. Lincoln's admirers did not want him to suspect they were passing along used goods. "Honored Sir," begins a September 30, 1864, letter from William F. Warburton Sr., a Philadelphia hatter. "I herewith send you a fine hat made expressly for you, and shall feel pleased if you will accept and wear it. . . ." (He didn't: the hat was the wrong size, and Lincoln returned it; Warburton, showing a determination that seems characteristic of hatters, made him another.)

Lincoln, in contrast to Kennedy and reflecting his far more humble origins, was delighted with the free hats. Brooklynite George Lincoln conveyed a "handsome silk hat" from a New York hatter to the president-elect, and reported that "in receiving the hat Lincoln laughed heartily" and commented to Mary Lincoln, "Well, wife, if nothing else comes out of this scrape, we are going to have some new clothes, are we not?"

Though at his first inaugural Lincoln looked out on "a sea of silk hats," by then the demise of the fashion had already begun. The highly publicized visit to the United States in 1851 of Hungarian patriot Lajos Kossuth, who wore a broad-brimmed felt hat, undermined the rule of silk toppers.

In his 1863 *Life without Principle*, Henry David Thoreau, who professed to loathe anything approaching fashion, concludes that the new hat was Kossuth's only lasting contribution to America. "That excitement about Kossuth, consider how characteristic, but superficial, it was!" he wrote. "For all fruit of that stir we have the Kossuth hat."

"[Kossuth] caused a sensation—not so much by his words and actions as by his hats," wrote fashion expert Colin McDowell. "Here was an authoritative national figure who eschewed the top hat and wore instead a dashing soft hat of great Romantic appeal."

The "slouch hat," a medium-brimmed hat with a lower crown, was embraced by Civil War generals in the field (though its name refers not to officers lounging in their campaign hammocks, but to Charles II's time, when the hats' broader brims slouched down). At the same time another hat arrived that would become immediately popular: the derby. The derby—or bowler—was a hard hat, like a top hat, but instead of being a cylinder it was streamlined, like an egg.[5] Bowlers seemed modern, fast, and went well with the lounge suit, a shorter, less-fitted garment than the tight frock coat, and called a "suit" because unlike frock coats it was typically matched to a man's vest and pants.

Both the bowler and the suit were bred in the English countryside by relaxing aristocrats who wanted something a little more comfortable than tall hats, stiff detachable collars, and swallowtail coats for their leisurely Saturday afternoons.

Men's fashion in the second half of the nineteenth century was largely a tale of these comfortable country fashions slowly invading the city. Purists resisted. King George V—who, like many British royals, was fashion-conscious to the point of lunacy—detested derbies, calling them "ratcatchers' hats" and refused to let them in Buckingham Palace. As late as 1909, the English trade journal *Tailor and Cutter* was denouncing the practice of wearing derbies in town.

---

[5]There is a marvelous, scholarly book—*The Man in the Bowler Hat* by Fred Miller Robinson—fully exploring the rich history and iconography of the derby, and I will yield the field to him in this regard.

Resistance was in vain. The derby, embraced by middle-class men everywhere, perfect for crowded trolley cars and windy train platforms, pushed the top hat from being a hat worn by men across the range of the economic scale to a hat worn mostly by the well-to-do.[6] While commuting mechanics, clerks, and office managers switched their top hats for derbies, the wealthy clung to them, although the presence of an alternative seemed to release a pent-up hostility toward the fashion—a dislike expressed at first, not by the envious underclass, but by the top hat wearers themselves.

New York writer Edward Hamilton Ball begins his 1890 essay "The Rise of the Top Hat" with this bold declaration: "Though the universally execrated tall chimney-pot or stove-pipe hat is a modern affair, yet there have been throughout the centuries foreshadowings of its stiff hideousness. . . ."

It was as if gentlemen, lulled for most of the nineteenth century by consensus regarding the fashion, began to awake to what was perched atop their heads as the century dwindled. Oscar Wilde, in a conversation about the clarifying effects of the narcotic liqueur absinthe, said that after the third glass "you see things as they really are, and that is the most horrible thing in the world." To illustrate this clear-eyed horror, he used something even sober men were gazing at particularly closely:

"Take a top hat," he continued. "You think you see it as it really is. But you don't because you associate it with other

---

[6] A faint echo of the wearing of top hats by working men is found today among downtown hansom horse cabdrivers and the occasional chimney sweep.

things and ideas. If you had never heard of one before, and suddenly saw it alone, you'd be frightened or you'd laugh."

By the last decade of the nineteenth century, men were indeed laughing at their top hats, which they also called "plug hats," a term whose etymology is clear if you recall what a black rubber tub stopper looks like. In Mark Twain's 1889 novel, *A Connecticut Yankee in King Arthur's Court,* a radical criticism of the social order wrapped in humorous fantasy, the narrator encounters Sir Ozana le Cure Hardy. "He was in the gentleman's furnishing line, and his missionarying specialty was plug hats. He was clothed all in steel, in the beautifulest armor of the time—up to where his helmet ought to have been; but he hadn't any helmet, he wore a shiny stove-pipe hat, and was ridiculous a spectacle as one might want to see. It was another of my surreptitious schemes for extinguishing knighthood by making it grotesque and absurd."

It took men a long time to put their fingers on exactly why top hats were "grotesque and absurd." Though Twain picked up the habit of wearing top hats in London, according to his friend William Dean Howells, "he seemed to tire of it" and not only went back to his soft Southern hat, but began speaking against toppers, objecting to the hats, not on the basis of comfort, but out of a vague sense that wearing them somehow was morally wrong. In December 1906, the author went to Washington to testify before a congressional hearing on copyright reform. The subject of his dress came up after he shocked onlookers by throwing off his cloak to reveal a white suit, something that was just not worn in December, especially not with white shoes.

"When a man reaches the advanced age of seventy-one

years, as I have," he said, "the continual sight of dark clothing is likely to have a depressing effect."

Twain explained his lack of a top hat this way:

"It is true that I dressed the Connecticut Yankee at King Arthur's Court in a plug-hat but, let's see, that was twenty-five years ago. Then no man was considered fully dressed until he donned a plug-hat. Nowadays, I think that no man is dressed until he leaves it home. Why, when I left home yesterday they trotted out a plug-hat for me to wear."

Even the articulate Twain, however, couldn't quite describe what, precisely, was the matter with top hats. He continued:

"'You must wear it,' they told me; 'why, just think of going to Washington without a plug-hat!' But I said no; I would wear a derby or nothing. Why, I believe I could walk along the streets of New York—I never do, but still I think I could—and I should never see a well-dressed man wearing a plug-hat.[7] If I did I should suspect him of something. I don't know just what, but I would suspect him."

He ended his vignette by noting that the only man on the Pennsylvania ferry wearing a top hat was Howells, who accompanied him.

"I tell you he felt ashamed of himself," Twain said. "He said he had been persuaded to wear it against his better sense. But just think of a man nearly seventy years old who has not a mind of his own on such matters!"

That brief comment of Twain's contains the basic contra-

---

[7] As with Kennedy's claim to not have bought a hat in fourteen years, Twain's "never" was a pose, feeding his own myth, since just the year before he had been photographed not only wearing a top hat, but doing so on the streets of New York.

dictions—the demands of formality versus the sneaking sense of something amiss, the expectations of others versus the impulse to follow one's own desires—that heralded the end of top hats over the first half of the twentieth century and hats in general in the second half.

By the beginning of the twentieth century, to return to Wilde's observation about top hats inspiring fear and amusement, some men indeed found top hats frightening. Consider Henry Irving Dodge's 1906 novel, *The Hat and the Man,* a fast-paced mix of Victorian melodrama, ham-handed social commentary, and a horror plot straight out of Stephen King about the monstrous transformation of the narrator's father by his white beaver top hat.

Though poor, Nick Farnum had been "a genius, a poet, kindly and gentle." Unhappy with his station, "one day, he went into his laboratory and locked himself in and worked and worked, night and day, and then emerged with—the hat." The narrator—his eldest son Nicholas—relates his sobbing mother's confession of what happened after the Frankenstein-like creation of the hat:

> That day he began to change. All of his imagination gradually went from him, he laughed at poetry, and spurned music and art. He would talk of nothing but facts. Finally avarice possessed him, and he lost all respect for the rights of others. . . . The schemes he had formerly rejected with indignation were now the most attractive to him. He made money—yes, he made money.

And now, in a transport of agony, she cried, "Nicholas, however it was accomplished, the day your father put that

hat on, that day Satan entered into his life, and made of mine a hell. By its destruction only will his soul be saved and my deliverance be accomplished."

I raised my hand and swore by God to destroy the hat.

Nicholas's father passes away, bequeathing his vast estate—and with it the love of his beautiful ward, Madeline— to his firstborn son, provided he wears his infernal hat for an entire year. Philip, the righteous younger son, selflessly offers to fulfill their father's dying request. But Nick Jr., trying to shield his brother from the "agent of evil," agrees to the terms, and is transformed into a monster of Mammon similar to his father, leading to a climax with every melodramatic cliché at full cry: the raging thunderstorm, the imploring Madeline, the weeping ghost of mother, the steadfast noble Philip, and the final banishment of the fiend.

I lowered the gun and, turning it stock-to, extended it to Philip.

"Here!" I cried, "in the name of God, take my life and save my soul."

He seized the gun and putting it to his shoulder swerved the barrel to the right and fired point-blank at the hat. At that moment Madeline flung her arms around my neck and snatched me violently back as the great mirror, loosed from its ancient fastenings by the shock, fell shattered at my feet.

My vision cleared and I turned to Madeline, who still clung to my neck. Yes, it was she, sweetheart and mother, come to save me. And here was Philip, whom I loved. I saw it all now. I sought Madeline's eyes, but in them was a look of sudden horror. Her glance passed me and I turned. Where the mirror had been, and formed of the glass that still remained standing, was a gigantic silhouette, an old man with a high hat. And as we looked, the father of all blasts struck the mansion, and the glittering image, scintillant of malice, moved outward and fell shattered upon the hearthstone, mingling with the fragments of the hat.

One needn't be Sigmund Freud to detect a certain amount of hostility toward top hats in a passage such as that.

Around the time Dodge's novel was published, the term *high hat* began to be used as a synonym for *snobbish* and, as if making way for the hat's symbolic self, the actual wearing of top hats began to recede. Still, the top hat did not yet carry the automatic class symbolism it was soon to acquire. While editorial cartoonist Frederick Opper is remembered for putting top hats on his huge-bellied, grinning figures labeled "The Trusts," he also placed a top hat on a small figure representing "The Common People." Uncle Sam was given a top hat, spangled with stars and stripes, not for his riches, but because he was a lean, hardworking, no-nonsense Yankee who took care of business.

Just as Kennedy was blamed for the decline of hats that took place well before his arrival in the public eye, so the life-or-death imperatives of World War I were credited with washing away a rigorous formality that was already in decline before the war broke out. In the decade before August 1914, men caused controversy by dining in the most exclusive London hotels while not dressed for dinner, and top hats were set aside in the most traditional locales.

"An American in London only fifteen years ago invariably

felt a wave of relief as he saw a soft hat," wrote Percival Pollard in 1909. "For then he knew another American was approaching. To-day you may see all manner of hats in Bond Street."

Pollard, a sharp-eyed critic described as having been "born sneering," pauses to note another crucial factor in the death of top hats. After mentioning "immaculate bowlers perched far back upon the heads of glorious Bond Street dandies in lounge suits," he observes, "in the increase of the latter combination you may find the real rival to the frock coat and top hat convention. The London tailor, patterning after the Fifth Avenue model, has finally turned out what we call on this side a sack suit that completes a man as well-dressed as any who ever robed himself for a wedding . . . we of Fifth Avenue have by now almost routed the frock coat and top hat."

Top hats and frock coats seemed matched: they complemented each other, the tails of the coat thought to "balance" the height of the hat. The decline of one meant the decline of the other, since a bowler hat looked odd on a long coat, and top hats seemed overkill on a short one. Top hats and frock coats dwindled as a pair, each pulling the other down.

Few things are more difficult to imagine than the certainties of the day being swept away, however, and as soon as Pollard declares the frock coat and top hat "routed," he hedges, adding "there will always be frock coats . . . just as there will always be funerals and weddings" before yet again noting "a century of British convention has crumbled when, to-day, the Bond Street exquisite who parades his long coat and his high hat appears somehow outmoded, rococo."

As more men stopped wearing top hats, those who continued to wear them felt increasingly out of step and under scrutiny. The symbol of upper-class conformity had turned into a peccadillo. London newspaperman Alfred George Gardiner discovered this uncomfortable truth while walking to church one day around 1916:

A few days ago I went to a christening to make vows on behalf of the offspring of a gallant young officer now at the front. I conceived that the fitting thing on such an occasion was to wear a silk hat, and accordingly I took out the article, warmed it before the fire, and rubbed it with a hat pad until it was nice and shiny, put it on my head, and set out for the church. But I soon regretted the choice. I had no support from any one else present, and when later I got out of the Tube and walked down the Strand I found that I was a conspicuous person, which above all else I hate to be. My hat, I saw, was observed. Eyes were turned toward me with that mild curiosity with which one remarks any innocent oddity or vanity of the streets.

Gardiner nervously searches for reassurance from a passerby and is punished by whom he finds:

I became self-conscious and looked around for companionship, but as my eye travelled along the crowded pavement, I could see nothing but bowlers and trilbys and occasional straws. "Ah, here at last," said I, "is one coming." But a nearer view only completed my discomfiture, for it was one of those greasy-shiny hats which go with frayed trousers and broken boots, and which are the symbol of "better

days," of hopes that are dead, and "drinks" that dally, of a
social status that has gone and of a suburban villa that has
shrunk to a cubicle in a Rowton lodging house. I looked at
greasy-hat and greasy-hat looked at me, and in that
momentary glance of fellowship we agreed that we were
"out of it."

Safely at home, Gardiner tosses his hat into a closet, vowing to leave it there for all social events save an invitation from
the king. In his subsequent analysis, he blames "the psychology of the war." "The great tragedy has brought us down to
the bed-rock of things and has made us feel somehow that
ornament is out of place," he writes. "The top-hat is a falsity
in a world that has become a battlefield."

But he goes on to make the important distinction that the
war is not the primary cause, but merely "a knock-out blow"
to the tottering top hat, pushing men in a direction they are
eager to go. "Men have been only too glad to use the war as
an excuse for getting rid of an incubus," he writes. "We had
better not make too great a virtue of what is, after all, a comfortable change. Let us enjoy it without boasting."

A year after the 1918 armistice, the Prince of Wales, a
much-admired fashion plate, visited America. Touring Mount
Vernon, he came face-to-face with a photograph of Edward
VII, taken during his visit to the United States in 1860.

"I see grandfather wore a plug hat," the young prince
mused. "I wonder if I should have done the same."

That comment evoked a long, wistful editorial in the
November 16, 1919, *New York Times*. "There was a time
when everybody who was supposed to amount to something

wore a black coat and a tall hat," it said. "It was necessary. It was duty."

The writer cites the popularity of American straw hats as eroding the top-hat habit in England, but also blames the war. "We all know that the war broke up the strictness of the habit of evening dress," he wrote.

That same year came a second blow to the top hat in the United States: Prohibition. The standard urban evening of socializing at vast champagne dinners in glittering hotel ballrooms was replaced by furtive outings to dim, illegal basement bars.

"There were only a few speakeasies where a man could safely liquor up in formal garb," wrote *New York Times* columnist Meyer Berger. "Tweeds and business suits seemed to blend better with Scotch and soda, or visa versa."

During Prohibition, the top hat came to symbolize something that had little to do with wealth and nothing to do with elegance. "A high silk hat with a black mourning weed was at one time the symbol of blue-nosed clerical sanctimoniousness," observed man-about-town Lucius Beebe, "and as such was adopted by Rollin Kirby in his now famous 'Thou Shalt Not' prohibition cartoons."

By the end of the Harding administration, even the hat trade was predicting the end of the top hat. C. Harris, the secretary of the American Association of Wholesale Hatters, announced to the group's fifteenth semiannual convention in Atlantic City on January 10, 1923, that the era of sensible clothing following the war had doomed the top hat.

"For many years past there has been a gradual decline in the popularity of the high silk hat until at the present time what was once the most popular form of headgear is now on the high road to extinction," he said. "Whether this change has been influenced by the assertions of medical men that hard hats produce baldness I do not know."[8]

As top hats dwindled, they were replaced not only by the bowlers that initially cut into their popularity, but by a newer sort of hat, the fedora, a descendant of the slouch hats of the Civil War era. The fedora was a soft hat—a hat whose brim could be adjusted and crown creased to suit the wearer's taste—and its popularity can be seen as symbolic of the end of the equestrian age in America. Top hats and bowlers were both stiff hats; the bowler's creator had stood on the first one to test its strength. They were intended to protect the head of a man on horseback from low-hanging branches, which were not a problem to men in automobiles.

Just as the top hat seemed streamlined and modern to Leigh Hunt eighty years earlier, so the fedora was in step with what was seen as a general and welcome loosening of outdated Victorian rigidities.

"The 'tall hat' in this country, as in England, already has become a rare spectacle, and therefore a rather comic one," wrote the *New York Times* in 1923, predicting the top hat would end up "in the limbo of forgotten things." "Not much

---

[8]Scientists stoked the myth that hats cause baldness. In 1845, the *Boston Medical and Surgical Journal* presented the tendency of hair to linger at the back and sides of the head as proof that hats killed the hair under them. Dr. J. O. Conn, a surgeon at the United States Public Health and Maritime Hospital Service, published an article in 1909 in the *New York Medical Journal* claiming that tight hat bands were the "sole cause" of baldness in men. The false-hood held wide currency for decades.

beauty can be claimed for any kind of modern headgear for men, but the soft felt hat does have some possibilities of grace and picturesqueness, and certainly it is more comfortable than any of its rigidly unyielding rivals. Its associations, as yet, are perhaps a bit careless—even 'Bohemian'—but these are disappearing. As always, what 'everybody' does or wears is right, and the soft hat soon will have that claim to general approval and respect. . . . Thus, too, does the age progress from mere convention to good sense."

Another factor working against top hats had nothing to do with fashion. Whether stiff or collapsible, top hats were entirely handmade. Machines couldn't perform the complex tasks of finishing silk plush hats. As the boom years of the early 1920s unfolded, men's hats in general were enjoying wide popularity in the United States. But those in the silk hat trade complained that young men were balking at the lengthy apprenticeship their craft demanded, and the number of new workers dwindled. Thus, even at those rare moments when top hats threatened to surge back in popularity, the supply wasn't there. In 1924, for instance, Princeton sophomores had to cancel their traditional top-hat parade celebrating their ascension into the upper classes because they could not get their hands on six hundred top hats (though some of their elders saw this as more evidence of the laxity of youth, arguing that the sophomores could have rounded up the hats had they really tried).

One place in the 1920s where top hats were still religiously worn was in diplomatic circles, where the need to flawlessly represent one's home country while at the same time display respect for other nations demanded the zenith of formality be observed. That meant a high silk hat. "Diplomats would be as forlorn without one as they would be without their medals," the *New York Times* noted in 1928, adding simply, "The President of the United States has to wear one."

This diplomatic necessity posed a dilemma for one nation supposedly casting off the chains of class oppression. When it came time for the new Soviet Union to send a representative from the workers' paradise to the international finance conference in Genoa in 1922, the Bolsheviks fiercely debated the need for diplomat Georgii Tchitcherin to wear a silk top hat. The world eagerly followed the controversy.

"The Soviet Executive also decided that Tchitcherin must wear a silk hat," the *London Morning Post* reported. "The Commissary for Foreign Affairs emphatically protested against such bourgeois prejudice, but after a stormy meeting at which long speeches in favor of and against the silk hat were made by members of the moderate (pro-toppers) and extremist (anti-toppers) groups of the Communist Party, a division was taken which gave the pro-toppers an overwhelming majority and a resolution was passed making the wearing of a silk hat by Tchitcherin compulsory."

Americans, troubled by the implications of the Russian revolution, could not help being amused and relieved by this episode. The Soviet embrace of "the complete and shining symbol of homage to the conventions, to the thought itself, of the bourgeoisie" was hailed as a "good omen," and editorial writers praised "the harmonizing and uplifting influence of that true symbol of statesmanship—the silk hat."

Symbols cut both ways. If the top hat represented the dignified authority of government—the photos of Woodrow Wilson meeting his fellow leaders at the Versailles conference show a cluster of top hats—it could just as easily be used to symbolize the state's darker qualities. At the end of *The Trial,* Franz Kafka's 1923 novel of bureaucratic persecution, K's two assassins arrive on the evening of his thirty-first birthday in the form of a pair of men in "frockcoats, pallid and plump, with top-hats that were apparently irremovable."

"Tenth-rate old actors they send for me," K thinks, looking at his guests before asking them: "What theatre are you playing at?" Hats did not a dignitary make. While the top hats were still expected on the heads of diplomats and world leaders, the guardians of culture were not willing to extend the privilege to just anybody who happened to hold an office and have access to a silk hat. New Year's Day 1926 saw the inauguration of Jimmy Walker as mayor of New York City. Walker, a brash product of the corrupt Tammany Hall political machine, practically strutted into office. "Up the age-worn stone steps of the city hall he came, a slim, debonair young man, the acme of confidence and self-possession beneath a glossy silk topper and swinging a cane," wrote the *New York Daily News.* Seeing the Tammany tiger back on its throne after more than twenty years in exile prompted the *New York Times* to express scorn at the crowds of coarse yet momentarily top-hatted Democratic bosses, directing a bit of the psychoanalysis so popular at the time toward the "Tammany *arrivistes.*"

"To Tammany the stovepipe at is an outward and visible sign of an inward and spiritual grace," the *Times* wrote. "This symbolism has long dominated members of Tammany present at national conventions, or locally in evidence at the wedding of the daughter of some political magnate, or at the funeral of a lamented boss. Keen observers have long noted the phenomenon and wondered what its explanation might be. The thing seems simple. The silk hat is, to the untutored Tammany mind, the mark of a man not only struggling upward but 'arriving.' "

Joining attacks on unworthy wearers of the hat were assaults on the hat itself. No longer castigated as merely uncomfortable or unattractive, by the 1920s the top hat was excoriated for the people it represented. Top hats were a "vicious, vile and ugly symbol of the ungodly Victorian," thundered Westminster Abbey's Canon Donaldson in 1927.

Unsurprisingly, more men stopped wearing them, even in diplomatic circles.

In 1930, a London delegation to an international law conference in the United States returned home aghast. "We never had a chance in America to use our toppers—they were excess luggage," a delegate complained in the *London Telegraph,* which commiserated, "It menaced the very principle of the top hat, that it is a vestment of ceremony." The group had their top hats and swallowtail coats at the ready but, informed that President Hoover would receive them in a "sack suit," prudently left them in their hotel and greeted the president on his own terms.

That same year, an article in the *New York Times* headlined, "Melancholy Doom of the Silk Hat," noted sorrowfully that "the silk hat is on its way to extinction, along with the American bison."

The stock market crash and following Great Depression permanently chained top hats to wealth and its follies. Writers castigated the top hat in even harsher terms, as an object of class envy, though their tone suggested that this was nothing new.

"The hat remains to this day a symbol of arrogant wealth that is to the masses what a red flag is to an ill-tempered bull," Berger wrote in 1936. "The villain in the plush-and-brocade melodrama was hissed most warmly when he wore a silk headpiece. The hat was something the pit customers could hate with all their hearts."

As the Depression continued, a return of top hats would be now and again predicted; for all their negative associations, top hats coming back would still be a welcome sign of economic recovery. In Britain, the unexpected coronation of King George VI in May 1937 inspired momentary optimism among London haberdashers that top hats would once again be the rule of the day.

They wouldn't. At best, diplomats—such as John F. Kennedy's father, Joseph, whose generous support of Roosevelt had bought him the ambassadorship to Great Britain—continued to make calls in them. And the upper reaches of society still required them at operas and balls.

But politicians back home, their livelihoods depending on their ability to accurately gauge the public mood, knew better, and were quick to turn away from top hats. New York mayor Fiorella H. LaGuardia avoided top hats, even when propriety seemed to demand one. "Mayor LaGuardia sticks democratically to his black felt," read the caption of a photo of the mayor among dignitaries—all in top hats save himself—in the reviewing stand at a Saint Patrick's Day Parade. New York governor Alfred E. Smith, beloved in his brown bowler, was said to have lost support because he put on what he called, idiosyncratically, "a piffer," and joined the "high hat Liberty League crowd."

President Franklin D. Roosevelt looked sharp in a top hat and wore one from time to time at important events, such as the opening of the 1939 New York World's Fair. Yet he felt the need to claim that not only did he hate top hats, but he would avoid certain dinner parties rather than wear one.

Maybe that was sincere. Roosevelt had an affection for certain battered old fedoras he considered "lucky." He wore one particularly crumpled old felt hat during his first three presidential campaigns before donating it to a charity auction. He wore it with the brim turned up all around, providing an effective common-man counterbalance to his high-toned style and upper-crust speaking voice.

Roosevelt is the first president on record to blanch at the idea of wearing a top hat to his inauguration. After he defeated Hoover—who did not endear himself to the public by being seen wearing a top hat during the unsettling first years of the Depression—FDR faced a far more formidable adversary: Maximilian Fluegelman.

Max Fluegelman was president of M. Fluegelman Inc., the largest silk hat maker in New York City, which made it the largest silk hat maker in the country. An ambitious Romanian immigrant, he had crafted the inauguration silk hat for the past six presidents, going back to FDR's cousin, Theodore Roosevelt, whom he had known as police commissioner of New York. Fluegelman made sure that incoming presidents wore his hat and made sure that the press knew about it. He loved telling the story of how Woodrow Wilson once personally phoned him to complain that a top hat was too large. Fluegelman, showing a hat salesman's smooth repartee, joked, "Mr. President, maybe your head has shrunk a little," and Wilson replied, "Hardly. The head never shrinks when you're president. If anything, it may get a little bigger."

When he wasn't fitting presidents, Fluegelman did what he could to keep top hats in the public eye. Should a newspaper report the fashion's demise, he replied with a bristly letter to the editor.

"It is true that the silk hat is not selling in the quantities that it did forty or fifty years ago," he wrote in September 1930. "It is true that up to about ten years ago the silk hat dropped somewhat out of use during a semi-barbarous clothing era. But the fact is that ever since the war, and particularly in the last two years, silk hats and opera hats have come back on the tide of fashion more decidedly than any other article of headwear."

By then there were only twenty or so men trained to make silk hats in the country, and most of them worked for M. Fluegelman Inc. For a while Fluegelman tried to drum up publicity by giving a free top hat to the first June groom to get married at the New York City Hall, and though that made the newspapers, more often than not his company's name was omitted, and the result, rather than an increase in sales, was an increase in politicians pestering him for free hats. Eventually he dropped the practice.

Making sure the new president wore a silk hat at his inauguration, however, was an effort too crucial to be abandoned. In early 1933, Fluegelman went to Hyde Park to fit FDR, bearing a conform-measurer, a head-measuring apparatus that an observer described as "a hellish-looking device with movable wooden flanges. It is placed on the head and the flanges stretch until they take the shape of the skull; then a cork-lined flap on top of the device is snapped down and a lot of spikes mark the shape of the head on a piece of paper."

Roosevelt balked at putting the contraption on his head and said he might prefer a soft hat for the inauguration anyway.

"I have made silk hats for every president since Theodore Roosevelt, and you're going to wear one, too," Fluegelman, a hefty, mustachioed man, told him.

"But I really think I'll wear a soft one," FDR protested.

Fluegelman promised the president-elect he would make him two hats: the standard silk, with the finest white lining and FDR's name inscribed inside in gold letters, and a formal gray homburg.

"But the soft one was of such a frivolous shade of pearl gray," observed *The New Yorker,* which recorded the scene, "that Roosevelt didn't dare sport it on that dour day when he took the oath."

Despite being both wealthy and liable to wear a top hat himself, by his 1936 re-election campaign FDR, too, was using top hats as a metaphor for the hated rich. Here is a joke that FDR wrote and inserted into a campaign speech to illustrate Republican reaction to his blizzard of reforms:

In the summer of 1933, a nice old gentleman wearing a silk hat fell off the end of a pier. He was unable to swim. A friend ran down the pier, dived overboard and pulled him out; but the silk hat floated off with the tide. After the old gentleman had been revived, he was effusive in his thanks.

He praised his friend for saving his life. Today, three years after, the old gentleman is berating his friend because his silk hat was lost.

Notice that FDR never mentions the words *rich* or *wealthy* to describe the foundering old man. He didn't have to. "Wearing a silk hat" said it all.

Still, Roosevelt wore the new top hat that M. Fluegelman Inc. sent him for his second inaugural in 1937. That year the date of the ceremony shifted from March 4, when it had taken place since Washington's second inaugural in 1793, to January 20, a miserable, rainy day of piercing cold. The change was a victory for practicality over tradition, made to reduce the outgoing president's period as a lame duck, prompted by the agonizing interregnum in 1933, when in the span of four months the banks collapsed, FDR was shot at by a lunatic in Miami and narrowly missed,[9] and a desperate public began turning to the president-elect for hope and guidance long before Hoover left office.

FDR wore his third Fluegelman hat to his 1941 swearing-in. Former vice president John Nance Garner, who was being replaced by Henry Wallace, would have done well to have subjected himself to Fluegleman's conform-measurer. He borrowed his top hat from a friend, but it proved too tight to wear, and he was forced to hold it throughout the ceremony.

For his perfunctory wartime inauguration on January 20, 1945, an ailing FDR not only dispensed with his top hat, he

[9]Hit and mortally wounded was Chicago mayor Anton Cermak who, dying, bravely told Roosevelt, "I'm glad it was me and not you."

didn't wear any hat whatsoever at the ceremony, which was moved for his convenience from the Capitol steps to the White House South Portico. Roosevelt had less than three months to live, though he gamely removed his navy cape to deliver his 559-word inaugural address, the second shortest in history, with the requisite show of vigor. He stood, leaning heavily on the arm of his son James, and was in so much pain during the fifteen-minute ceremony that James worried he wouldn't be able to finish the speech. In the depth of war, no fuss was made over FDR's fashion choice. It was not considered a break in the top hat tradition and was quickly forgotten, though the press did note without comment the presence of just two top hats in the inauguration crowd: one on New Hampshire governor Charles M. Dale, the other on comedian Georgie Jessel.

If World War I helped crack the tradition of top hats, then the end of World War II found them, to borrow Leigh Hunt's description of cocked hats a century earlier, "sunk into the mock-heroic." Max Fluegelman died in 1945. New York's once-vibrant silk hat industry was reduced to a handful of elderly hatters carrying on as best they could at M. Fluegelman Inc. The company's limited postwar business depended heavily on the presence in New York of the United Nations headquarters and its South American diplomats, who strove to demonstrate their legitimacy through a tendency to "cling to strictly formal headgear for public appearances." Even then, sales ranged between two to four tops hats a month. The hansom cabdrivers taking tourists and lovers around Central Park also wore top hats, for nostalgia value, but their income demanded that they purchase their top hats used for a dollar or two, rather than new from M. Fluegelman Inc. for forty dollars. Every thrift store and secondhand shop offered top hats, thanks to the generalized shedding of silk hats by the well-to-do at midcentury. This abandonment of top hats can be seen reflected in the popular culture of the time by cartoon hoboes, sad clowns, and snowmen wearing silk hats, their tops inevitably half punched out. (This group of unexpected top hat wearers should be distinguished from the American Indians and bone-nosed Africans who were given top hats by humorists a half century earlier as an attempt at some kind of wry comment on class.)

Otherwise, what remained from a century and a half of popularity were two dueling images: Fred Astaire and the top hat as the final frosting in the complete ensemble of deco Manhattan sophistication, and, as a grim antipode, the Soviet propaganda model of the top hat as decadent dunce cap atop the bloated head of a piggish capitalist, clutching moneybags emblazoned with dollar signs. He could hardly be portrayed without it.

Elegance and money. You can see the top hat used to convey each idea in the commercial world. Planters put a top hat on its Mr. Peanut character to lend an air of sophistication to a product that struck people as hopelessly low class—food for animals and the poor—particularly when compared to actual nuts such as cashews or almonds. And Parker Bros. stuck a top hat on its little mustachioed Uncle Bucks character in Monopoly to show that he has grown rich on real estate.

Somewhere between the two symbolic extremes, however, room did remain for sincere use, such as at the inauguration of

Harry S. Truman in 1949. The event was noted for its extravagance—the Republican Congress, certain of a Dewey victory that would end sixteen years of Democratic rule, had splurged when appropriating money for the festivities, largess which Truman gleefully spent.

Truman was a fastidious man who never went outdoors without a hat, worn perfectly level on his head. That said, he was not immune to his share of husbandly grumbling about the demands of diplomatic fashion. "I hate to go," Truman wrote to his wife just before leaving for the Potsdam summit conference in 1945. "I have to take my Negro preacher coat and striped pants, tails, tux, winter clothes, and spring ones, high hat, soft hat and derby. It'll be a circus sure enough."

But, for Truman, duty trumped personal preference. A man needed his hat. The day Franklin Roosevelt died, Truman was tracked down via telephone enjoying his 5 PM bourbon with Sam Rayburn in the Capitol. Told he should get to the White House as "quickly and as quietly" as possible, Truman left Rayburn's office at a run, then took a brief detour upstairs to his office in order to retrieve his hat. He wasn't going to face the weight of the world naked.

That was characteristic of Truman. He once sold hats in a men's furnishing store and believed in wearing the right hat for the right occasion. He was "famous . . . for the astonishing variety of his hats," from jaunty golf caps to wide summer Panamas, with the stray pith helmet and Shriner's fez tossed in. There was no reason he would fail to wear a silk top hat at his own hard-won inauguration, and did so without protest or apparent contemplation. And there was still a general nostalgic warmth regarding toppers.

"After all," Henry Luce's *Time* magazine reasoned, trying to find a ray of light in Truman's unexpected inauguration, "it was the nearest thing the U.S. had to a coronation, a rare chance for the republic's leaders to turn out in a top hat."

Thus it fell upon Dwight D. Eisenhower, who had already influenced fashion with his namesake short jacket, to truly break with tradition in early 1953.

Consistent with his Kansas farm roots and self-effacing personality, Eisenhower had requested his inauguration ceremonies be "plain and simple." The parade, Eisenhower decreed, would be no more than two hours long. He described the ceremony as "almost a sacred affair" and ordered it be presented with the utmost dignity.

Thus he was appalled to find himself facing a "three-day extravaganza" featuring two balls and a parade with not one but three elephants and "10 miles of floats, cowboys, Indians, State Governors, an Eskimo dog team and almost anything you can mention."

Embarrassed at how plans for the snowballing public spectacle diverged from his initial promise of solemnity, Eisenhower told friends that he had to draw the line somewhere. He drew it at hats.

On January 12, 1953, he convened the first cabinet meeting ever held by a president-elect—a luncheon at New York's Hotel Commodore. Eisenhower read his inauguration address and, when it met with dutiful acclaim, he told the group that he didn't read it to them for their praise, but for their criticism. They should "tear it to pieces."

When it came time to discuss the festivities, however, Eisenhower, sitting at the head of the U-shaped table, was less interested in feedback. "I know more about this parade business than most people," he began. He told the assembly—including vice president–elect Nixon and Secretary of State–designate John Foster Dulles—that he had put up with many things to be elected president, and he would no doubt have to put up with many more, but he'd be damned if he was going to parade down Pennsylvania Avenue in a top hat. The idea of wearing a less formal hat had already been floated, he continued, and though certain members of Congress voiced their disapproval, it was going forward anyway.

"We got a bit of a blink from some of the Congressional delegations, saying they must wear silk hats," Eisenhower said. "They are going to be the silk-hat boys. And we will wear dark Homburgs."

Several incoming cabinet members, some of whom had already bought their top hats, objected to this breach of tradition, resulting in a "prolonged discussion of what type of hats to wear." Eisenhower, in good military style, later smoothed over the debate.

"I have not had a single incoming Cabinet officer or any of the Senators or members of Congress disagree with the proposal, even by a lifted eyebrow, for simplifying man's formal dress," he claimed.

And by the time he sat down to write his memoirs, dissent had almost vanished.

"There was talk about headgear," Eisenhower wrote of the Commodore meeting. "I suggested that we wear simple Homburg hats. It was said that tall silk hats were the tradition, and I answered that if we were worried about what had been done in the years before, we could wear tricornered hats and knee breeches."

Ike's decision, made public exactly one week before the event, "caused high consternation among officials who will attend the ceremony" who "not wishing to appear out-of-step or overdressed" ditched their top hats and went scrambling for homburgs. For several days after the announcement, newspapers continued to print clothing store advertisements offering silk hats "for the men who will attend the inauguration." Eisenhower defended his move.

"I am not attempting to change the styles for America," Eisenhower wrote in a memorandum. "But I believe the above would be more practical and businesslike than to cling too closely to the styles of 1900. It would certainly be more convenient in getting in and out of modern automobiles."

The press approved. "All he did was decide to wear a comfortable hat," reasoned *Business Week*. "Like many another American male before him, he'd reached the conclusion that he'd look and feel silly in a high silk hat."

One particular American did object, strongly—the outgoing president—though it is unclear how much of Truman's reaction was offended fashion sense and how much was wounded pride.

Reporters immediately tried to bait the volatile Truman with Eisenhower's decision, but Truman batted away the issue when it was brought up at his 324th and final presidential press conference.

"I don't want to get into any hat controversy," he said, managing a chuckle. "I will wear anything that is decent and that I can go outdoors in."

Underneath this pleasant mask, however, Truman was seething. "The president should wear the most formal of formal clothes when he's going to the inauguration," Truman complained, years later. There was more to this than hats, of course. He and Eisenhower initially had a good relationship after World War II, with Truman even considering stepping aside and running as Ike's vice presidential candidate. But eventually Eisenhower declared himself a Republican, and though Truman wasn't running, the Republicans tried to tar him as an incompetent and a Communist appeaser. Truman had lashed out at Eisenhower during the campaign, mocking his vow to go to Korea if elected, and condemning him for not supporting General George C. Marshall when Joseph McCarthy and his henchman, Indiana senator William Jenner, called him a traitor. Eisenhower, for his part, delivered a series of snubs to Truman, which would culminate in his refusing the customary pause for coffee at the White House just before the inauguration. Truman felt that as the sitting president, *he* should set the fashion tone at the inaugural, not the usurper. The feud and Truman's well-exercised sense of outrage inflamed the insult of not being consulted on the hat business into a hurt he nursed for years. "I sincerely hope you'll wear a homburg hat and a short coat as you did in 1953 at the inauguration," he sneered in the midst of a sarcastic blast at Eisenhower written just before Ike's second inauguration in 1957, one of the many choleric letters Truman penned and then in a cooler moment decided to file instead of send.

If Eisenhower's homburg was nettlesome to Truman, it was seen as a disaster by the die-hards at M. Fluegelman Inc. Mortimer Loeb, Max Fluegelman's successor and brother-in-law, had already manufactured a top hat for Eisenhower: he made it before the election, perhaps an act of hubris, and kept it on display in a glass case in his store, awaiting the general's head size. Just weeks before Eisenhower's announcement, Loeb was happily chatting with the press about the history of top hats, confident that Eisenhower would wear one. When the president-elect decided he wouldn't, Loeb recognized the moment as a mortal blow and frantically tried to get through to Eisenhower to make a personal appeal.

"We thought we could convince him not only of the inherent beauty of silk hats but of their propriety on such an occasion," Loeb said. But he was kept from pestering Eisenhower directly. "After talking to several of his aides, we realized that the General was definitely off silk," Loeb said. Trying to salvage the situation, he offered to custom-make a homburg for Eisenhower, but again was rebuffed. "His aides said not to bother," Loeb recounted sadly. "He already had plenty of hats."

M. Fluegelman Inc. remained gracious, however, even in defeat. "We don't hold any grudge against the General," Loeb said. "We just feel he's breaking a fine tradition, that's all."

The hat industry put a brighter spin on the matter, noting the boost in popularity of homburgs inspired by Eisenhower, even in hinterlands such as Iowa and North Carolina "where *nobody* ever wore a homburg before." The Hat Research

Foundation's Warren S. Smith suggested that Eisenhower actually wasn't dressing down from top hats, but up from the typical dishabille of the Democrats.

"For the past 15 or 20 years, the trend in Washington has been all toward casualness, if casualness isn't too kind a word," he said. "The New Deal influence, I call it. Those sloppy Harvard Law School graduates! All day long with no garters,[10] and maybe even no necktie, and at night they'd be wearing any kind of hat with their tails."

The inauguration was Eisenhower's introduction to the limits of presidential power. The dignified two-hour parade of his imaginings in real life clocked in at a little more than five hours—twenty-seven thousand marchers, including cowboy Monte Montana on horseback, who, with the permission of the Secret Service, tossed his lasso around Eisenhower's shoulders.

In the audience watching the carnival was a twenty-three-year-old *Washington Times Herald* reporter who would become First Lady precisely eight years later. Jacqueline Bouvier had a date that evening with Jack Kennedy to attend Eisenhower's inaugural ball, and she recorded the holiday aspects of the crowd, with its picnic lunches and hot dog venders, in an article illustrated by her own whimsical drawings. Her main interest was clearly with the well-heeled European guests, the "mustachioed ambassadors," and their "sleek black Rolls Royces." She also noticed their headgear.

"Homburg hats were definitely the order of the day," Bou-

---

[10] In the years before elastic hosiery was perfected, men wore garters to hold up their socks.

vier wrote. "Yet two of the most dapper ambassadors were hat-less. French Ambassador Bonnet and Belgian Ambassador Sil-vercruys sat bareheaded in a box together, bundled up in coats and mufflers. Behind them, Spanish Ambassador Lequerica was resplendent in a fur collared coat, and, of course, a homburg."

A lone tall silk hat was seen at Eisenhower's inaugural, perched in mute protest atop the head of seventy-five-year-old Senator Carl Hayden, the famously loyal, famously closed-mouthed Arizona Democrat, one of the members of Joint Congressional Inaugural Committee who had blinked when Eisenhower first proposed homburgs.

Still, the top hat was not quite dead. At the opening of the 1954 season of New York's Metropolitan Opera, hatcheck attendants counted forty-one silk hats in the checkrooms, and estimated there were another seventy-five other toppers "hiding out in the boxes." At the first White House state dinner given for the diplomatic corps that fall, 20 percent of the men wore silk hats, the rest wore homburgs, in a nod to Eisenhower, or arrived bareheaded.

Hope flickered among the embers at M. Fluegelman Inc. At mid-decade, Meyer Berger checked in on Loeb and found him "still dazed by the shock of 1953's rebuff," but clinging to the dream that Eisenhower would see the light regarding top hats for his second inauguration.

"Maybe by then," Loeb said wistfully, "he will change his mind."

He didn't.

* * *

Given Eisenhower's public break with precedent, the trail was blazed for one of those former "sloppy Harvard" graduates,

John F. Kennedy, to abandon it, had he desired. If he didn't dispense with a hat altogether, as was his widely acknowledged preference, the path of least resistance would have been for Kennedy to follow Eisenhower's lead and wear a homburg. Deciding to wear a top hat at his inauguration was the least likely option, but made sense in retrospect.

Though Kennedy had been urged by incoming cabinet members Arthur Goldberg and Abraham Ribicoff to wear a hat as a favor to his labor supporters, it was his tailor, Sam Harris, who advised him as to what kind of hat that should be.

Harris, a "high-class East Side tailor," had fitted Kennedy for a dozen years, and was kept out of the limelight all that time. But November's flap over Kennedy's raft of Savile Row suits made it seem a good idea to give his American tailor a higher profile. Harris was trotted out before the press, describing the cut of Kennedy's suits—ultraconservative—claiming credit for pushing Kennedy toward something a little sportier and, to Kennedy's embarrassment and horror, mentioning that his inaugural suit had to be let out a bit because Kennedy had put on weight.

He also took credit for the style of Kennedy's inaugural outfit. Harris told *Newsweek* he "advised Kennedy on the proper uniform for the inaugural—Oxford gray coat, light pearl gray waistcoat, and worsted gray striped trousers." Traditionally, an ascot tie would be worn with that, but Kennedy preferred a four-in-hand. And though Harris did not sell hats, he told Kennedy there was only one hat to wear with that ensemble. The inseparable bond between the top hat and the long coat, which had done so much to pull the top hat down half a century earlier, was now pulling it out of its gathering oblivion for a final moment in the spotlight.

"You're going to wear a topper," Harris said.

"Okay," Kennedy replied. "I'll wear a topper."

Kennedy's decision, his sudden lurch from vigorous hatlessness to the most formal hat in existence short of a miter, was front-page news, though news that was passed along without any attempt at analysis. Nobody asked Kennedy to explain his decision, though reporters did run the choice by Harry Truman, who was still mad at Eisenhower. Stopped on his morning walk by reporters the day after Christmas 1960, Truman said that it was going to be good to finally have a "working president" in the White House. Asked if Kennedy's choice of hat was the "right headgear" for the inauguration, Truman said it was, then took the opportunity to again chastise Eisenhower for his fashion lapse, though he couldn't bring himself to mention his successor's name.

"The other fellow didn't know what headgear to wear," he said. "It didn't make any difference. He got inaugurated anyway."

Since Kennedy's mild acquiescence, quoted by Harris, is his sole recorded comment on the matter, a little speculation as to motive might be in order. Throughout his career Kennedy had deflated the obvious liability of being seen as a son of wealth by taking a jesting view of himself: at the 1958 Gridiron dinner he joked in a speech that his father had warned him not to buy a single vote more than was necessary. "I'm not paying for a landslide," Kennedy had the old man say. Thus, wearing a top hat, the ridiculed symbol of the rich, could be seen as the kind of slyly self-deprecating in-joke Kennedy savored. He hadn't worn a top hat at his elegant Hyannis Port wedding eight years earlier.

But Kennedy's humor did not extend to donning costumes. It is possible that he particularly disliked the homburg, a hat associated with seniority—in hat ads, the young men were given fedoras, while dignified older men, inevitably shown with white hair and thin mustaches, wore homburgs. With sufficient coaxing Kennedy might pose wearing a fedora, but he never put a homburg on his head with photographers around. The hat was also closely associated with Eisenhower, and Kennedy tried to distance himself from his predecessor, going so far as to avoid being photographed golfing, a recreation that Ike had been criticized for indulging to excess. Kennedy eyed the putting green Eisenhower had installed outside the Oval Office but never used it.

Or perhaps Kennedy, the astute politician, sensed a national thirst for elegance and pageantry, sharpened by two terms of down-home living with good old Ike and his Zane Grey novels and his dinners with Mamie eaten off TV trays.

"By 1960, the country was parched for ceremony," wrote Wilifred Sheen. "After eight years of stag lunches at the White House and golfing weekends with businessmen and nothing but businessmen; or, to put it another way, after so many years of looking at John Foster Dulles—the country fairly craved color and gaiety."

Kennedy also belonged to an upward striving Boston clan of Irish-Catholic Democrats. Top hats ran in his family.

"My father wore top hats and always looked great in them

and also my grandfather Honey Fitz," said Senator Edward Kennedy. "My mother just loved them!"

They were exactly the kind of "arrivistes" that the *New York Times* had mocked for their affection for wearing top hats to formalize occasions, and while realization of this no doubt would have horrified Kennedy, wearing a top hat to a special event was viewed as typical behavior for an Irish-Catholic politician. When Mamie Eisenhower saw her husband in his top hat on the day of the Kennedy inauguration, she burst out laughing and said, "He looks just like Paddy the Irishman!"

Kennedy wouldn't have indulged that impulse toward grandiose formality—at least not consciously. He may simply have liked top hats, despite his general avoidance of ordinary headwear. There is evidence of this. In 1959, Kennedy was named by the Harvard Alumni Association to its Board of Overseers, a position he coveted in the hopes of being the first Catholic named to the board (he wasn't; he was the second). Kennedy's private secretary, Evelyn Lincoln, records his reaction to being told the news:

"A smile spread across his face . . . then with a twinkle in his eye, the Senator said to me, 'This means that I will have to wear a top hat at the commencement exercises next June. Be sure to order one for me.'" She did.

"When I brought the hat into the office the Senator was away," she continues. "But each of the men in the office tried it on and everyone thought it looked all right. When the Senator came in he put it on and rushed to a mirror. In a moment he came back beaming. Like a little boy wearing his first 'grown-up' clothes, the Senator sat at his desk the rest of the afternoon and never once took off that top hat." The following June, he wore his top hat, with striped trousers and a cutaway coat, to the 1960 Harvard commencement exercises. And in her description of the commotion-filled days before the inauguration, Evelyn Lincoln refers to Kennedy's top hat as both "precious" and "beloved."

That does not sound like a man who hated top hats. And one should remember that to Kennedy, who as a young man accompanied his father to London when the elder Kennedy became ambassador to the Court of Saint James, a top hat was indeed among "his first 'grown-up' clothes." Nor was he the only Kennedy to own his own top hat. A close look at the photos of Bobby Kennedy at his brother's inauguration reveals that his hat is not new from the box, but well worn and marred with scuffs. While Ted Kennedy "wasn't all that comfortable wearing a top hat" to the ceremony, he saw it as "part of that special celebration that seemed right for the occasion."

It might also have been a matter so trivial to the president-elect that, with all he had on his mind, he didn't give it much thought. A few days before the inauguration, according to Evelyn Lincoln, he paused from dictating letters and put on a hat that a well-wisher had sent.

"Now this hat fits," he said. "What are we going to do about my hat?" Lincoln reminded him that he had his top hat from the Harvard Board of Overseers or else "some hat men were going to meet with him in New York in a few days."

The hat industry's representative indeed arrived at the Carlyle Hotel in New York, where Kennedy went to relax just before the inauguration. William Schnautz, a Norwalk, Connecticut, hatter in the Cavanagh division of the Hat Corporation of America, left Kennedy two hats. He told the phalanx of reporters camped in the lobby the hats were gifts from the Hat Corporation of America and the United Hatters, Cap and Millinery Workers. They were size $7^1/2$; a $7^5/8$ hat Schnautz had sent previously was too big. One was five and a half inches high, and the other ("our new model") was five inches high.

If Eisenhower or Nixon felt any Trumanesque bitterness regarding Kennedy's decision, they wisely kept it to themselves and agreed to wear toppers. The rest of the Republicans, however, decided to "come as they please," and a few took the opportunity to engage in public pondering over whether to follow Kennedy's lead. Illinois Republican senator Everett Dirksen said he "could come either way" but that he'd leave his decision to "a higher authority," meaning his wife. Invariably, Republicans found a reason to dress down, most preferring dark business suits, one columnist noted, "as to a wake." Senator George Aiken, a Vermont Republican, said he feared his constituency would misunderstand if he dressed up, though he did let a trace of sour grapes seep through. "We'll wear our own clothes," he said. "This is an inauguration, not a coronation."

Democrats also refrained from fancy dress. "I just don't like those tail coats," said Representative Carl Albert, a Democrat from Oklahoma and the future Speaker of the House.

The return to top hats offered a chance for eccentrics to preen in the publicity they loved. In Chicago, White Sox owner Bill Veeck announced that though he had received an invitation "all engraved—very official" to the inaugural ball, the formal dictates would prevent the famously casual Veeck from attending.

"Not only do I not have a tie," Veeck said, "I don't have a high hat either. So I'm ruled off on two counts." The *Chicago Daily News* snapped at the bait by printing a doctored photograph of Veeck in top hat and white tie so "those attending the Inaugural Ball in Washington can see what they'll be missing." Actually, Veeck looked quite dapper.

On the sunny, cold morning of his inauguration, Kennedy returned from church and changed into his inauguration suit. The rumor—now generally accepted as fact—was that he wore long underwear under his formal clothes to keep out the cold. There was a momentary crisis, not over hats, but over his detachable wing collar. Because of his weight gain, the collar set out didn't fit. A flunky was quickly dispatched to get one of his father's collars, but by the time he returned a larger collar had been found in the back of a bureau drawer. Properly dressed for the occasion, Kennedy stepped out of his front door. Wearing light leather gloves and a dark overcoat, his shiny black silk top hat firmly atop his head and his wife, Jacqueline, by his side, holding a fur muff, Kennedy left his home on N Street, bound for his new residence, the White House.

Chapter 3

"Somebody had to do something."

As frail, white-haired, eighty-six-year-old New England poet Robert Frost began to speak, the inauguration threatened to veer toward disaster. Already, a motor used to raise and lower the podium had shorted out, sending smoke wafting from under the dais during Richard Cardinal Cushing's benediction. Concern flashed over the faces of Mamie Eisenhower, her husband, and Jacqueline Kennedy. But John F. Kennedy kept his features set in a smile as security men eventually smothered the fire, though his hand rubbed reflexively—again and again and again—over the nap of the top hat he kept balanced on his knee. Afraid that the smoke might be from a fizzling bomb, the cardinal read his prayer with agonizing slowness, determined that it would be he and not Jack Kennedy who took the blast.

Kennedy wanted culture in his White House and intended to establish that fact immediately, in the first minutes of his inauguration. That's why Frost was there. No one had ever included a poet in a presidential inauguration before, but that did not deter Kennedy—he knew the public would embrace Frost's presence, and once again he was right. Kennedy had asked his favorite poet to compose something new, specially for the ceremony. Frost at first declined, observing that "occasional poetry" was not his strong suit. He instead suggested reading his "The Gift Outright" but ended up writing a new dedicatory poem whose opening lines indicate his original instincts had been sound. "Summoning artists to participate," he read, haltingly. "In the august occasions of the state . . . seems something for us to celebrate."

That's as far as he got. The sunlight was blazing—mockingly so, given the harsh twenty-two-degree cold and razor wind—and it blinded the old man. He struggled to read his own words. As Frost muttered at the microphone, and the dignity of the occasion teetered toward farce, Lyndon Johnson sprang to his feet, stepped forward, and gallantly tried to shield the poet's pages from the sun with his top hat, on the poet's left, while another man on the platform stepped around and tried to do the same thing, with a fedora, from the right.

The hats didn't help, and the poet waved the vice president away. Frost ended up salvaging the moment by shifting to "The Gift Outright," a better poem he could recite by memory.

Still, Johnson's attempt at shading the pages was the sort of spontaneous practical application that hats were perfectly suited for. One of the basic functions of a hat is to act as a shield—from the sun, from the rain, from the wind. So it was natural to extend that use. A man who wanted to sleep in a public place—on a train, in a bus station—would tip his hat forward, over his eyes, to afford himself a little darkness. The same gesture helped when the world became too overwhelming. Even Kennedy was once spotted by James Reston doing just that, covering his eyes with his hat "like a beaten man" after his exasperating meeting with Khrushchev in Vienna.

Hats could also shield more than the light. They could conceal your identity: the brim could be pulled down low, almost like a mask. If that wasn't sufficiently anonymous, you could simply remove the hat and cover your entire face with it. When famed New York low-life photographer Weegee stuck his Speed Graphic in the back of a police van, two crooks there shielded their faces with their hats before he could click the shutter. Criminals today are forced to hike their shirts or jackets awkwardly over their heads when confronted with press photographers, but for decades hats were a ready device to keep one's mug out of the newspapers. "No, no Bill," a man in a 1950s *New Yorker* cartoon admonishes his companion who is covering his face with a hat as they descend the stairs of a building toward a gaggle of press photographers. "You're a commissioner now."

Guilty faces were not the only signs of sin hats covered. If the brim of a hat is a shield, then its crown is a bowl and it, too, could conceal much. Generations of young women learned to avoid sitting next to men on trains and buses whose hats were perched too precisely in the middle of their laps. Policemen put their own hats to similar use when apprehending naked culprits, with the arresting officer's cap affording a fig leaf of modesty until a blanket could be found.

A hat could also be an accomplice to theft, carefully placed over something you wished to take later when the coast was clear. Or, caught red-handed, your loot could be placed on your head and quickly hidden under your hat, such as Tom

Sawyer does when Aunt Polly catches him filching food in the basement in *The Adventures of Huckleberry Finn* (the loot, unfortunately for Tom, is butter, and he ends up forced into a warm room crowded with farmers, the butter slowly melting atop his head, a gag that Twain repeats with a candle in *Innocents Abroad*). In medieval times, people would conceal money in their hats. They were also ideal for smugglers: when the steamship *City of Washington* docked at New York in October 1883, customs officers arrested a passenger and found packages containing 533 diamonds, rubies, sapphires, and other precious stones hidden in his hat.

Right side up, the crown of a hat hid things. Upside down, it held them in open view as a container. It is said that John L. Sullivan, the Gilded Age boxer, used his custom-made Collins & Fairbanks top hat to chill bottles of champagne. John Adams used his to hold corn for his horse's feed, and Walt Whitman was observed using his as a bowl for his own dinner, though we assume that the meal was something like apples or hard cheese and not beef stew. But who knows? In *Oliver Twist*, the Artful Dodger produces a breakfast of hot rolls and ham out of the crown of his hat.

Hats could hold dinner *after* consumption as well. Lucius Beebe related the following in his *San Francisco Chronicle* column:

New York first nighters of the Thirties still recall the Broadway opening at which an afternoon newspaper critic, who was widely known for his addiction to the bottle, was taken in wine during the performance and staggered up the aisle using his opera hat as a receptacle for emesis. A witty old lady in a front seat remarked audibly that "she did wish those critics would wait til they got to their office to write their reviews."

Hats served as buckets in more dire emergencies as well. When three debutantes and their dates left a charity ball at Chicago's Century of Progress fair in June 1934, they headed up the lake in a thirty-foot motor boat. The boat sprang a leak, but the group, "bailing frantically" with their hats, kept the boat afloat long enough to make the beach.

The most famous user of a hat to store and carry things was Abraham Lincoln who, like many backwoods lawyers, traveled too much on horseback to let the volume of his hat go to waste. "My hat, where I carry most all my packages," he wrote in a letter in 1849. He used it as a desk and filing cabinet, tucking papers inside—a habit he acquired when he was postmaster in New Salem in 1833, carrying the mail around in his hat, distributing it to the people he met.

If a thought struck Lincoln, he would write it down "on a small slip of paper and put it in his hat, where he carried quite all his plunder, checkbook for the bank account, letters answered and unanswered, handkerchief, etc.," according to William Herndon, his third law partner.

This system had certain drawbacks, such as the acquisition of new hats.

"I am shamed of not sooner answering your letter," Lincoln wrote to Richard S. Thomas in 1850. "When I received the letter I put it in my old hat, and buying a new one the next day, the old one was set aside, and so the letter was lost sight of for a time."[1]

It is tempting to credit (or blame) the practice of lawyers removing papers from their hats—sometimes a considerable number of papers and sometimes with a dramatic flourish—as the inspiration for the popular magician's act of pulling bouquets, rabbits, and other objects out of a hat. But with Louis Comte pulling rabbits from his hat onstage in Paris as early as 1814, the idea might very well have flowed the other way, from art to life.

Lawyers and magicians were not alone in keeping things in their hats. Doctors often kept their stethoscopes in their hats. Sigmund Freud had a field day with a patient who dreamed of her physician removing his stethoscope from his hat, which of course Freud viewed as a snakelike object being withdrawn from an article of clothing. Other professions made use of hats, too. "Up to the late 1870s country children knew of quaint, fearsomely respectable real estate men, lawyers and money lenders who used their tiled beavers or tall silks as filing cabinets and safes," the *New York Times* wrote in 1931. "Years afterward, in melodrama, the villain who entered to foreclose the mortgage would still draw the pernicious documents from the recesses of his stovepipe."

The article, written to mark the safe's centennial, noted that there were none in America prior to 1831. Valuable doc-

---

[1] There is a story that Lincoln removed the Emancipation Proclamation from his hat the day he presented it to his cabinet but, alas, the story is not substantiated in the historical records.

uments had to be kept close at hand, much in the way early-nineteenth-century Kentucky real estate king Thomas Duckham kept track of his acquisitions:

> He is still remembered by a few who saw him in later years—a strange figure—a little elderly gentleman still using as headgear an old-fashioned beaver stovepipe hat. This was his safe, in which he stored the title deeds to his property. The deeds lay next to his head, curved and bent to fit his skull, and became molded so with the long years of confinement.

As a container, a hat was good for drawing lots: filled with slips of paper and held above eye level, a rough fairness could be guaranteed. According to the CBS producer who ran the TV debates between Kennedy and Nixon, that's how the panelists were selected. Names of contending reporters were written on bar napkins and then drawn out of a hat. The practice continues, particularly in political circles, where the law sometimes requires deadlocks to be broken by chance. In 2001, the Illinois secretary of state picked the ninth member of a committee evenly divided between Democrats and Republicans by drawing a name out of a replica of the hat that Lincoln wore to Ford's Theatre the night he was assassinated.

A hat was also was a collection plate. "Christmas is coming, the geese are getting fat," begins the English beggar's rhyme. "Please to put a penny in the old man's hat / If you haven't got a penny, a ha'penny will do / If you haven't got a ha'penny, God bless you!"

At the end of a street performance, a musician would doff his hat in acknowledgment of the applause and then pass it around for coins. "We would pass the hat and divvy up," remembered Louis Armstrong, of his days playing trumpet on street corners.

Beggars, now also generally hatless, have shifted to paper cups. But the familiar habit of passing the hat at the end of a street performance has survived the decline of hats; headgear remains a useful prop for entertainers, something that can be juggled and flipped and deftly propelled off one's foot onto one's head. A hat also remains a quick way to give personality to a character; there was a forgotten vaudeville entertainment known as "chapeaugraphy," which consisted of creating a variety of types of hats and characters by twisting a simple crownless brim, a technique that was the basis of entire performances and produced its share of stars.

Another primary function of the hat was to identify a person—not only by its style and cut, but by its mere presence. A hat suggested there was a head underneath. In tall brush, members of the Lewis & Clark party would reveal their positions, or try to, by placing their hats on the ends of their muskets and holding them high in the air. Winston Churchill did the same thing while touring bombed-out sections of London during World War II, removing his hat, putting it on the end of his cane, and then holding it high over his head so people could see him.

The trick of putting a hat on a stick or a rifle muzzle and using it to draw the fire of an enemy seems like a bit of movie cleverness today, but it was actually used in the days when priming and loading guns took some time.

"In the Peninsular war, one of the 93d and a French infantryman came upon one another in a wood," wrote John Doran. "As their pieces were unloaded, they both rushed to the cover of a tree, in order to put their muskets in deadly order; but this done, neither was inclined to look out, lest the other should be beforehand with him, and let fly. At length the Highlander quietly put his feathered hat on the end of his piece, and held it a little beyond the tree, as though a head was in it, looking out. At the same moment the impatient Frenchman reconnoitered, saw his supposed advantage, and, from his rifle, sent a ball through his adversary's bonnet; thereupon the bonny Scot calmly advanced with his loaded piece, and took his enemy prisoner without difficulty."

A traveling salesman wouldn't have to spend too many nights alone with a pack of playing cards to come up with the game of tossing cards into a hat. While still played at children's birthday parties, the game, like the top hat, survives mostly as an image, an immediate way to convey that a character is bored and killing time.

In the film *Groundhog Day,* the characters played by Bill Murray and Andie MacDowell at one point sit in a hotel room and toss cards into a hat. Yet Murray is bareheaded for the entire movie—except for a single moment when he is jokingly costumed as the High Plains Drifter—even though much of it takes place outdoors on a very cold February 2. Since he is playing a TV weatherman, that detail is true to life: TV reporters tend to avoid wearing hats on camera, despite standing outside in extreme weather, since they have found that any hat they wear is an invitation for comment and ridicule.

Another little game with symbolic value was tossing your hat onto a peg. Hats needed to be hung up, and flinging one's hat successfully onto a hook from a small distance was a feat that a man could look upon with satisfaction, a minor triumph to start the day at the office. In movies and TV shows, the successfully tossed hat was a code to show that fate was smiling upon a certain character. James Bond, arriving at headquarters to receive his latest assignment from M, would toss his hat squarely onto the hat stand in Miss Moneypenny's office, a wink to the audience that whatever troubles might be in store for Bond, he would come through with aplomb.

While a deck of cards or a hook was not always available to play with, a man's hat usually was, and that was probably its greatest practical value of all. A hat was like a cigarette: it gave a man something to do with his hands. It could be adjusted, or taken off and fiddled with, its brim rubbed, its top molded, its lining gazed into, a speck of dust removed from its crown. Many a nervous swain, in movies and in real life, crushed his own hat into a ball trying to stammer out his feelings for his beloved.

A man out in public always had something to do if he had a hat with him. After several failed attempts to make small talk with the icy, bitter Herbert Hoover during the ride to the Capitol for his first inauguration, Franklin D. Roosevelt turned his attention to his hat.

"I said to myself, 'Spinach!' Protocol or no protocol, somebody had to do something," FDR later told his secretary, Grace Tully. "The two of us simply couldn't sit there on our hands, ignoring each other and everybody else. So I began to wave my own response with my top hat and kept waving it until I got to the inauguration and was sworn in."

Twenty-eight years later, hats were still good for filling awkward moments. A few minutes before Robert Frost's appearance, Nixon—who wore his top hat with a decidedly jaunty tilt—and Eisenhower were ushered out to the grandstand, and the military band launched into "Hail to the Chief," honoring Eisenhower for the last time. Both men stood, hesitant; it was not yet the moment for them to be escorted to their seats. So they removed their tall silk hats and held them over their hearts. Decorum didn't demand it; there are no rules for civilians uncovering their heads during "Hail to the Chief," but it must have felt right for the two, and nobody seemed to mind.

* * *

For all the usefulness of a hat, from holding apples to fanning fires to giving an outlet for restless hands and fingers, the utility of wearing one was counterbalanced by an enormous practical problem: Where do you put your hat when you take it off? The guests in the reviewing stand behind Kennedy either wore their top hats or held them in their laps. Kennedy, rising to speak, set his top hat on his coat, which he had removed, folded, and placed upon his chair.

After his rousing inaugural speech, with its famous exhortation to "Ask not what your country can do for you, but ask what you can do for your country," Kennedy and his entourage headed up the stairs of the stands, out toward the car that would ferry them to the Capitol, where they would review the inaugural parade. With them was Kennedy's newly acquired military aide, Major General Chester V. Clifton, who had scooped up Kennedy's hat and overcoat while he was speaking. On the stairs, Kennedy surprised his aide by taking his things back from him and giving them to a Secret Service agent.

"General, you don't have to carry anyone's coat and hat," Kennedy said. "That's not your job."

This was a generous gesture on Kennedy's part, the sort of thoughtfulness that made him adored by many who served him. The taking of a man's hat was the definition of servility. It was what inferiors did. The butler greeted you at the door, took your hat and coat, and showed you to the parlor. By taking his hat from the general, Kennedy was removing him from the universe of coat handlers and drivers and elevating him to a station closer to his own.

The dilemma of parking your hat was compounded by these social overtones. A man could not thrust his hat at another man without the risk of being seen as arrogant, nor could he quietly take another's hat without appearing subservient. And yet, there was also a peculiar kind of honor in guarding a great man's hat.

"To offer to hold one's hat is showing a kind of chivalrous veneration, similar to the act of holding the stirrup of a knight in the good old times," hatter Henry Melton wrote in 1865.

One hundred years, minus six weeks, prior to Kennedy's inauguration, a little tussle took place at Lincoln's first inaugural. Arriving at his seat on the podium, Lincoln faced the quandary of what to do with his tall hat and ebony cane. "He looked around, hesitated and peered, then pushed the cane into a corner of the platform railing," Carl Sandburg wrote in his epic biography of Lincoln. "His hat, too, needed a place. Young Henry Watterson, a press writer from Louisville, put out his hand for the hat, but Senator Douglas, just behind, outreached Watterson, received the hat from Lincoln's hand, and held it a half-hour."

Douglas was later heard to comment, "Well, if I can't be president, at least I can hold the president's hat."

During the centuries when men always wore their hats—on the street, indoors, at the table—taking them off was not much of a problem. But men began removing their hats, as a sign of sincerity,[2] or while eating, or because they were in somebody's home. They had to put them somewhere.

Sitting, a man typically just held onto his hat—in his lap, or crossing his legs and using his knee or foot or the back of his chair as a hat rack. This was such an ingrained habit that it held true at the highest levels. It is common to see photographs of, say, Winston Churchill and Franklin Roosevelt conversing, sitting on chairs on a lawn, each still holding onto their hats, even though they are surrounded by a sea of attendants. One can assume that had either of them wanted to give his hat to a subordinate, that person would have dutifully held it, but the leaders kept hold of their hats of their own accord out of habit.

---

[2] A man giving a speech typically took his hat off, out of respect for his audience, though impromptu stump speeches were sometimes delivered while covered, since leaving your hat on meant that you wouldn't be speaking long. Thus those who claim that Kennedy's not wearing a hat during his inaugural speech was somehow significant are betraying ignorance of the convention they are discussing, though it is an ignorance that many of Kennedy's contemporaries shared.

Deciding what to do with one's hat wasn't as difficult in workplaces or homes, where there was usually a convenient side table or rack ready to receive it. But public spaces, where hats could be stolen, lost, swapped, or crushed by other hats and coats, posed a far greater challenge.

Arriving at a private party, the host or his servants could be counted on to take control of a hat, put it somewhere safe, then return it.

Not that this always went smoothly. While Kennedy's inauguration was disrupted by a storm, previous inaugurations during America's raw youth were famous for tempests generated by the guests. The drunken riot in the White House for Andrew Jackson's inauguration is well known, but that was only the most extreme of a number of stampedes, scrambles, and assorted bad behavior that followed presidential inaugurations.

Take the 1849 inaugural festivities of Zachary Taylor. According to a British witness, the guests acted as if they "had not eaten in days. Men tore the meat off turkey skeletons—women dug jeweled hands into cakes—champagne drenched gowns and suits."

The guests behaved so boorishly and stayed so late that the servants abandoned them, dumping their hats and coats in a mass in the middle of the nearby City Hall lobby.

"There was a general scramble for the wraps," writes historian Paul F. Boller Jr. "But it soon became clear that the only hope was to 'try on till you got a coat to fit.' Young Abraham Lincoln, who had just finished a term as congressman, never did locate his hat, and he finally left bareheaded. 'It would be hard,' wrote one of the guests, 'to forget the sight of that tall and slim man, with his short cloak thrown over his shoulders,' setting out on a long walk home in the snow without a hat.' "

The problem men faced guarding their hats while out on the town only grew in the decade after the Civil War, as cities expanded and the popularity of visiting theaters, staying in hotels, and eating in restaurants increased. Here there were no servants to take charge of hats. Men were on their own.

Typically, a restaurant would have a large coatrack and umbrella stand at the entrance, but this was no protection against mistake or theft. Stealing hats was a particularly appealing crime. Hats were extremely portable, tended to resemble one another, were often very expensive and, since they were frequently exchanged by accident, any thief caught red-handed could always play innocent by pleading mere carelessness.

In *Secrets of the Great City,* Edward Winslow Martin's 1868 gem of fascination with "the darker sides of city life" masquerading as a cautionary tale, the catalog of New York swindles and scams includes professional thieves who prey on hotel restaurants.

"These adventurers often practice the hat game," Martin writes, "depositing when they enter the dining-room, a worthless chapeau, and taking up, when they pass out, a valuable one—by inadvertence, of course."

Such thefts were bad for business, resulting in both disgruntled customers and lawsuits. Martin's glance at the measures one hotel restaurant took against hat thieves captures an early incarnation of the hatcheck business, which would grow enormously profitable while playing a role in the demise of the headgear it was supposed to protect.

"The Metropolitan Hotel has a colored man in its employ stationed at the door of the dining-rooms, who has proved thus far too much for the efforts of any of these gentry," Martin writes. "Consequently this hotel has been, in this respect, particularly fortunate."

Few establishments could be expected to hire a man to watch hats, however. So the obvious solution was for men to keep an eye on their hats themselves. Men at the theater would do just that, holding their hats on their laps. Some opera houses had little shelves under the seats on which to slide collapsible opera hats. In a restaurant, patrons would dump their hats and coats on a nearby open seat, which worked for the customer, but had the effect of seriously diminishing the seating capacity of the establishment.

This sparked the creation of hatcheck concessions, which A. J. Liebling traced back to 1904 and a young man named Harry Susskind, who gazed through the window of Captain Jim Churchill's, a large, crowded restaurant on the corner of Broadway and 46th Street.

"He noticed that the male patrons laid the overcoats and hats on chairs and balanced their walking sticks precariously against tables," Liebling wrote. "This presented a loss of income to Captain Churchill, a retired police officer, since obviously if every third or fourth chair was occupied by an overcoat, the space available for customers was reduced by a third or a quarter."

The sight gave Susskind, who minded the hats at the Hotel Astor, an idea, and he made a bold offer to the restaurant owner. He would set up a booth to check the hats and coats of Churchill's customers as they entered the restaurant. This would free up seats, please patrons and—as the clincher—Susskind would pay three thousand dollars a year for the privilege. Captain Churchill gladly took the offer.

Three thousand dollars was a lot of money in 1904, but Churchill's was a big restaurant, and Susskind's plan proved lucrative. There was no product made or sold, no skilled service performed beyond the acceptance and return of hats. Every man had a hat.

Tips of nickels and dimes poured in. According to Liebling, Susskind cleared twenty-five thousand dollars[3] his first year at Churchill's and was soon opening concessions around the city. Eventually he became a millionaire, as did his two brothers, who joined him in the business.

Susskind could have avoided much eventual controversy and ill will had he simply charged men a fee for keeping their hats. But he didn't, probably because the stowing of hats had previously been free, and men would have balked at paying for what they considered a basic element of hospitality: imagine customers at a restaurant today being asked to pay for a napkin. So the service was ostensibly without charge, a tip being the only compensation.

Not that the tip was voluntary in the usual sense of the word. Hat checking may have begun as a convenience, but it quickly turned into a "genteel kind of banditry." The patron who refused to leave a tip could expect anything from a dirty

---

[3] Hard to imagine after doing the math. Susskind would have to clear nearly seventy dollars a day, 365 days a year. That's seven hundred men handing over a dime—a generous tip in 1904—every single day. Whatever the true figure, the concessions were undoubtedly profitable. By the 1950s, the hat check at the Waldorf-Astoria Hotel was renting for ninety thousand dollars a year.

look to a tongue-lashing from the hat checker. Nontippers might not get their hat back at all. Hats belonging to stiffs were sometimes "lost" in crowded cloakrooms.

"If they don't give me something, then I hold on to their hats until they do give me something," a Detroit hat boy testified during a 1910 trial over the division of tips in a restaurant hat check.

Nor could a customer escape tipping simply by declining to hand over his hat. If a man tried sneaking by the hat check, hat in hand at a New York restaurant in 1911, "it would be but a few minutes before the news spreads and an attendant is soon before him to exchange a check for the hat—they will even go so far as to take a hat without a word and bring back the check before one realizes that the chapeau has vanished."

Compounding public unhappiness over the coercion behind checking hats was Americans' extraordinary ambivalence about tipping, an unease that peaked around World War I. In *The Itching Palm*, a 1916 book by William R. Scott denouncing the practice, tipping is presented as an un-American import of aristocratic Europe, a "moral disease" and a "willingness to be servile for a consideration" that exerts a "mesmeric influence" over its addicts and constitutes no less than "democracy's deadly foe." Scott compares tipping to slavery and the extortions of the Barbary pirates, and presents a long list of quotes from the Bible he claims support his cause.

Scott was no isolated loon. Concern over tipping was widespread enough at the time that half a dozen states tried to make the practice illegal and several succeeded, briefly. Organized opposition also sprang up, in the form of groups such as the Anti-Gimme League and the Society for the Prevention of Useless Giving.[4] Charles S. Whitman, the future governor of New York, was the New York City district attorney when he appeared before the latter group and condemned tipping in general and hat checks in particular.

"I object to having a man take my hat and hang it up for me and then accept a coin," he said. "I am strong and big enough to hang up my own hat."

Whitman's macho phrasing reveals a vulnerability soon to be exploited by hatcheck concessionaires. He said he objected to a *man* taking his hat. But *women* proved to be another matter entirely, and soon the hatcheck boys populating *The Itching Palm* were mostly gone, replaced by hatcheck girls, whom the average man felt somewhat better about gracing with a coin or two. It was an innocent—or sometimes not so innocent—form of flirtation. The hatcheck girl greeted the customer warmly; by name, if he had been there before and tipped well. She might help him on with his coat or, if she was ambitious and it was a slow night, notice a loose button on his coat and repair it.

Hatcheck girls came to occupy a particular niche in American culture in the 1920s and 1930s. They were both helpful and alluring—halfway between a sister and a slut—and their toehold on the bottom rung of the nightlife world of fancy clubs and restaurants made them perfect grist for all sorts of modern Cinderella stories in books, movies, and, occasionally,

---

[4] The group was founded by society women in New York in 1912 to discourage the giving of Christmas presents among the lower classes, which the wealthy matrons considered wasteful and a strain on the limited means of the poor.

in real life. A number of society matrons, such as candy heiress Helen Brach, started life as hatcheck girls, who for thirty years or so were part of the set piece drama that was nightclubbing. Taking his date out for an elegant evening of dinner and dancing put a man through a gantlet of servitors that only began with the hatcheck girl. There were cigarette girls and photo gals, women selling gardenia corsages, gum, and stuffed animals on sticks, not to mention doormen, bathroom attendants, busboys, waiters, bartenders, and parking lot attendants, each in his or her own way encouraging the belief that the man who avoided shelling out for any and all was a tightwad not worthy of his date's attention.

And that was only the capstone of a day busy with hat checking.

" 'Check your hat, sir?' is the expensive refrain he hears from morning until midnight," wrote the *New York Times* in April 1928, elaborating:

When a man stops in at the barber shop in the morning he is greeted with a solicitous "I'll take your hat, sir." Into the willing palm drops a dime. At luncheon a cloakroom damsel smiling lures his gray felt from his head and there goes another dime. Or if he lunches in an eating house of the type where signs on the wall bid him look out for his own hat, and he hangs it where he can see it, a voice at his elbow murmurs as he rises from his pie and milk, "This is yours, isn't it, sir?" Of course it is. He slips an extra nickel under the edge of his plate. . . . If he is dining out, the story repeats itself. Should the occasion be a banquet or a wedding requiring a high silk hat, the price of storage goes up in accordance. . . . There is the girl at the theatre, the boy at the club and the porter on the train. To cite all of the places where parking a hat costs a dime would be to reveal the life history of modern man.

If checking hats was an art form, its prima donna was Renée Carroll, the "hat check queen" at Sardi's, the famed theater-district restaurant in New York City. Carroll was a brash redhead, with a sharp tongue and an easy manner with the rich and famous, and her methods explain why it was estimated that 99 percent of men tipped their hatcheck girls. Though not particularly good-looking, the "snap-eyed, voluble" Carroll kept her clientele in line with a careful mix of flattery and bullying. For tippers, there was the carrot of being recognized.

"When I accept a coat," she wrote in her 1932 memoir, *In Your Hat,* "I look at the label immediately and read the man's name that his tailor usually writes just inside the inner coat pocket. I call the gentleman by his name and remember it afterward, refusing to give a check for his coat and insisting on knowing faces and garments every time. This, of course, flatters the gentleman who, in turn, tips better."[5]

For nontippers, Carroll had a ready arsenal of sarcastic lines and gestures. She would hand quarters to steady nontippers

[5] Perhaps inspired by hatcheck girls less skilled than Carroll, "The Hat Check Problem" is a complex mathematical puzzle asking, if N number of men leave N hats with a hatchecker who forgets which hat belongs to which man and instead returns the hats randomly, what are the odds that one man—or all, or none—will receive his own hat back? Surprising to the layman, rather than decreasing as the number of men in the problem goes up, the odds of getting your hat back actually stabilize.

(though this did not necessarily shame them. Pulitzer Prize–winning playwright William Saroyan would wordlessly pocket the quarter, so she stopped giving it to him).

She slathered on guilt. Hatlessness was no excuse. When French star Maurice Chevalier showed up at Sardi's without a hat, Carroll told him that she had just paid to see him in the movies the night before, and was it fair that he was now refusing to pay her the "customary fee"? Chevalier meekly went back to his car, got his hat, and checked it, tipping a dollar.

Words were not even necessary for a hatcheck girl to make her feelings known. This is how fellow hatchecker Blanche Holland described the reception given a nickel tip in the 1940s.

"Some girls, however, extend the palm of their hand with the offending coin on it, and then look incredulously up at the man's face," she writes, in her own published confessions. "In most cases he immediately says, 'I beg your pardon. I thought I gave you a quarter.' Then, an exchange is hastily transacted."

"If you give a hat check girl less than a quarter, she'll give you a look that you will carry around with you for the rest of your night-clubbing days," Dorothy Kilgallen wrote in 1942. "Brother, it's a dirty one!"

Carroll had Sardi's customers so spooked that men would routinely tip her, even if they didn't have hats to check. Playwright Ward Morehouse forgot to tip Carroll in his rush to make a steamship, so he sent her a five-franc note from Paris and a letter of apology.

Any illusion of familiarity between tipper and hatcheck girl was regularly punctured by the revelation that the women didn't keep the money. Rather, they were paid modest salaries, with the tips going to the owners of the concession. That is, most of the tips did: any business involving an often solitary, underpaid employee collecting an undetermined amount of cash without distributing any kind of product or receipt can expect a lot of theft, and the owner of hatcheck concessions struck on a variety of creative stratagems to reduce pilferage, from uniforms without pockets to locked tip boxes to cloakroom spies tipping with marked bills to the most effective, knowing how much revenue a certain hat check should pull down and firing those whose receipts consistently fell short.

Beginning around 1917, the public was routinely scandalized—with declining degrees of shock as the years went by and a certain collective knowledge developed—to learn that the girls whose palms received their coins didn't get to keep them. Think of all the generous dime and quarter and even half-dollar tips delivered with a wink to a smiling young lady who, it turns out, never saw the money, despite the fiction encouraged by the concessionaires. ("Take care of the girls!" one owner would cry to his departing customers. "Take care of the girls!") Hat checking already seemed coercion as it was; with the true economics revealed, it was nearly fraud. And it didn't help that on one side were often pretty, always poorly paid young women and on the other middle-aged businessmen, sometimes quite wealthy and frequently with ties to organized crime. (Hatcheck concession owners were also more often than not Jewish, which inspired some writers at the time to betray their biases in a subtle mockery, of their accents, of their methods, and of the idea that running a hat check was a legitimate way for a man to earn a living.)

State legislatures got involved. In New York and Illinois it became illegal to deprive an employee of her tips (or his tips, as the practice was also widespread among those who hired porters). These laws were inevitably challenged by concession-aires, or the "tipping trust" as they were called, and courts found them an unconstitutional infringement of the rights of individuals to enter into business arrangements.

Not that the law mattered much, particularly once Prohibi-tion arrived in 1919 and organized crime began to move into restaurants and nightclubs in full force. The appeal of a lucra-tive, inventory-free cash business such as hat checking was irresistible to mobsters, and provided a handy means for tak-ing over legitimate establishments as well, since a standard way to start a fancy nightclub was to sell the hatcheck conces-sion, first, and then use that considerable sum of money to launch the club. This put the hatcheck concessionaire in a per-fect position to buy out the owner at the first sign of financial difficulty—almost inevitable in opening a new nightspot.

Gangsters skulk in the background of Renée Carroll's memoir. Her book was clearly intended as a gossipy, insider's look at the stars of Broadway and Hollywood, but it begins with mob kingpin Arnold Rothstein offering a tip of a thousand-dollar-bill to Carroll, who receives the concession at Sardi's as "a sort of birthday present to me" from one of her mobster pals.

Carroll actually owning her hatcheck concession made her an extreme rarity and allowed her to live on Central Park, wear mink and diamonds, and become famous during the twenty years she worked at Sardi's. Besides her book, she sparked a movie, *Hat-Check Girl* with Sally Eilers, as well as a short-lived Broadway musical, *Bright Lights*. Carroll was a fixture on radio programs, wrote articles for magazines, and appeared in advertisements.

* * *

The abundance of hat checks didn't mean they were everywhere. Men still had to often fend for themselves, and in the fanciest of places. In 1943, Norman Rockwell visited Roosevelt at the White House and produced four pages of sketches about those waiting in the anterooms of the Oval Office. It is illuminating to look at the sketches and take note of the men's hats—some two dozen hats over the four pages. The waiting men cope with their hats in a variety of ways. A Scotsman in a kilt wears his, as does a press photographer. Hats are piled on tables and in laps, propped against a briefcase and hooked on the arm of a chair. This, despite the presence of what Rockwell labeled "The Visitors' Hatrack," a six-foot-long affair that Rockwell drew including a grinning attendant poised with a hat and brush.

After World War II, the nightclub scene went into a gradual decline, spurred by the growth of television, rock and roll, and suburban flight. Hatcheck girls were no longer painted as glamorously as in Carroll's day. The fact that they didn't get their tips was widely known. "When you throw down a quarter for checking your coat and hat, you probably know the girl doesn't get it—it goes to the concessionaire," began an article by Blanche Holland in *Coronet* magazine. Customers would try handing over two coins, saying that one was for the girl, one for the boss; the boss still got both. Rather than ride around in customer's limousines, as Carroll always seemed to be doing, hatcheck girls now presented themselves more realistically.

"Although the movies portray the 'hatchicks' as beauties in

scanty apparel, in real life they are different," wrote Holland. "The typical girl is usually the same type you see in most offices and department stores. She wears simple dresses with white collars. Rarely are they chosen for looks; charm and personality are more important. . . . From experience they know that most of the customers who try to date them are either married men, out-of-towners, or just playboys on the loose. . . . Inadequate salaries, long hours on calloused feet, and the necessity of humoring drunks and smart-alecks are just a few minor woes of the checking business."

Sympathy for the hatcheck girls was muted by realization of what checking your hat almost every day cost. It was estimated that a businessman who ate his lunch in restaurants paid out the equivalent of a ten-dollar hat every three months if he tipped well, and every six months if he tipped poorly. Recognition of the cost, plus awareness that the women didn't keep the tips, soured men on the idea of checking their hats and, to some, the idea of wearing hats themselves. It was enough of a problem that, in 1951, Lee Hats introduced a hat that could be rolled up and tucked into a coat pocket, with the central appeal being to avoid the cost of checking hats. It was a great success, and while some cite the expense of checking hats as a factor in their decline, it should also be noted that coat checks did not seem to diminish the wearing of coats.

Annoyed hatmakers were always using the coat argument to point out the unfairness of hats getting the blame, since people never complained about checking their coats. Actually, the dual purpose of the checks made sure that hat checks survived longer than hats did, continuing to guard hats even as they dwindled.

Checking your hat was also important for another reason, beyond the risk of humiliation inflicted by the hatcheck girls. If there was one thing even worse than the trouble of looking after your hat or the routine extortion of the hatcheck business, it was the crushing, metaphysical shame of losing your hat.

Chapter 4

"Never run after your own hat."

John B. Hynes served what was at the time the longest stretch anyone had been mayor of Boston. Beginning in 1950, he stepped into the shoes of the beloved James Michael Curley, who ended his term in prison, and managed a decade in power before leaving office in 1960. Like most everyone who mattered in Boston politics, he was at the inauguration of their homegrown hero on January 20, 1961, but unlike most, the *Boston Globe* asked him to write a column about the experience. Here is the somewhat breathless opening paragraph of that column (the ellipses are his):

It is done . . . It is the first page in a new chapter of history . . . The lad of destiny . . . The youthful hero in war . . . The slim statesman in the first flush of early manhood and now . . . in the full flower of life . . . The leader of 180 million of his fellow Americans . . . The new President of the United States . . . The gifted son of the mother state of the Union . . . John F. Kennedy . . . May he reign over a peaceful and progressive land.

Hynes's awestruck contemplation of the lad of destiny was interrupted when "the swirling winds" blew his top hat off his head as he left mass at the Shrine of the Immaculate Conception. Hynes set off "with an agility of a man half my years" in pursuit of the hat, "which seemed destined to land in the nearby Maryland Hills." He was losing both the race and his breath when fate, perhaps not wanting to tarnish Hynes's enjoyment of the day, interceded. Hynes was saved when "a vagrant and friendly bush [held] out its hands to capture my errant headpiece."

He returned the hat to his head, maybe a little more tightly than before, and continued on to the festivities.

Losing your hat was not like breaking a shoelace or misplacing your keys. It was not a neutral event. Losing your hat *meant* something. Not by accident did Hynes turn his attention away from the inauguration of the president of the United States to give a detailed account in his column of the loss and recovery of a hat.

That was typical. Hat loss did not go unrecorded. People cared about such things. It was news. Consider an incident that occurred during the primaries. Eleven months before the inauguration, Richard Nixon was on a roll. Five hundred people turned out at the train station on a cold February day to greet him when he arrived in Milwaukee to deliver a speech in the midst of the Democratic primary. His Lincoln Day address would be, the vice president promised, a "major policy talk."

He would also hold strategy discussions—Nixon called them "skull sessions"—with key Republican leaders.

The latest Gallup poll showed Nixon well ahead of Kennedy in a hypothetical head-to-head race, particularly among women. A newsman's straw poll of stewardesses crewing Nixon's plane into Chicago on his way to the Milwaukee speech showed them behind Nixon three to one, citing his dark good looks.

Like Kennedy, Nixon was keenly conscious of his image. As per his orders, there were no Cadillacs in the Nixon caravan waiting for him at the Milwaukee station. No Cadillacs for him, no mink coats for his wife, Pat. The Republican Party was a party of the people.

When the Nixons stepped off the 11:15 train, the reporters approvingly noted Pat's feathery red hat and red scarf, and her charcoal gray wool coat—the "Republican cloth coat" her husband made famous in his Checkers speech. They saw Dick Nixon's dark blue overcoat, blue suit, blue shirt, and light blue necktie. They also noticed his bare head.

"He was hatless," the *Milwaukee Journal* reported. With Richard Nixon that could mean only one thing: Someone had taken his hat. Again.

"Nixon loses another hat," read a headline on the front page of the *Chicago Daily News* the next day, speculating that the hat had been stolen.

"The second one in two months," complained Nixon, who was sure he had had it when he boarded the plane.

The previous November, Nixon had left his gray fedora in a Wisconsin Rapids police car after being driven to a speaking engagement. Rather than return the hat—Nixon's favorite—

Sergeant Franklin Smith "regarded the hat as a lawful souvenir" and let his nine-year-old daughter, Deanne, pose for newspaper photographers wearing it. The vice president was forced to ply his hat's new owners with presents—a silk tie for Sergeant Smith, an autographed photo for Deanne—before the officer took the hint and returned the fedora.

To today's sensibilities, the media attention to Nixon's lost hat might seem puzzling. Why would it get such prominent coverage? And during a presidential campaign, no less. The *Chicago Tribune* also put Nixon's loss on the front page. The *Journal* ran the headline "Nixon Will Get His Fedora Back" on a subsequent page-one story. Why the updates?

This wasn't because losing your hat was a rare occurrence. Lost hats were common. In 1960, the same year Nixon lost his hat on his way to Milwaukee, the Ohio Turnpike Authority reported that more hats were lost on its 241 miles of highway than any other item—six thousand hats the previous year, compared to the runners-up: four thousand pairs of sunglasses and fifteen hundred thermos bottles. Hats were left behind, they blew away in the wind, they were swapped in cloakrooms, they were stolen, sometimes brazenly plucked off somebody's head through an open train window as a subway car pulled out of the station.

Though unexceptional, losing your hat was nevertheless a Bad Sign. There was definitely the mark of cosmic disfavor to it. Herman Melville couldn't send the *Pequod* and her crew to the bottom in *Moby-Dick* without first having a sea hawk swoop down and snatch Ahab's hat, then drop the hat, a distant speck, into the ocean. A hint to tell the astute reader what was coming.

Thus, of the galaxy of information that could be relayed

about an event like the vice president coming to town for a foreign policy speech, the hat loss was singled out and explored in full detail. There was no need to explain why; the readers understood. If losing your hat wasn't a portend of doom, then it was a note of ridiculousness. There was something funny about it—to other people, that is.

"Never run after your own hat," Mark Twain quipped. "Others will be delighted to do it; why spoil their fun?" You can almost see the smirking passerby behind that statement, chuckling, then helping unfortunate hat owners retrieve countless dusty toppers after their tumble through the streets. Or not helping them. Losing your hat had a way of separating you from the rest of society and transforming you into an object of ridicule.

"There are very few moments in a man's existence," Charles Dickens wrote in *Pickwick Papers,* "when he experiences so much ludicrous distress, or meets with so little charitable consideration, as when he is in pursuit of his own hat."

The word *own* stands out in both Twains's and Dickens's statements, neatly underscoring the real shame of losing your hat. Chasing after somebody else's hat was an act of benevolence. Chasing after you own hat was an act of humiliation.

While the person losing his hat was set apart from everybody else, for onlookers, a hat on the move was a free comic spectacle, a joyful, unifying public event. "They could all imagine that the hat was theirs," wrote World War II–era essayist James Norman Hall, describing the reaction of the crowd that saw his hat lifted off his head by a blustery April

wind and deposited directly under the wheels of several Fifth
Avenue buses:

> All the pedestrians waiting at the corner—there must have
> been half a hundred—saw the hat leave my head, and they
> watched with amazement and delight the freak the wind
> played with it. When they saw it plop down precisely in
> front of the wheels of the busses and beheld it being flat-
> tened to a thinner and thinner wafer, the laughter I speak of
> sweetened the air and brightened the day. My fellow pedes-
> trians forgot their individual cares and worries. The tense,
> preoccupied expression vanished from their faces as fore-
> thought and afterthought vanished from their minds. They
> were living in one vivid moment offered them by Chance
> and a gust of east wind. I was conscious, even at the time,
> that a sense of brotherhood had come to them. A deep and
> rich vein of common feeling had been uncovered as sud-
> denly as my head had been, and for a moment all differ-
> ences of rank, circumstance, and political or other opinions
> had been swept aside as though they had never been. They
> were united in the holy bonds of carefree, convulsing
> laughter. . . .

All had lost hats, seen others lose hats, read of men losing
hats, watched comedians lose hats, and sung lustily about lost
hats. Cartoon characters lost their hats: Casper Milquetoast
loses his hat, blown by a breeze onto a lawn where he can't
retrieve it, kept at bay by the KEEP OFF THE GRASS sign. "Oh
well," he thinks, with characteristic humility. "I had to buy a
new hat anyway."

By the time of Kennedy's inauguration, comic songs had been mocking the suddenly hatless for more than fifty years. In E.E. Harder's 1907 "The Hat That Sailed Away," the unlucky singer loses his hat again and again—while tipping it to greet a woman, at the ballpark, walking down the street, and speeding in an automobile. In George Lamy's "The Night I Lost My Hat," the expensive five-dollar topper is squashed by a fat lady, who laughs dismissively when she realizes what she's done.

Hats being squashed by fat ladies—or smashed by tough guys or blown away in the wind or grabbed around the brim and yanked down around a man's shoulders—was a common comedy bit through most of the twentieth century. The 1927 Laurel and Hardy comedy *Hats Off*—called the "Holy Grail of Laurel and Hardy movies" since no copies of it are known to exist—culminated in a massive hat-smashing spree that began with the two heroes and spread to an entire town.

"Why it is funny to see a man with a red nose put an end to the career of a straw hat by simply stepping on it is one of those mysteries which will probably never be solved until the last custard pie has been thrown," wrote the *New York Herald and Tribune* in 1925, in an article noting the practice of Broadway hatters taking the battered old straw boaters left behind by customers buying new hats and selling them to theaters for a dime apiece.

"Dozens of vaudeville teams use 'em," said one Times Square hatter. "Some dancers step on 'em, some comedians fall on 'em and some jam them down over their ears. Jugglers take a few; there's a demand for 'em all year, and we're being called on every day to fill the demand. . . . There's a team in the Follies that breaks one every performance; that's eight a week; and then there's Jack Rose, he breaks eight or ten at every performance."

The destruction or loss of a hat remained a consistent gag from silent movies to farce comedies such as the Three Stooges films, and points to the essential slapstick nature of hat loss. Men lost wallets, too, but your wallet did not fly out of your pocket and go skittering down the street, to the delight of onlookers. Almost any activity posed its own particular peril to a hat.

"Boating is a mortal enemy to new hats," wrote Leigh Hunt. "A sail-line, or an inexperienced oar, may knock the hat off; and then fancy it tilting over the water with the tide, soaked all the while beyond redemption, and escaping from the tips of your outstretched fingers, while you ought all to be pulling the contrary way home."

Note the word *new* in the above. While favorite old hats such as Nixon's certainly were lost in real life, hats lost in story or song inevitably are fresh from the box and expensive, a maddening blow to pride and pocketbook. In James Norman Hall's aforementioned essay, part of the humor comes from a protracted buildup as he rashly buys an extravagant fifteen-dollar hat and walks uneasily down the street under it, feeling unworthy of its opulence in the minutes before it blows away.

Casey's "brand-new hat" is stolen at Murphy's wake in the boisterous Irish ethnic song "I Had a Hat When I Came In," sung by young men into the 1940s. The loss sends Casey on a rampage, breaking up the furniture and nearly waking the corpse as he rages:

I had a hat when I came in
I hung it on the rack
and I'll have a hat when I go out
or I'll break somebody's back!
I'm a peaceful loving man I am,
and I don't want to shout, but
I had a hat when I came in,
and I'll have a hat when I go out!

The financial loss of a hat, though fuel for comedy, was no laughing matter. Depending on the condition of your bank account, losing your hat could be a catastrophe.

In George Gissing's 1888 novel, *A Life's Morning*—considered a classic of grim realism—a weary clerk named James Hood rides a train to a nearby city on a business trip, only to find himself in the midst of an exchange between drunken soldiers and cattle drovers, all conducted in "racy vernacular not to be rendered by the pen." Hood is leaning his head out the window "to escape the foul language" when one of the soldiers lurches against him and his hat is suddenly gone. The soldier grins inanely. "The drovers were enjoying the joke beyond measure." Hood tries to get some kind of compensation from the soldier, who only comes up with a few coins; certainly not enough for a hat.

At the station Hood, "a shy man," steps hatless onto the platform suffering an "agony of embarrassment."

The novel was praised by none other than George Orwell, who admired Gissing's work as "a protest against the form of self-torture that goes by the name of respectability." Orwell declares:

In "A Life's Morning" an honest and gifted man meets with ruin and death because it is impossible to walk about a big town with no hat on. His hat is blown out of the window when he is traveling in the train, and as he has not enough money to buy another, he misappropriates some money belonging to his employer, which sets going a series of disasters.

An iron logic drives Hood to embezzle his employer's money, which he is carrying, so he can buy a replacement hat. What else can he do? "It was impossible to go through Hebsworth with an uncovered head, or to present himself hatless at the office of Legge Brothers."

Fiction, no matter how realistic, is not life. But without question, situations similar to Hood's arose in the real world, such as the August day in 1900 when Samuel Bramley, a member of Engine Company No. 4 in Trenton, New Jersey, went on an excursion to the Atlantic City seashore with a group of grocers.

"While sitting in the train with his head part way out of the window," the *Trenton Times* reported, "a strong breeze carried his straw hat out of sight." His fellow passengers laughed at his misfortune. Bramley, "a good natured chap," shrugged it off and took a nap. Perhaps because he was hatless, he "followed" rather than accompanied the group to the beach, where as luck would have it there was a vendor selling caps. He bought one and enjoyed most of the day before a gust of wind carried that hat off, too, to the renewed delight of his friends.

Bramley, on the train trip back, "whispered to the conductor. No one heard the remark but in a few minutes afterwards the conductor returned with a P.R.R. cap for the hatless unfortunate."

The suddenly hatless who were unable to borrow a railway cap or unwilling to steal could find themselves rooted to the spot. This paralysis, which we saw in literary form afflicting the Caller in *The Lost Silk Hat,* invaded the real-life dreams of Sigmund Freud, who had nightmares about losing his hat. Though he had declared it "quite unquestionable" that hats were phallic objects, Freud did not view these dreams as reflecting castration fears, but rather as a variety of what he called the "not being able to do anything" dream, where a person is confronted with a situation demanding immediate action, yet is somehow frozen. In one of Freud's dreams, he finds himself being led into "a large hall with machines standing in it." The place reminds Freud "of an Inferno with its hellish instruments of punishment." As in Dante's *Inferno,* Freud sees a colleague receiving his due. Freud is in this awful place, he recalls, because of suspicion that he stole something. In the dream, before anything dire happens, he is recognized as an honest man and told he is free to go.

"But I could not find my hat and could not go after all," he wrote, concluding, "My not being able to find my hat meant accordingly: 'After all you are *not* an honest man.'"

One wishes Freud were around to explore the implications of Nixon's repeatedly losing his hat. The loss certainly fit into the generally hapless tone of his campaign, set when he committed himself, unwisely, to visiting every one of the fifty states, including newcomers Alaska and Hawaii. Beside wasting his energies in distant, low-electoral-vote backwaters, the pace ground him down. He injured his knee getting out of a car, it became infected, and he was hospitalized just a week before his infamous pale, sweating, nervous performance in the first TV debate in September 1960.

That was only the capstone of a variety of humiliating snafus and snubs afflicting Nixon's campaign. Eisenhower, who had maintained his sunny, avuncular image in part by delegating the dirty work to his vice president, turned on him at the end and probably cost Nixon the tight election by not only failing to campaign on his behalf until the last minute, but actually undermining his candidacy. Asked by a reporter what input Nixon had contributed to his administration over the previous eight years, Eisenhower replied, "If you give me a week, I might think of one."[1] The idea of being frozen, hatless, and unable to continue forward meshed perfectly with Nixon.

Motivated by the triple inspiration of public ridicule, financial loss, and inability to go about one's business, with the possible portend of doom thrown in, men were inspired to do whatever they could to hang onto their hats. The U.S. Patent Office contains thousands of hat-related patents, a great number of them bizarre devices intended to prevent hat loss, from hooks with grippers on them to prevent hats from being knocked off in crowded cloakrooms, to hats with springs inside the crown to tightly grasp the wearer's head in a gale.

None of these devices caught on, however, either because they were awkward or uncomfortable or didn't work well or

---

[1] In his memoirs, Nixon poignantly explains that what Eisenhower meant was that the reporters should give him a week so he could have time to compile a list of Nixon's many contributions.

merely drew attention to the owner's timidity. Here, the perversity of social convention worked against a man. The most basic, obvious way to keep your hat with you was a simple lanyard, connecting hat to wearer. To this day, fine men's hats sometimes have a button inside to be used with such a cord, which was then attached to the buttonhole of the lapel. Yet even in the heyday of the hat you almost never saw anyone using hat lanyards because, like children's mitten clips, there was thought to be something precious and juvenile about them.

This is beautifully illustrated in the first Norman Rockwell painting to ever appear as a cover on the *Saturday Evening Post*. In the 1916 painting, done in shades of gray and red in keeping with the *Post*'s limited ability to reproduce color at the time, a meticulously dressed boy, in suit, tie, and bowler hat, pushes a wicker baby carriage past two boys his own age—about twelve—fresh from a baseball game, dressed in dusty flannel uniforms. The baby-carriage-pushing boy stares straight ahead, his face frozen in a pout of grim shame, while the two ballplayers gleefully mock him, one tipping his cap, the other pressing a finger to his chin. Ever the master of the subtle detail, Rockwell heaps embarrassments upon the unlucky baby-carriage boy: he is wearing kid gloves and a carnation, the baby's bottle is sticking from his breast pocket, the foot of the unseen baby is arched at an angle that suggests a tantrum, and, the crowning ignominy, the boy's derby is securely fastened, no doubt at his mother's insistence, to his lapel by a sturdy black cord.

Why aren't such precautions seen as masculine? Perhaps they are viewed as cowardly attempts to escape moderate risks that the true man faces and conquers. While protections against actual perils—helmets, steel-toed boots, work gloves—are dramatic and necessary enough to be admirable, measures against minor setbacks are not. Thus real men do not wear sock garters, or galoshes, or plastic hat covers. Men do not keep their coins in change purses; women do. These were also safeguards men were "supposed" to use, at the urging of first mothers and then wives, and so casting them aside is a statement of masculine independence. In James Thurber's classic short story "The Secret Life of Walter Mitty," the items that the beaten-down, fantasizing Mitty is ordered by his wife to purchase while she is having her hair done are, significantly, puppy biscuits and overshoes. "I don't need overshoes," Mitty protests. "We've been all through that," his wife says, dismissively. "You're not a young man any longer." Under her gimlet eye, he puts on his gloves. When she leaves, he takes them off again.

This element of youthful rebellion—the inspiration behind entire schoolyards worth of boys leaving their coats flapping open in the cold—should be considered as a factor in the decline of men's hats, which were both a largely unnecessary protection and required by hectoring social convention. Such contrariety was definitely at work in Kennedy's avoidance of hats. White House doorman Preston Bruce handled the reserve of extra raincoats and galoshes for Kennedy at the first-floor entrance, but sometimes Kennedy wouldn't put them on.

"He was like a little schoolboy," Bruce said.

Not to make too much of the doorman's comment, but the observation does help make sense of a range of trademark Kennedy activities, from the win-at-all-costs football games to the constant teasing of associates, and from the serial sexual escapades to his casual attitude toward his appearance—at least initially—and possessions, which he constantly misplaced. Discarding the hat he was supposed to wear was in perfect keeping with all this. By not wearing a hat, he didn't have to worry about the emasculating experience of losing it. "A hat was one more thing [for Kennedy] to have to keep track of and not lose or leave behind," said Senator Edward Kennedy. "It was just easier not to wear one at all."

* * *

Protecting your hat while preserving your masculinity was indeed a challenge. Cowboy star Fred Barrows hit on a method that was both practical and manly. Inside the sweatband of his white Stetson was stamped boldly "Fred Barrows PUT IT BACK YOU BASTARD."

Writing your name inside your hat—albeit with less pugnacity than Barrows—was common. Top hats inevitably had their owner's name embroidered in them since, like fur coats, they all tended to look the same. From time to time, fads also emerged where hats would be given distinctive linings; bright colors or paintings of scantily clad women were popular. But those fads were brief, particularly the naughty paintings (which was understandable, considering all the people—parson's wives and aged relatives and such—who might have occasion to look inside a man's hat when he arrived with his wife for tea). Usually men's hats were lined in white.

Thus men often ended up with someone else's hat, and that could be seen as sort of a consolation prize for losing your own. "In dry, windy Amarillo," wrote Evelyn Lincoln, "they say, if your hat blows off you just reach up and pull down another one." Still, a person wanted his own hat, not some-body else's, as shown by this early letter from a young John F. Kennedy to his Choate pal, LeMoyne Billings, after Kennedy arrived at Harvard and found they had swapped hats.

"You are certainly a large-sized prick to keep my hat," Kennedy joked, "as I can't find my other one and conse-quently am hatless. Please send it as I am sending yours."

Tales of swapped hats often made it into the newspapers, such as that of Warren I. Lee, a Brooklyn attorney who, after dining at a London restaurant, arose and took the wrong hat—one belonging to another American, Alfred E. Payne. When Payne finished, he had no option but to take Lee's aban-doned hat. The matter was sorted out when, back in the United States, Payne visited a third man, Walter B. Seymour, who recognized the name in the hat as a lawyer he knew, and arranged a meeting to swap the hats back again.

In London in July 1899, Mark Twain attended a luncheon that included an English clergyman. He wrote to his friend William Dean Howells:

I must break off and write a postscript to Canon Wilber-force before I go to bed. This afternoon he left a luncheon-party half an hour ahead of the rest, and carried off my hat (which has Mark Twain in a big hand written in it). When the rest of us came out there was but one hat that would go on my head—it fitted exactly, too. So [I] wore it away. It had no name in it, but the Canon was the only man who was absent. I wrote him a note at 8 p.m.; saying that for four hours I had not been able to take anything that did not belong to me, nor stretch a fact beyond the frontiers of truth, and my family were getting alarmed. Could he explain my trouble? And now at 8.30 p.m. comes a note from him to say that all the afternoon he has been exhibiting a wonder-compelling mental vivacity and grace of expression, etc., etc., and have I missed a hat? Our letters have crossed.

Chapter 5

"Your hat is YOU."

Mark Twain's joke about himself and the Canon swapping personalities along with their hats was an old one, even then, and leads us to one of the oddest aspects of hat-wearing. Hats were sometimes viewed as if they were nearly animate.

"It is sleek as a lapdog," Leigh Hunt wrote of a new hat. "It comes home more like a marmot or some other living creature than a manufacture."

Viewing hats as animals was something of a rarity. But considering them a kind of man was not. You picked it out, bought it, wore it, shaped it to your head, handled it, caressed it, sometimes for years. A hat was part of you. It practically *was* you, as clearly demonstrated in a strange practice that popped up in the 1920s and 1930s—that of men sending their hats as proxies on globe-trotting trips.

At the time, air travel was just beginning to shrink the planet, and the public became fascinated with the idea of going around the world via commercial routes. Newspapers were sending reporters to follow the tracks of Phineas Fogg in

Around the World in Eighty Days, and they wrote dispatches from the exotic locales reached by transcontinental flights and steamship voyages. These accounts resulted in the average person feeling more homebound than ever and, perhaps inevitably, a few of the men who were not world travelers wanted to get in on the action. They did so by sending their hats.

In 1922, P. J. Fagan, of Wilkes-Barre, Pennsylvania, rather than dispose of his summer straw hat when the autumn arrived, instead bought it a ticket to New York on the Delaware & Hudson train line. Thus began an odyssey that saw the hat, eventually dubbed "Hobo the Hat," fly to Honolulu, where it was greeted by the governor, then on to Hong Kong, then to Japan, where it was received by "high officials," and other points in the Far East. The hat kept going and had circumnavigated the world three times when greeted by famously prolix ex-senator Chauncey M. Depew at a ceremony in New York in 1925.

"A startling thought occurs to me," said Depew, in his welcoming speech. "We have machines to take thought in the shape of words out in the air, why not a machine to extract from a hat the thoughts of its wearer?"

Hobo the Hat was not unique. Other hats joined the community of globe-trotting headgear.

"I'm never going to be able to go," Albert E. Wickey, a retired Missouri freight handler, shouted to the pilot as he stepped from a Saint Louis crowd watching an American Airlines plane warm up for a flight to Fort Worth, Texas, in 1936. "But will you take my hat for a ride?"[1]

---

[1] This is one version of the story. According to another, perhaps more probable, rendition, friends of Wickey's conspired to send the hat after plans for a postretirement trip fell through.

Wickey, who had never ridden in an airplane, despite handling airport baggage for seventeen years, tossed the old green felt hat and the pilot caught it, beginning an adventure that would see the hat travel the continent, head down to the Caribbean, then over to South America, where it crossed the Andes. In Rio de Janeiro the hat—dubbed, significantly, "Wickey"—was taken aboard the Graf Zeppelin for the transatlantic crossing to Germany. The hat visited London, Africa, India, and Australia, among other places. It ended up in Alaska, where a steamship took it from Juneau to Seattle, to begin the trip back home. American Airlines flew Wickey the man to Newark, New Jersey, to get Wickey the hat. It was the first time the bespectacled sixty-year-old had ever left the Midwest. The hat was covered with tags and messages such as, "Spent night in French Legation in Guatemala City, calling at all night clubs." Wickey, both hat and man, saw the sights of New York City, spoke on the radio—the man, that is—and then returned home together to Saint Louis.

A hat standing in for its owner was extraordinary, yet wasn't just an oddity of the air age. Just as the phrase "wearing many hats" uses hats to symbolize professions, so a man's hat was representative of himself. Thus Horace Greeley became "The Old White Hat," celebrated in a number of campaign songs.

> *We follow where the White Hat leads,*
> *We rally round it freely*
> *Hurrah, hurrah for Chappaqua*
> *Hurrah for Horace Greeley!*

A scoundrel might be referred to as a "bad hat," and not all men measured up to the hats they tried to wear. When Benjamin Harrison ran for president in 1888, the Republicans invoked the memory of his grandfather, President William Henry Harrison, in the song "Grandfather's Hat Fits Ben." This inspired one editorial cartoonist to produce a brutal caricature of Harrison as a little round homunculus slumped in a chair, dwarfed by his grandfather's enormous white hat.

Going back even further into history, there is William Tell, the legendary Swiss archer forced to shoot an apple off his son's head. While that much is well known, much less familiar, except to theater fans, is why Tell found himself challenged. Gessler, the despotic Austrian governor of the Swiss town where Tell resided, placed his hat on a stick in the town square at Altdorf and ordered the passerby to bow to it, as a recognition of Austrian authority. Tell, in refusing to bow to the disembodied hat, drew his famed punishment.

The Austrian governor was using his hat as a stand-in because travel was difficult and dangerous, and people were gone from their posts for months at a time. Sometimes, just as Wickey did, those unable to make a journey dispatched hats instead. For those who could not make it to the Vatican, for instance, the pope would bless hats and send them to worthy individuals (though, it should be pointed out, as devout Catholics today know, popes blessed a wide range of items beside hats, including diapers for royal newborns).

The hat was seen as a symbolic man not only in politics, folklore, and faith, but by the intelligentsia. Freud wrote a paper called "The Hat as a Symbol of a Man" as a supplement to his famed *The Interpretation of Dreams*.

"It may seem strange, perhaps, that a hat should be a man, but you will remember the phrase '*Unter die Haube kommen*,'"[2] Freud writes of telling a patient, using a German expression that means "to find a husband," but literally translates as "to come under the cap."

Freud believed that hats represent men because of their proximity to the head. "It may be that the symbolic meaning of the hat is derived from that of the head," he wrote, "in so far as a hat can be regarded as a prolonged, though detachable head." He also thought of hats as representing the genitals of both sexes but then, to Freud, hats are not unique in this.

Freud's analytical counterpart in literature, Sherlock Holmes, draws a man's life story out of "a very seedy and disreputable" hat he encounters in *The Adventure of the Blue Carbuncle*. After examining the hat, he astounds Dr. Watson by describing the hat's owner as if he were standing in front of him, including the state of his bank account, home life, and the fact that his wife no longer loves him. (Echoing something that William Penn wrote two hundred years earlier: "The hat choketh because it telleth tales; it telleth what men are.")

Indeed, in the era before fingerprints, a hat was considered evidence of its owner's identity. The *Buffalo Gazette* of August 26, 1869, tells of a man framing another for his crime by stealing his hat and leaving it at the scene of an attack. John Wilkes Booth, after assassinating Abraham Lincoln at Ford's

---

[2] This is a curious explanation, as *haube* means "cap" in the sense of a woman's bonnet, and the idiom refers to women covering their hair with caps after marriage. How this supports a hat being the symbol of a man is unclear, though Freud obviously thought it did.

Theatre, leaped to the stage and lost his hat. The hat was retrieved by a witness, and given to authorities to lend what aid it could to his capture.

Even from far away, a hat could distinguish its owner.

"A cow-person adopts a particular block, shape or brim early in life, and sticks to it," wrote J. V. Knight in 1927. "His particular way of creasing it is his totem, his thumbprint. . . . When countenance of man and markings of pony are indistinguishable on long trails, the rider is spied afar off and known by the shape of his hat."

A hat can be set upon a head in countless ways, and men of fashion were much admired, not only for the kind of hat they wore, but how they wore it. In 1926, the Associated Press wrote that the Prince of Wales and Admiral Earl Beatty both "[give their] headgear an original tilt which the young bloods for years have been trying unsuccessfully to imitate."

For at least four hundred years, from the time of Shakespeare to today, wearing your hat at an angle has been considered youthful, rakish, or jaunty, and it might be worthwhile to pause a moment and wonder why. The obvious answer is, because you were supposed to wear your hat straight. Countless etiquette books hectored on the importance of this, and so tipping your hat, either back on your head or to the side, was a way of challenging the edicts of manners and fashion while staying within their parameters, somewhat the way Catholic schoolboys will wear their shirts untucked and their tie knots slipped to their sternums, rebelling against their school uniforms while still wearing them.

Men not only wore hats at distinctive angles, but created

their own styles to match their personalities. In 1926, David Lloyd George, Britain's chancellor of the exchequer, started designing his own hats.

"He likes one with individuality," reported one account. "As there was no maker here who could form a hat to suit him, the Liberal statesman took the matter in his own hands." The unique Lloyd George hat was bright blue "designed to stand out in contrast with his abundant gray locks."

While hat companies frowned on men customizing their own hats, they were eager to blur the distinction between a man and his hat.

"Your hat is YOU," wrote C. A. Mallory, president of the Mallory Hat Company, in promotional material. "Your hat, by its quality and individuality; poise and pitch; angle and droop can be made to take on as many varying moods as the face underneath. . . . It commends or condemns you. It bestows characters or becomes a caricature. Hence, it should not be selected at random, but chosen with care, to be a reflection of the wearer's taste, position and personality, instead of a reflection upon them."

In their desire to make their products seem warm and friendly, hat companies came very close to personifying their hats. They sometimes gave them the names of people. "Grow old with Heywood the hat," suggested Knapp-Felt hats, as if hat and owner would marry. Of another hat, they claimed, "Denny is as likable and informal as its name."

"The Stetson is part of the man," was a slogan for years, and here a man's desire to keep his hat, and his identification with it, come together. Where your hat went, you were supposed to follow. Hence, the idiom of tossing your hat in the ring—once a sign that you were about to climb in after it and enter a boxing contest. "My hat is in the ring," Teddy Roosevelt announced in 1912, popularizing the phrase. You had committed yourself because your hat was committed. After that, what choice did you have?

Even Kennedy was susceptible to this sense of hat-wearing, at least metaphorically. The day before he was assassinated, Kennedy spoke at the dedication of the Aerospace Medical Health Center at Brooks Air Force Base in Texas. After defending his space program on a practical level, for the advances it would bring to understanding physiology and protecting the environment, he spoke of the intangibles of space. He ended his speech this way:

> Frank O'Connor, the Irish writer, tells in one of his books how, as a boy, he and his friends would make their way across the countryside, and when they came to an orchard wall that seemed too high and too doubtful to try and too difficult to permit their voyage to continue, they took off their hats and tossed them over the wall—and then they had no choice but to follow them.
>
> This Nation has tossed its cap over the wall of space, and we have no choice but to follow it. Whatever the difficulties, they will be overcome. Whatever the hazards, they must be guarded against. With the vital help of this Aerospace Medical Center, with the help of all those who labor in the space endeavor, with the help and support of all Americans, we will climb this wall with safety and with

speed—and we shall then explore the wonders on the other side.

You needed to avoid losing your hat, not only because it was socially necessary, expensive, and an embarrassment if you didn't, but because your hat was a part of you, your emissary, as it were. It contained some vital element of yourself, as if your soul had leached into it. Because of this intimate connection between men and their hats, hats were considered a particularly venerated memento. In a display of presidential memorabilia, the top hat that Lincoln wore the night of his murder was labeled as "one of the Smithsonian Institution's most treasured icons." And the miters of departed cardinals and popes receive places of veneration in churches where they officiated.

Two nights before Kennedy's inauguration, just before Lyndon Johnson's party, a Back Bay political hack named Charles H. McGlue stood in the crowded lobby of the Statler Hilton Hotel in Washington, D.C. He removed his hat—old, battered, and grease stained—held it aloft, and began an impromptu speech.

"This is James Michael Curley's hat!" McGlue thundered, his broad Boston *a—haaaaat*—immediately drawing an audience of party-bound Texans in their ten-gallon-hats, as well as others in a town suddenly enamored with colorful Boston political characters.

"I wish James Michael could have been here," he continued, clutching the hat as if he thought somebody might try to snatch his prize away. "It would have done his heart good."

But Curley, four-time mayor of Boston and a former governor of Massachusetts, beloved despite his two jail terms for corruption—the Massachusetts legislation passed a special law to allow him to continue to hold office while in prison—had died two years earlier. Still, it was as if the archetypical Last-Hurrah Boston pol was there, in hat form.

"The next best thing I could do was to wear his hat," McGlue said, telling how Curley had taken the hat from his own head and given it to him, to pay off an election bet—hats, being both valuable and present, were a common stake in spur-of-the-moment wagers.

Life was transitory, and at times hats would have to make do.

"James Michael Curley won't be here to see John F. Kennedy inaugurated as President of the United States," the *Boston Globe* wrote the next day, "but his hat will be."

Chapter 6

"What! Do you stand with your hat on?"

After the inauguration, President Kennedy was driven from the Capitol to the White House, where a presidential reviewing stand had been set up. His car led the parade at a walking pace while he struggled to decide what to do with his top hat.

"During the drive to the White House, the new President wasn't quite sure whether he preferred wearing it or not," the *New York Times* observed. "At 10th and Pennsylvania Avenue, he put it on; at 11th, he took it off, at 12th, he put it on again."

His hat was back on his head when he reached the reviewing stand, where his father was waiting.

Joseph Kennedy had taken a low profile in the election. He had stayed out of sight, working his network of powerful contacts, concerned that he might appear to be a shadowy force behind a candidate many considered a playboy and a lightweight. His past, the popular perception of which could be reduced to a simple shorthand—bootlegger, stock manipulator, philanderer, anti-Semite, appeaser of Hitler—was not the kind of résumé that enhances a relative's political chances. The elder Kennedy was not photographed next to his son during the entire campaign, not until the election was won.

Yet, in a very real sense, it was Joe Kennedy's victory. The tough, win-at-all-costs millionaire had been pushing his second son toward the White House for fifteen years, ever since the death of his eldest, Joe Jr., a pilot who lost his life after volunteering to fly a dangerous, almost suicidal mission during World War II. Joe was the son who was supposed to be in the White House. Jack wasn't as handsome or as vigorous or as smooth as his older brother had been, and might have ended up as a writer had Joe Jr. lived. But his father put the full power of his domineering personality, the range of his influence, and enormous quantities of his money behind the effort, and now that son was president.

When John F. Kennedy arrived at the reviewing stands and saw his father, something happened that various onlookers viewed in different ways. Some saw the president salute his father.

"I remember the moment when my brother was riding in the inaugural parade and his car approached the presidential reviewing stand where my parents were sitting," says Senator Edward Kennedy. "Jack stood up in the car and tipped his top hat to my father. It was a very meaningful moment for them both."

Others saw the old ambassador rise and tip his hat to his son first, a tribute that also deeply touched those who saw it.

"It was an extraordinary moment," Kennedy's sister, Eunice Shriver, later said. "Father had *never* stood up for any of us before. He was always proud of us, but he was always the authority we stood up for. Then, just as Jack passed by and saw Dad on his feet, Jack too stood up and tipped his hat to Dad, the only person he honored that day."

Of all the symbolic functions of a hat, its removal in recognition of someone or something was the most significant. The question of who should uncover his head and under what circumstances has been a matter of controversy for thousands of years, and contributed to practices in all major religions and a few minor ones. The doffing of hats is discussed repeatedly in the Bible, was debated among the Founding Fathers of the United States, and closely monitored in the distant halls of forgotten kings, and, one day in the 1930s, caused a moment's consternation between Mr. Jack Pfefer, wrestling impresario, and one of his clients, King Kong, the Abyssinian Gorilla Man.

"Take off your lousy hat, you bum!" yelled Pfefer, to the Gorilla Man, who had shuffled into his office with his hat in place. King Kong "obediently took off his hat."

Pop historians like to trace the tradition of lifting one's hat as a form of greeting to knights in armor raising their face guards to be recognized as a friend, but present no specific factual basis for this belief, and it sounds more like one of the stories nineteenth-century hatters made up to lend their product romantic appeal. Knights wore armor for battles and tournaments, not for traveling down the road. Even if they did, they would of course have their coat of arms emblazoned on their shields, not to mention a cluster of flags and heraldic banners that would identify them from a half mile away. And a suit of armor was in many cases as individual as a fingerprint. Raising face masks hardly seems to have been necessary.

Even if knights, though identified by their armor and trappings, did occasionally raise their face guards in a "look, it's really me in here" gesture to confirm that a ringer wasn't hiding inside all that metalwork, or just so they could speak and be heard, crediting the tipping of hats to knights would still strain credulity, particularly when the rarity of armored knights, confined to a very limited time and place in history, is compared to the universal practice of peons and peasantry around the world and throughout the ages flinging themselves onto the ground at the approach of nobles. Removing your hat is a natural prerequisite for becoming horizontal, and this, no doubt, was a far more important factor in the development of uncovering as a sign of deference than knights in armor.

Besides, the removal of head coverings to show respect predates medieval times by a millennium, and keeping one's head covered for the same reason is older still. To wear a head covering in public as a deference to God and the neighbors is an ancient practice that can be seen today in the ever-present skullcaps and turbans of observant Sikhs, Muslims, and Jews. The reason for this widespread custom traces back to prehistorical notions regarding hair, which was considered a focal point of eroticism and mystic power, the display of which betrayed wantonness in women and unseemly vanity in men. Thus women, particularly married women, covered their hair in public, and men covered most of theirs as well, especially when they were at prayer.

"In the view of the ancient Jews, one could not trifle with the mysterious demonic powers who were out to do man harm, therefore, the hair could not be uncovered without inviting mischief from them," wrote Jewish scholar Nathan Ausubel.

The Old Testament is filled with references to people covering their heads when they go to worship the Lord, such as 2 Samuel 15:30: "And David went up by the ascent of Mount Olivet, and wept as he went up, and had his head covered, and he went barefoot: and all the people that was with him covered every man his head, and they went up, weeping as they went up."

Eventually, the special requirements of prayer became an everyday custom for the pious. Chumah ben Joshua, a Babylonian rabbi of the fourth century, would not walk "four steps" bareheaded, explaining, "God's radiance is above my head."

"The great men among our Sages would not uncover their heads because they believed that God's glory was around them and over them," Moses Maimonides wrote in his Guide for the Perplexed at the end of the twelfth century.

Just as Jews adopted a number of practices in order to be different from their neighbors—circumcising males, for instance, beyond its ritual value, was also an easy way to tell who was on the team and who wasn't—so nascent Christianity sought to distance itself from its parent religion by adopting methods that were the opposite of what Jews did. If Jews went about with their heads covered, then the new faith would go uncovered.

"Every man praying or prophesying, having his head covered, dishonors his head," Paul wrote in Corinthians 11. "For a man indeed ought not to cover his head, forasmuch as he is the image and glory of God."

This may have been fine in the Middle East, but as Christianity spread to chilly Europe, Paul's general admonition against hats fell by the wayside except during moments of piety. Men took their hats off to pray, whether in church or before meals, and during the centuries when men wore their hats at all times whether indoors or not, they slipped them off for grace at dinner.

Divinity was not the only power to be recognized, however. Men removed their hats to pray; they also removed them to extend honor to earthly powers. This became particularly important as hats went from simple hoods and cowls and other head coverings worn for warmth, to elaborate displays of wealth and station. The more a hat grew in grandeur, the more important it was that it be removed in the presence of one's betters. If a hat's gold buckle and large feathers showed your rank, then it followed that you would defer your rank to the authority that granted it.

British history is replete with stories about the doffing of hats to kings. John Doran relates the following old tale—perhaps better described as a joke—about Henri IV, in disguise, being asked by a peasant boy if he could ride behind him and be taken to see the monarch. Henri said yes, and the boy climbed aboard his horse. Doran writes:

> "How shall I know the king when he is among so many nobles?" said the rustic, as he rode *en croupe* behind the sovereign, of whose identity he was ignorant.
>
> "You will know him," said Henri "by his being the only person who will keep his hat on."

At length the two arrived where the king's officers

awaited him, and they all uncovered as he trotted up to them.

"Now good lad," said he, "which is the king?"

"Well," exclaimed the boy, "it must be either you or I, for we have both got our hats on!"

This constant doffing may have been at times as bothersome to the royalty as it was to their subjects. Shakespeare presents some princely exasperation in *Hamlet,* when Osric, the fawning young lord, approaches Hamlet and Horatio to convey Claudius's fatal suggestion of a sword-fight between Hamlet and Laertes. Osric of course uncovers before his prince, who tries in vain to get him to put his hat back on. "Put your bonnet to his right use," says Hamlet. "Tis for the head." The courtier refuses, first claiming it is hot. Hamlet uses Osric's obsequiousness to twist him around into agreeing that it is cold, then tries again to get him to remove his hat. "I beseech you, remember . . . ," Hamlet says, pointing at the hat. But Osric begs off because, hot or cold, he would be uncomfortable wearing his hat before the son of a king. "Nay, good my lord," he says, "for my ease, in good faith."

After Osric minces offstage, Hamlet and school buddy Horatio laugh at the whole hat business. "This lapwing[1] runs away with the shell on his head," says Horatio.

The insincerity of hat greetings runs through Shakespeare. "Since the wisdom of their choice is rather to have my hat than

---

[1]The lapwing is a bird, at the time considered foolish, and said by folklore to begin life wearing part of its shell as a hat.

my heart," says Coriolanus, "I will practice the insinuating nod, and be off to them most counterfeitedly."

By then tipping a hat to one's betters was known as "hat honor," and in 1600s England it was courtesy of the strictest sort. Failing to remove your hat to superiors, whether sincerely or not, could land you in prison, or worse. Ample evidence of this is preserved in the records of George Fox, the founder of the Quaker movement.

Fox felt that God was not to be found in the grandeur of churches, with their pompous clerics and gaudy ceremonies, but as an "inner light" hidden within each person. He went about England in the 1650s preaching, urging his growing "Society of Friends" to seek this "still small voice" in their own hearts, and encouraging them to dress simply and speak respectfully, even to the humble, but to refuse to tip their hats to anyone, in recognition that ultimate authority and honor reside with God.

"When the Lord sent me forth into the world, He forbade me to put off my hat to any, high or low," Fox wrote. "And as I travelled up and down I was not to bid people Good morrow, or Good evening, neither might I bow or scrape with my leg to any one; and this made the sects and professions to rage."

And rage they did. Fox decries the wrongs inflicted on himself and his fellows, while unable to resist savoring the hypocrisy such abuse revealed.

"Oh, the blows, punchings, beatings, and imprisonments that we underwent for not putting off our hats to men!" he wrote in his *Journal*. "Some had their hats violently plucked off and thrown away, so that they quite lost them. The bad language and evil usage we received on this account are hard to be expressed, beside the danger we were sometimes in of losing our lives for this matter; and that by the great professors of Christianity, who thereby discovered they were not true believers."

That Fox was able to preach his heresies at all reflects the extraordinary moment in history when he appeared on the scene. Up to that point in Britain almost any religious or political dissent would have been quashed—all printed material was censored, for instance. But the royal government had collapsed. Oliver Cromwell and his men had taken power. The king, Charles I, was beheaded in January 1649—he refused to remove his hat during the trial and resulting execution, not out of any nascent Quakerism, but as a snub to his captors—and the next month the House of Lords was abolished. The Quakers joined all manner of radical groups—Ranters, Diggers, Seekers, Muggletonians—all ready to stand up and lead the society dissolving around them. It was natural in such a world that those who retained authority would cling to whatever prerogatives remained, and their indignation leaps from Fox's *Journal*.

"What! Do you stand with your hat on?" one judge thunders. Fox would typically be hauled into court for violating the statute against five or more people meeting together, though sometimes he was just arrested upon entering a town, on reputation alone. But it was not so much his alleged crimes as his determination to keep his hat on before the court that inflamed judges and landed him in dungeons. Thousands of Quakers were arrested, hundreds were shipped into slavery or died, either during assaults by mobs or in jail. While certainly victims of a harsh period, they were also practicing an

early form of civil disobedience by denying the hat honor.
Fox's *Journal* captures the unease he liked to cause, almost as
a kind of ministry. Notice the moment he chooses to speak in
his description of an appearance before the court in Lan-
caster:

> The session was large, the concourse of people great, and
> way being made for me, I came up to the bar, and stood
> with my hat on, they looking earnestly upon me and I upon
> them for a pretty space.
>
> Proclamation being made for all to keep silence upon
> pain of imprisonment, and all being quiet, I said twice,
> "Peace be among you."
>
> The chairman asked if I knew where I was. I said, "Yes,
> I do; but it may be," said I, "my hat offends you. That's a
> low thing; that's not the honour that I give to magistrates,
> for the true honour is from above; which," said I. "I have
> received, and I hope it is not the hat which ye look upon to
> be the honour."
>
> The chairman said they looked for the hat, too, and
> asked wherein I showed my respect to magistrates if I did
> not put off my hat. I replied, "In coming when they called
> me." Then they bade one take off my hat.

As the years went by, Fox's steadfastness earned him a certain grudging respect. Late in the 1660s, he found himself
before another official. "When the mayor came, we were
brought into the room where he was, and some of his officers
would have taken off our hats, perceiving which he called to
them, and bade them let us alone, and not meddle with our

hats; 'for,' said he, 'they are not yet brought before me in judicature.' "

By then, England had tired of the chaos of revolution and brought back its king. Charles II returned to London on May 29, 1660, in a procession estimated to number twenty thousand people. It took seven hours for the parade to pass, and it was noted that the new king, whose father had kept his hat on going to the block eleven years earlier, showed distinct humility in raising his crimson-plumed hat "to all in the most stately manner ever seen."

That even a king could uncover to commoners demonstrates the changes that were brewing in the world. Yet change was slow, and while the seeds of democracy were taking hold and the rigidities of rank weakening, the well-bred remained deeply concerned with balancing their own station against that of the person they were attempting to pay respect.

* * *

Around 1748, a teenage George Washington sat down and wrote out a list of 110 "Rules of Civility and Decent Behaviour in Company and Conversation," cribbed from old French etiquette manuals. Rule No. 26 was:

In Pulling off your Hat to Persons of Distinction, as Noblemen, Justices, Churchmen &c make a Reverence, bowing more or less according to the Custom of the Better Bred, and Quality of the Person. Amongst your equals expect not always that they Should begin with you first, but to Pull off the Hat when there is no need is Affectation, in the Manner of Saluting and resaluting in words keep to the most usual Custom.

Washington's next rule showed the urging of inferiors' hats back onto their heads—and their perpetual reluctance—that Shakespeare noted a century and a half earlier was still an issue.

> 27th: Tis ill manners to bid one more eminent than yourself be covered as well as not to do it to whom it's due Likewise he that makes too much haste to Put on his hat does not well, yet he ought to Put it on at the first, or at most the Second time of being ask'd; now what is herein Spoken, of Qualification in behaviour in Saluting, ought also to be observed in taking of Place, and Sitting down for ceremonies without Bounds is troublesome.

Telling someone to put his hat back on was a privilege reserved for the superior of the two parties involved, and while youths such as Washington shouldn't be in a rush to put their own hats back on, they were out of place to delay if their betters requested they do so.

There were other reasons to raise your hat, in addition to showing deference. Lifting your hat was a signal—to start a race, to fire a cannon, as well as a way of saying, "I'm here."

In Jonathan Swift's *Gulliver's Travels,* in the land of the giants, the now-tiny Gulliver finds himself drinking hard cider with an enormous farmer and his family. He slips:

> I happened to stumble against a crust, and fell flat on my Face, but received no Hurt. I got up immediately, and observing the good People to be in much Concern, I took

my Hat (which I held under my Arm out of good Manners) and waving it over my Head, made three Huzza's, to shew I had got no Mischief by my Fall.

The withholding of hat honor, used by the Quakers in England as a dramatic statement of belief, helped the Continental Congress reassert itself during a period when it had fallen into disrepute. When George Washington, having led the successful Revolutionary War against the British, went before Congress on December 23, 1789, to resign his commission as commander in chief, the Congress—after much prior discussion—chose to receive Washington seated and with their hats on, as a sign of their independence as a body, removing their hats in tribute only after Washington had submitted his resignation and recognized their authority.

Meanwhile, getting people who appeared before Congress to remove their hats—and keep their voices down—was viewed as a sign of the growing acceptance and decorum of a body whose authority the bumptious states questioned for years, as revealed by this passage in a 1795 letter from James Monroe to Thomas Jefferson, trumpeting the improvements:

"The effect which the change has produced is great indeed . . . ," Monroe wrote. "The contrast which a tranquil body, in whose presence no person is allowed to wear his hat, or speak loud, a body who have little to do,[2] & who discuss that little with temper & manners, is so great when compared

---

[2] After the constant crises of the Revolution, lack of pressing business was seen as a distinct luxury.

with the scene often exhibited by its predecessor, that the spectators look on with amazement & pleasure."

Keeping your hat on was a way of expressing your rights as an individual in the face of authority—or, in the case of Congress and George Washington, the rights of an authority in the face of a powerful individual. But it was also an insult, a way of "cutting" someone you had fallen out with. After a letter became public from John Adams ridiculing Pennsylvanian John Dickinson for giving a "silly cast" to political discussions, Dickinson walked by Adams in the street without acknowledging him. As Adams recorded in his diary: "He passed without moving his hat or head or hand. I bowed and pulled off my hat. He passed haughtily by."

A person's fall from favor could be instantly assessed by how he was greeted. "Not a hat was moved," read an account of the hostile reception given Elbridge Gerry in Boston upon his return from France. News had leaked out that the French took an unseemly liking to Gerry, who was supposedly pressing them hard for America's interests.

Such rudeness is timeless but stings enough to make it seem a fresh affront and a sign of crumbling manners. Two decades after Adams bemoaned his snub, Jefferson used the same practice to contrast what he remembered as the pleasant political dealings of his earlier years to the harshness of the current day. He wrote to Edward Rutledge in 1797:

> You & I have formerly seen warm debates and high political passions. But gentlemen of different politics would then speak to each other, & separate the business of the Senate from that of society. It is not so now. Men who have been

intimate all their lives, cross the streets to avoid meeting, &
turn their heads another way, lest they should be obliged to
touch their hats. This may do for young men with whom
passion is enjoyment. But it is afflicting to peaceable minds.
Tranquility is the old man's milk.

Jefferson's mention of the "touch" of a hat introduces a
subject given considerable attention in the following century.
Exactly how do you lift your hat? Jefferson was probably
being sarcastic, because a touch was not enough when greeting equals, just as an overzealous raising of the hat was considered either a mockery or the sign of a boor, as well
described in *Bad Breaks in Good Form,* an 1897 etiquette
guide:

> Gentlemen should not recognize ladies by removing their
> hats and describing a gymnastic curve with them. A bow
> proper consists in simply lifting the hat so as to permit the
> inclination of the head. Observe how many idiots clutch
> the hat, describe a half circle with a radius equal to the
> length of the arms, and then gravely restore their head
> covering.

Those tempted to smile at the nineteenth century concern
over how high to raise your hat should remember that this was
a pedestrian and equestrian culture, and thus people had a
more intimate relationship with strangers they passed at a
walking or riding pace. How and when one tipped his hat
depended on the circumstance: a farmer traveling an empty
country road might tip his hat to all he passed, while in

crowded cities you only tipped your hat to people you knew. Of course it wasn't that simple. Deciding if the person approaching you should be greeted with a tip of the hat was frequently a cause of distress as well as an occasion for empty gesture, as captured by the description in Marcel Proust's *Remembrance of Things Past* of the "terrified" men attempting to greet the elegant and wealthy Charles Swann as he strolled with Odette, "a woman of the worst type" whom he has unwisely married:

> Young men as they passed looked at her anxiously, not knowing whether their vague acquaintance with her (especially since, having been introduced only once, at the most, to Swann, they were afraid that he might not remember them) was sufficient excuse for their venturing to doff their hats. And they trembled to think of the consequences as they made up their minds to do so, wondering whether this audaciously provocative and sacrilegious gesture, challenging the inviolable supremacy of a caste, would not let loose the catastrophic forces of nature or bring down upon them the vengeance of a jealous god.
>
> It provoked only, like the winding of a piece of clockwork, a series of gesticulations from little, bowing figures, who were none other than Odette's escort, beginning with Swann himself, who raised his tall hat lined in green leather with a smiling courtesy which he had acquired in the Faubourg Saint-Germain but to which was no longer wedded the indifference that he would at one time have shown. Its place was now taken (for he had been to some extent permeated by Odette's prejudices) at once by irritation at having to acknowledge the salute of a person who was

none too well dressed and by satisfaction at his wife's knowing so many people, a mixed sensation to which he gave expression by saying to the smart friends who walked by his side: "What, another one! Upon my word, I can't imagine where my wife picks all these fellows up!"

By the beginning of the twentieth century, concern over tipping your hat to superiors had been eclipsed by concern over tipping your hat to ladies. But rank still complicated the duty of doffing your hat. When Mark Twain visited London in 1907, the London newspapers reported that he had kept his hat on during an audience with the king and queen, not to mention slapped the king on the back while they were talking, a rumor that even the iconoclastic Twain was quick to put to rest.

"I'll tell you just what took place," he told an American newsman. "When I renewed my acquaintance with the Queen I took off my hat and made my lowest bow. 'Put on your hat; put on your hat,' said the Queen, fearing, I supposed, I'd catch cold. But I didn't obey her, and we continued our conversation, I remaining uncovered.

"Presently, the Queen told me again to put on my hat, and her tone was such that I couldn't, with gallantry, longer disregard her injunction. Almost immediately thereafter I was presented to King Edward, and, remembering the Queen's command, kept my hat on. I didn't feel at liberty to do anything different."

The old codes of manners lingered on into the first half of the twentieth century, even as Americans jumped into cars and stopped greeting each other in the street. Nearly four pages of

Emily Post's 1922 "Etiquette" are devoted to when a man lifts his hat and when he takes it off completely.

Doffing a hat, to Post, meant a man "lifts it slightly off his forehead and replaces it." He is to do this, she continues, without either smiling or looking at "the object of his courtesy" since "no gentleman ever subjects a lady to his scrutiny" (a reminder that etiquette books are indicative of how people were *supposed* to act and how some *might* have acted as opposed to evidence of how most people actually behaved). She warns that a gentleman "should never take his hat off with a flourish, nor should he sweep it down to his knee" while allowing that, if one is greeting a very old person, an exaggerated gesture where the hat ends up upside down at waist level might be needed "to show adequate respect."

When the object deserving respect was the flag, passersby helped enforce the doffing of hats, just as they had in seventeenth century England. Emily Post writes, "It is not necessary to add that every American citizen stands with his hat off at the passing of the 'colors' and when the national anthem is played. If he didn't, some other more loyal citizen would take it off for him."

Post was not just postulating some white-glove ideal. When John Brantzer, a Lithuanian immigrant living in Brooklyn, failed to take his hat off for the American flag as it passed by in September 1925—perhaps because he was drunk—he was set upon by an angry mob. A policeman rescued him and charged him, not the mob, with disorderly conduct. He was fined twenty-five dollars in Coney Island Court.

As the pace of modern life overwhelmed etiquette, the rules were adjusted trying to accommodate the two. Hats were to be removed in elevators, Post decreed, but not in corridors because "a public corridor is like the street, but an elevator is suggestive of a room." In foreshadowing the hectic urbanity that would dispense with hat etiquette altogether in a few decades, Post excluded the elevators in office buildings from these standards because "the elevators in such business structures are usually so crowded that the only room for a man's hat is on his head." Although such behavior could be seen as an oversight, even decades later.

"You know you're the only one who takes his hat off in the elevator," pert Miss Kubelik says as a compliment to C. C. Baxter in *The Apartment*. "The characters you meet!"

During the heyday of hats, etiquette writers did not suggest that a hatless man was somehow offending people by not having a hat to tip. But as hats declined, hatters tried to invert the idea that men should remove their hats for ladies into an argument for wearing the headgear: How could you doff your hat if you didn't have a hat? Those castigating Kennedy for killing an industry marveled how he got through his day without giving offense to the fairer sex.

"How can a hatless man properly greet a lady?" the British trade journal *Tailor and Cutter* demanded of President Kennedy in July 1963, a query that was picked up in the American press. "The deft touch of a raised hat, politely pinched between thumb and forefinger and held for a hesitant moment over the wearer's heart, would bring a bright spot of gallantry to those modern diplomatic moves which seem to have lost so much of their old world glamour in the current rush for time-saving practicalities."

Kennedy's relations with ladies seem not to have been damaged by his general lack of a hat. That said, in the early 1960s, hats were still an ideal vehicle to convey greeting—and to amplify it, as Lyndon Johnson's energetic waves of his large white hat demonstrated.

Hats also were used to wave farewell. After he was sworn in, Kennedy sat outside in the reviewing stand and watched the parade for three and a half hours, fortified by hot soup and hidden space heaters. Not being the sort to spend three and half hours watching a parade, however, even one in his honor, Kennedy had his military aide bring by a series of members of his new administration, so they could conduct sly, corner-of-the-mouth meetings while watching the floats pass.

Finally, with darkness settling, the parade ended. Kennedy bid farewell to the cheering crowds with a wave of his top hat. Then he went inside the White House where, the *Boston Globe* noted, "he has a four-year lease."

Chapter 7

"The government forbids habits to the contrary."

Several hundred members of the U.S. Army's Special Forces stood at attention in the sun at Fort Bragg, North Carolina, waiting. It was mid-October 1961 but unusually warm for autumn. The unit commanders scanned their lines, looking for "a chalk-white face that would indicate its owner was preparing to faint."

The president of the United States arrived in a convertible. As it stopped in front of the assembled men, John F. Kennedy stood up. Brigadier General William P. Yarborough stepped forward and saluted. Kennedy nodded in return and examined the men, all wearing the distinctive Special Forces green beret.

"Those are very nice," said Kennedy. "How do you like the green beret?"

"They're fine, sir," said Yarborough. "We've wanted them for a long time."

By the time Kennedy was president, the law was not something regularly applied to hats except in arcane matters of import quotas and labeling. As much as American hatters would have liked it to be otherwise, even if Kennedy had wanted to, he could not—as leaders in previous decades and centuries had done—simply issue an edict telling people what kind of hat to wear.

Except in the Army. Not only is the military more bound by rules than civilians are, but Kennedy was its commander in chief and, by coincidence, when he took office, one branch that would become very important to Kennedy happened to be embroiled in a dispute over hats.

The Army had established its Special Forces unit in 1952 in an effort to develop expertise at fighting the kind of unconventional, guerrilla war operations that even then were on the rise in the world. The Special Forces were called on to serve a variety of dangerous roles by the U.S. government and the following year reflected their renegade status by adopting their own particular headgear.

While the precise genesis of the green beret is complex and has long been the subject of disagreement among those involved, the short version is that the idea came out of the ranks in the early 1950s and found favor with the commander of the 77th Special Forces at Fort Bragg, Colonel Edson Raff, who thought that a distinctive hat would help build esprit de corps. He picked a green beret similar to that worn by the British Royal Marine Commandos.

The military is not designed to adapt to spontaneous fashion decisions made by colonels, however. Change comes slowly, particularly in relation to military uniforms: 1961 happened to also be the year the Army stopped putting watch pockets in its uniforms, nearly half a century after soldiers stopped carrying pocket watches.[1] Thus it was inevitable that the Pentagon would take "strenuous" objection to the berets. Special Forces continued to wear their berets in the field—which, by the nature of their missions, was out of view of top commanders—while badgering the brass for official approval.

Permission was denied for the next eight years. In a February 1959 disposition on the matter, the high command listed five objections to the berets: they gave the uniform "a foreign accent"; they were unauthorized; they were an unnecessary expense since enlisted men already were issued one wool and two cotton garrison caps; there were rules against unauthorized headgear; and, finally, were approval granted, other units would want their own special hats, too.

The spring after Kennedy entered office, a CIA scheme he inherited from Eisenhower—training Cuban exiles to invade Cuba—ended in utter disaster at the Bay of Pigs. Through sheer popularity, Kennedy endured that fiasco but he was not looking for another military humiliation right away in Vietnam. Kennedy had great interest in using the Special Forces to fight the covert war there that he was trying to keep covert. If a special hat made them happy . . .

The historical record is a little vague here. The military presents official approval of the green berets and Kennedy's visit as separate events, with the former taking place three weeks prior to the latter. But presidents do not usually just up and go places, and Kennedy's visit to Fort Bragg and the

---

[1] To be fair, business could be slow to recognize change as well; 1961 was also the year Van Heusen stopped selling detachable shirt collars.

Army's belated official approval of the green beret are undoubtedly linked. It cannot be coincidence, after eight years of refusal, that the Army happened to approve the berets the same month as a visit by Kennedy, who would later call the hats "a symbol of excellence, a badge of courage, a mark of distinction in the fight for freedom."[2] As it was, it took until December for the Army to publicly announce that it had decided to permit the Special Forces to wear a green beret.

* * *

Kennedy's involvement in the green beret matter was a rare reversal for him—rather than being pursued to wear a hat, he was instead pressuring others about a particular headgear. But throughout the years, rulers have used their power and authority to tell people what kind of hat they would wear. History is replete with sumptuary laws, designed to either keep average people from aping their betters—in Britain, anyone lower than a knight was prohibited from wearing a velvet cap by a 1566 law—or to prop up a nation's struggling industries.

Hatters did not begin lobbying governments for help in 1961. The practice goes back centuries and, in eras when leaders were not politicians but rulers, they supplied that help by law. An early ancestor of Alex Rose's United Hatters, the Incorporated Company of Hat Makers of London, convinced Queen Elizabeth in 1570 that imported wool was undercutting their business, and the result was a law that "Every person . . . shall wear upon the sabbath and holy days . . . upon

---

[2]During his own military career, Kennedy had no trouble wearing hats. "The one exception was his naval officer's cap," said Senator Edward Kennedy. "He was very proud to wear that."

their head a Cap of Wooll knit thicked and dressed in England." The law applied to everybody over the age of six, except nobility, who presumably couldn't be bothered.

The act was enforced, we know, because church records show fines being levied against those who violated it, though many who did so were not punished.

"The knitted caps so ordered to be worn were naturally known as Statute Caps and were worn by the conscientious and evaded by the fashionable until the Act was repealed in 1597," wrote Michael Harrison.

Even without pressure from hatters, kings would try to turn their fashion whims into law. The "martyr-czar" Emperor Paul I of Russia so liked the large cocked hat he wore that he forbade his subjects to wear a round hat and exiled offenders to Siberia. He was murdered four years later, and the law was swept aside. In general, kings trying to codify their style tastes were frustrated by an authority higher than their own.

"In 1664, Charles II solemnly ordained in council that a certain fashion of hats should forever after be worn by the court," J. N. Genin noted in his history of the hat. "But Fashion is more powerful than any king, and the shape of the hat retained its mutability of character in spite of the solemn edict of the Merry Monarch."

As the power of kings began to wane, laws related to hats applied more to their manufacture than to their style.

Across the ocean, the growing American colonies found the carrot approach useful in building the local hat industry. In 1662, the assembly of Virginia offered ten pounds of tobacco for every good wool or fur hat manufactured in the colony as part of a system of rewards for anyone with the initiative to manufacture something. That kind of inspiration worked, and hatting became one of the first American industries.

As the colonial hat industry grew, it drew the unwelcome notice of Great Britain. The British policy toward America at the time was to prevent the colonies from competing economically with the mother country while preserving them as a captive market. In 1731, Jeremiah Dunbar, surveyor general of His Majesty's woods, was asked to study the hat trade. He reported that New York and New England alone were manufacturing ten thousand hats a year.

That was too many for British hatmakers. The London Company of Feltmakers was able to extract from Parliament the particularly oppressive Hat Act of 1732, which not only forbade the colonies from exporting their hats abroad, but also banned them from selling hats to each other—it actually outlawed the physical loading of hats onto a ship or horse—while limiting any hatmaker to two apprentices and requiring those apprentices to serve for seven years.

In addition, it barred blacks from the trade. The fear—not unjustified—was that hats made by slaves on plantations would undercut and destroy the market for British hats, somewhat in the way American industry today has been ravaged by low-wage workers abroad.

The language of the act seems designed to cause offense, beginning with a bold declaration of which side of the ocean made better hats.

"Whereas the art and mystery of making hats in Great Britain hath arrived to great perfection . . . ," it begins.

While, from the distance of today, the Hat Act—along

with similar laws restricting the manufacturer of basics such as wool and iron—might seem the kind of outrage that led directly to the American Revolution, at the time it was of little concern, despite its severity. The British made scant effort to enforce the Act, giving rise to the suspicion that it was passed, not out of genuine legislative desire to suppress the nascent American hat industry, but merely to placate the complaining London hatters.

The historical importance of the Hat Act, and other attempts to quash American industry, is not the effect on the industries themselves—though there were a handful of Americans prosecuted under the Hat Act—but in the political message they conveyed.

"The three main British efforts against colonial wool, hats, and iron did little or nothing to hinder the Americans," wrote historian Theodore Draper. "Yet they taught the Americans an invaluable lesson—that the British were most vulnerable in their trade in manufactures. Wherever American production paralleled British production, or even threatened to do so, the British regarded the Americans as dangerous rivals, not as partners in a common enterprise."

This "fatal antagonism," Draper said, "ate away at the deference and loyalty which the colonists had been willing to grant."

It must be noted that the laws in England regarding English hats were stricter still—hatters had to be licensed, and were penalized fifty shillings a hat for every illegal hat sold. Hatmakers were required to stamp their name on the lining of their hats, and counterfeiting a hat stamp earned a death sentence.

Lest we consider such laws propping up local hat industries as relics of kingdoms in the hazy past, we should realize that similar measures were also considered in the United States and enacted in Europe in the twentieth century.

In the mid-1890s, when a bicycle mania hit the United States, all manner of businesses felt threatened by the sudden and enormous public interest in two-wheeled transportation. Watchmakers and jewelers complained they were going out of business because people were spending all of their money on bicycles. "The tailor, the hatter, the bookseller, the shoemaker, the horse dealer and the riding master all have similar tales of woe," *Scientific American* reported.

"Mad hatters claimed that bicycling kept people from purchasing hats because at the speeds attained by bikes, headwear was an impracticality," wrote pop historian Charles Panati. "One congressman introduced a proposal that would have required every bike rider to buy two hats a year."

While local governments had no difficulty beating back the bicycle menace with a number of laws that strike us as laughable today—such as requiring bike riders to dismount when approaching a horse—the pair-of-hats-a-year requirement didn't become one of them. Appeals to truthful advertising and sanitation were more effective, however, and the hatters were successful in reducing the market for so-called ash can hats—used hats collected by rag pickers and junkmen, cleaned, reblocked, and resold—by requiring them to be so prominently labeled as to scare off customers. It wasn't that these hats were inferior; on the contrary, hatters complained that, in tests, even experts couldn't tell a new hat from a reconditioned hat. The sticking point was that such hats could be sold more cheaply than new hats. Hatters claimed customers were being deceived. In the 1930s, not only were such hats required by law to be labeled "Used hat" or "Second-hand hat," but any retailer selling such hats had to display "a sign of such size that it may be legible from a distance of at least thirty feet reading 'Used hats' or 'Second-hand hats.' "

Nothing the United States did regarding hats came anywhere near the level of governmental action abroad. In Italy in the late 1920s, Benito Mussolini's Fascist Party was busy cementing its control over the smallest aspects of Italian life. It had already banned cats in Rome, blaming the feral packs of the Eternal City on "the persistent effort of foreigners."[3] On March 30, 1928, the Fascista abolished Catholic youth organizations. On the same day, it also issued a decree compelling all Italians to wear straw hats from April 1 to October 1. The hats, to be made in Italy of Italian design, were intended to break the "French monopoly of smart clothing" and were offered in a range of officially approved styles conceived by the Unione Industriale Fascista.

Mussolini liked to strut about in a wide variety of headgear.[4] The dictator would appear with his bald pate covered with everything from tasseled fezzes to streamlined helmets to berets festooned with eagles. His people would be hatted with equal variety, whether they liked it or not.

---

[3] This is a rare instance of fascist xenophobia supported by fact. In 1909, Mrs. Hill Tait, an Englishwoman, began giving twenty pounds a year to feed the cats of Rome. Upon her death, she left a bequest that established four refectories around the city where cats were fed daily. The effect on the cat population can be imagined.

[4] Italo Calvino called Mussolini's era the "cult of the Head."

"These are wide-brimmed hats with conical crowns and a dashing upward turn at the sides and back," the *New York Times* wrote in the spring of 1928. "These are mushroom-shaped helmets with creased crowns, straw caps with long visors, semi-stiff hats with melon crowns and colored ribbons—a variety of styles bordering on the Tyrolean."

College students were required to wear hats with linings showing the colors of their university and bands representing their field of study.

The rules applied to men, first, which provoked mockery of male Italian habits.

"The men's styles will come first, not only because in the Fascist scheme of things men are more important than women, but also because it was deemed good psychology to recostume in the beginning the dominating, purse-handling element of the Italian population," the *New York Times* tittered.

In nonfascist states, hatters turned to business to exert force that the government could not. In 1931, British hat-makers requested that banks and insurance companies compel their employees to wear hats to work. They also went to work on Prince Edward, whose "fondness for going out without a hat on annoyed both his father and the hat industry." Thow Munro, chairman of the Executive Council of the Textile and Allied Trades section at the British Industries Fair, complained to the prince who—diametrically opposed to how Kennedy would handle a similar situation thirty years later—apologized and started wearing hats more frequently. In 1932, he actively promoted the straw boater to help the hat-makers of Lutton.

Nothing that was happening in Europe or the United States in the 1920s compared to the transition that was going on in Turkey, a nation poised uncomfortably between the Western and Islamic worlds. The country offers up the zenith of compulsory hat-wearing and the most notable example of the symbolic power of a hat. Since the story is almost certainly utterly unknown to the average reader, it deserves to be examined in more than a cursory fashion.

* * *

In 1925, Turkey was thrown into turmoil by a charismatic young army officer named Kemal Atatürk, who seized power and attempted to drag his hidebound Islamic nation into the modern world by fiat and the force of his personality. He nationalized religious schools, secularized the legal system, dissolved various sects such as the dervishes, began adopting Latin script, and banned all manner of "fortune-tellers, magicians, witch-doctors, writers of amulets for the recovery of lost property or the fulfillment of wishes, as well as the services, dues and costumes pertaining to these titles and qualities."

And, as the literal capstone, he began a campaign against the traditional headgear of the Turkish faithful, the fez, and enacted laws to ban it and require his citizens to instead wear Western hats.

This extraordinary action needs to be put into a bit of Turkish context. The fez did not stretch into distant history but was itself less than a century old, having been introduced by Sultan Mahmud II in 1829—first for the army, then for the bureaucracy. The fez was also seen as a form of Westernization, compared to the turban—an ancient headgear so ingrained in Turkish society that men would carve their particular kind of turban on their gravestones, to display the station they had attained in life. The fez was considered an ideal replacement, since it had no brim, and would not impede Muslims from the required touching of the forehead to the ground during prayer.

This enforced switch, from turban to fez, was par for the course in Turkey.

"Political changes, especially the replacement of one dynasty by another, or even a new ruler's succession to the throne within a dynasty, were often signaled by a change in headgear," wrote Vamik Volkan and Norman Itzkowitz, an observation that could also be loosely applied to the United States in the mid-twentieth century.

Atatürk was a revered, almost mythical figure, and Islamic culture at the time was in such a state of self-doubt after its humbling encounters with the West that he could both lead Turkey and announce, again and again, that "there was only one civilization" and that was the West. The highest goal the Turks could pursue, he argued, was to emulate that one culture in every detail. "Civilization is a fearful fire," he said, "which consumes those who ignore it."

He began early summer of 1925 by imposing peaked caps on the military and police and going to the chief religious judge in Turkey to receive the proper Koranic approval for Turks to cast aside their fezzes.

The judge—the Kadi—settled on a passage in the Koran stating that if a Muslim buys a cow from a Christian who wears a hat, and the cow refuses to give milk unless the Muslim also wears a Christian hat, then the Muslim may wear such a hat in order to milk the cow. A bit of a stretch, perhaps, but thus were fedoras permitted under God's law.

Atatürk's first push for Western hats was modest and, not too surprisingly, made little progress. Turkish newspapers didn't even dare print the common, almost vulgar word for the infidel's hat—*shapka* in Turkish—preferring more oblique terms such as "civilized headgear" or "protector from sunshine" or "head-cover with a brim."

More dramatic action was in order, and Atatürk boldly waged a personal campaign to introduce Western hats in the late summer of 1925. He traveled to Kastamonu, one of the most conservative areas of the country, stopping at small towns and villages. Arriving in a Western suit of gray linen, a shirt, and tie and carrying a Panama hat, he made speeches and mingled with crowds, agape in silence at his outfit.

"The impact would be equal to that of an American president arriving in New York City dressed as a desert nomad, demanding that everyone follow his example," Volkan and Itzkowitz wrote.

"His audience," biographer Hanns Froembgen noted, "were horrified to see him appear in a hat."

Atatürk lectured them about the importance of adopting Western dress.

"A civilized, international dress is worthy and appropriate for our nation, and we will wear it," he said. "Boots or shoes on our feet, trousers on our legs, shirt and tie, jacket and waistcoat—and of course, to complete these, a cover with a brim on our heads. I want to make this clear. . . . ," he pointed to his Panama and called it by its shunned name. "This head-covering is called 'hat.' "

His performance was stunning. "The shock thus administered was profound," wrote A.L. Macfie. "But it produced the desired effect. In every part of Turkey, mainly in the more advanced areas of the west, thousands of men rushed to emulate their leader and acquire a hat."

Hat stores sprang up overnight. Price gouging was rampant. The prefect of Constantinople, Emine Bey, felt the need to decree a limit on profits—15 percent for ordinary hats, 25 percent for "fancy" hats.

By September, the wearing of turbans was restricted to Islamic officials. In October, a decree stipulated that top hats and tails be worn on ceremonial occasions.

That was not enough for Atatürk. On November 25, the "Hat Law" went into effect. "The hat is the common headgear of the Turkish people and the government forbids habits to the contrary," the law read. There was some legislative resistance. A retired general, Nureddin Pasha, made a speech in the National Assembly damning hats, and was summarily expelled.

Police went door-to-door advising people and gave warnings to fez wearers in the street, and the same religious watchmen who until recently had plucked Western hats off passersby as unacceptable marks of the unbeliever now knocked off fezzes.

Some Turks rioted, particularly in the hinterlands. In Erzurum, martial law was declared. In Marache, forty people were arrested after a mob paraded before the governor's house chanting, "We don't want hats." Harsher measures were also taken. Two fez wearers were hung at Kerasunt. Others were imprisoned at hard labor. A Turk who wrote an attack on hats on the walls of a building in Eastern Anatolia was also hung.

In all, approximately twenty death sentences were handed out to those resisting the hat law.

In the face of the gallows, Turks changed their ways. The Red Crescent, the Turkish version of the Red Cross, collected thousands of discarded fezzes and turned them into slippers for the poor and sick. Even rabbis, who were not covered by the law, shed their black gowns and tall cylindrical hats.

But giving up the fez was a simpler matter than putting on a Western hat. Fedoras could not be conjured out of the air. Shops were stripped of "anything in the way of headgear, provided it was furnished with a peak or brim." Some Turks had never seen a Western hat, and thus wore theirs backward, or sideways. Homemade hats were common. Much to the delight of British observers, "men were seen strutting through the streets in out-of-date women's hats which they had dug up in one of the Armenian shops." Meanwhile, European hatmakers raced to send shiploads of their out-of-date—and thus otherwise nearly unsellable—hats to Turkey.

Turkish newspapers which just a few months ago had shrank from printing the word *hat* now carried articles titled "How to Wear the Hat." Accustomed to the brimless fez, men kept knocking their own hats off accidentally.

In the West, the press, rather than happily welcoming Turkey into the supposed civilized world, took a more melancholy note of what was considered another in a string of "losses in the world's picturesqueness." If the Turkish embrace of Western dress is obviously a negation of their culture, then the Western response also reveals a certain discomfort with its own heritage.

"The color has disappeared from urban places," wrote John H. Finley from Constantinople in 1926. "They have taken on the dull gray uniformity of Western civilization." Three years earlier, Finley had been the only man in an enormous throng in Angora to wear a hat. Now, in two days of travel through two large cities, he found exactly one man wearing a fez.

"Even the muezzin in the mosque that once contained a special place of worship calls to prayer with a derby pulled down upon his ears,"[5] Finley wrote. "I spoke a few nights ago to a hundred or more Turkish boys gathered around a great bonfire who from all outward appearances might be a group of New York boys at the Palisades Interstate Park."

As always, there were also those who made the common mistake of extrapolating the trend of the moment to extremes. If fezzes were discarded, would not the faith be next?

"Islam is doomed," wrote William Rapp. "The East, in order to survive, has felt itself compelled to imitate the West."

Atatürk's edict was copied in Iran in 1931, when Shah Reza Khan Pahlavi outlawed the fez, also sparking deadly riots. By then, the growing hatlessness of the West was so apparent that an irony was detected.

"The simple fact remains that Asia is embracing the Occidental derby hat and the fedora even while these seem to be passing out of fashion among the Western nations," the *New York Times* opined in 1931. "An increasing number of men

---

[5]This account was later attacked as being fanciful, as religious leaders were exempt from the edict.

walk up and down Broadway bareheaded to the sun and the Winter storms. If any of them should be seized with the impulse to kneel down in prayer in front of the Paramount Theatre and strike the sidewalk with his forehead there is nothing on his head to prevent him."

Chapter 8

"Are you willing to destroy the beloved image of our country's leader?"

President Kennedy awoke in Chicago on Saturday morning, October 20, 1962. For all the public knew, nothing more was going on than a routine bit of campaigning for the rapidly approaching midterm elections.

He had left Washington the day before, stopped off in Cleveland, then visited the Illinois capital, Springfield, where he laid a wreath at Lincoln's tomb and attended a political luncheon. That afternoon he landed at O'Hare Airport. An estimated 100,000 people lined the Northwest Expressway as Kennedy was driven into downtown Chicago. They crowded the overpasses. Women screamed. Children ran down the green embankments along the highway, waving at the motorcade. Not all of the welcome was pleasant, however. In front of Kennedy's hotel, an anti-Castro picketer held a sign that read: LESS PROFILE, MORE COURAGE.

Friday evening Kennedy attended a hundred-dollar-a-plate Democratic rally for Sidney Yates, a veteran Congressman who had quit the House to challenge the Senate seat of powerful Republican incumbent Everett Dirksen. The next morning, Kennedy was supposed to fly to Milwaukee; a thousand people were already standing in the rain, waiting to greet him at Billy Mitchell Field. Then he would swing westward, hitting several states before ending up in Seattle to close the World's Fair.

He didn't go. Newsmen at his hotel, the Sheraton-Blackstone, noticed a flurry of activity. A Secret Service man was seen running. At a hastily called news conference, reporters were told that the president had a cold—an upper respiratory infection. His temperature was up a degree. He would not be flying to Milwaukee. He would, instead, on the advice of his personal physician, return immediately to Washington.

At the airport, Kennedy was overheard telling Mayor Richard J. Daley, "I feel okay. Just a little worn." Reporters recalled that, yes, his voice had seemed a little "husky" the night before at the fund-raiser at the McCormick Place. And he had been sweating. That was odd for him. The president stood in the drizzle at O'Hare and shook hands with Illinois and Wisconsin Democratic leaders before getting on his plane.

"KENNEDY ILL, CANCELS TOUR," the *Chicago Daily News* bannered across its front page that afternoon. "Cold Ends Visit Here."

The Associated Press moved on its wires a photo of Kennedy leaving his hotel, wearing a gray fedora with a wide black band and slipping into a white raincoat.

The next day the photo made the papers nationwide. It was natural that Charles H. Salesky would notice it in New York. He kept a collection of such pictures. Salesky had taken over as president of the Hat Corporation of America after his brother, Bernard, had died of a heart attack that February. Looking at the photograph, Charles Salesky saw an opportunity to make a point that had been so important to his late brother. On Monday, October 22, he dictated the following letter:

Dear Mr. President:

I was sorry to read that you had a cold and hope you recover quickly and completely.

The paper that reported the story also carried a picture of you wearing a hat and coat, and said you had donned them because of your cold.

As hat manufacturers, we naturally like to see you wear a hat. But we think there's a much better reason for you to wear a hat than as a protection against colds. We believe you really look good in a hat, and I've quite a collection of pictures that back up my claim. There are 25,000 workers in our industry who would be happy to see you wear a hat, not just as a covering but as the fashion accessory it is.

May I offer you the services of a stylist from either our Knox, Dobbs or Cavanagh Divisions, to come to Washington and prepare a hat wardrobe for you? If same is acceptable, you may rest assured that under no conditions will we take advantage of this for publicity purposes.

Respectfully yours,
Charles H. Salesky

That afternoon, news of what had been happening behind the scenes was released to a stunned nation. Eight days earlier, an American U-2 spy plane had taken photographs of Soviet medium-range ballistic missile bases being constructed near San Cristóbal, Cuba. It took two days for the news to reach Kennedy. The week that followed was, for him, a nerve-racking mix of the extraordinary and the mundane. It was probably his finest hour, as he contained the zeal of his military advisers to launch all-out war on Cuba—which would almost certainly have meant war with the Soviet Union—while picking his way toward a negotiated settlement. He held secret meeting after secret meeting with top aides, arguing over the options: full-scale invasion? limited air attack? naval blockade? In public, Kennedy maintained his normal schedule. He had lunch with Crown Prince Hasan of Libya. He marked the National Day of Prayer at Saint Matthew's Cathedral. But it was a facade.

Kennedy thought that the trip to Cleveland, Springfield, Chicago, and points beyond had been canceled. But when he asked aide Kenny O'Donnell if he had called it off, O'Donnell said, "I didn't call off anything. I don't want to be the one who has to tell Dick Daley that you're not going out there." Thus he was in Chicago when the rush of events forced him to hurry back to Washington.

The extraordinary thing about Salesky's letter is that he sent it anyway, even after news broke that afternoon of a grave international crisis inspiring Kennedy's bogus cold. Rather than drop his offer, or rewrite the letter, Salesky merely held the letter for a week, then mailed it, as written, on October

29, along with a note explaining that he had "thought it would be in very poor taste to mail it out" before the threat of nuclear annihilation had, for the moment, passed.

* * *

The hatters were still at it. Kennedy's wearing a top hat at his inauguration months earlier had not placated them at all; there had never been much chance of that. "True, Kennedy has announced he'll wear a silk topper to his inauguration," the syndicated "Inside News on Washington" column had noted in late November 1960, "but this does not delight the hatmakers. They are realists and know that the American Male isn't going to buy a topper just because the president did for one formal occasion. What they really want is for Kennedy to wear a hat—any kind of presentable hat. They are convinced that if he persists in going hatless, he'll be the excuse for hundreds of thousands of American males to do likewise to the detriment of the industry they're trying to promote."

With the stakes so high, no intercession of serious world events—the Bay of Pigs invasion, the Cuban missile crisis— was going to cause the hat industry to step back into the shadows. No sooner had Kennedy settled into the Oval Office than the drumbeat resumed anew, from both hatters and those with a vested interest in fashion.

In an editorial in its March 1961 issue, *Gentleman's Quarterly* offered a generally praiseful if creepily microscopic analysis of Kennedy's wardrobe: "He sticks to dark fabrics, usually worsteds, in oxford and cambridge greys and dark blues, most often plain, occasionally with faint stripes. He wears lightweight clothing, ten to eleven ounces in the fall and winter, six to eight-ounce tropical worsteds in the summer."

His one fashion flaw, in the magazine's eyes, was the lack of a hat.

"The only quarrel the clothing industry has with him—and it is the same complaint lodged in England against Mr. Anthony Armstrong Jones[1]—is his disinclination toward hats."

GQ tried to paint Kennedy's aversion to hats as a quirky anachronism.

"Young men today are returning to hats, but at the time the President was at Harvard, hats were considered 'out,' and Mr. Kennedy never seemed to pick up the hat-wearing habit," the magazine wrote. "Arthur Sarnoff, president of the Thomas Begg Hat Stores in Manhattan, reminds the President that a 'hat is terribly important for a look of prestige, and in spite of Kennedy's high office, it can still make its contributions.' "

GQ based the clincher of its argument not on fashion at all, but on a bald commercial plea that hatters had been making for years.

"Furthermore, should the President continue to avoid hats," it wrote, quoting Sarnoff: " 'The image that's established by a great national leader has its repercussions and could hurt a segment, however small, of our economy.' New England is the heart of the men's felt hat industry and many a citizen of Danbury, Fall River and Norwalk depend on hat-wearing Americans for their livelihood."

It was a weak argument, one that could be applied to literally anything—buy this because people sell it—and also a tau-

---

[1] Jones was a well-known British photographer, "a man of monumental, mythical charm," who, in 1960, married Princess Margaret and became Lord Snowdon.

tology: Hats must be purchased to shore up the hat industry so it can continue to make hats that people will have to buy to keep the hat business going so it can sell them more hats.

The editorial did note with approval Kennedy's increased appearance in hats in the press, and concluded, "they certainly become him. A hat makes him look older, less boyish. As Mr. Sarnoff says, 'the strength that is really there in his face is more evident.' So, Mr. President, the sake of your own appearance and simple patriotism both seem to dictate that a chapeau is well worth considering. And why spoil such an otherwise admirable sartorial impression?"

Sarnoff, an effusive man with "more hats than hair," was another vigorous defender of the hat in the grand old style of Max Fluegelman. He loved expounding on the traditions and history of hats, much of it fanciful, and his four Manhattan stores carried every type imaginable, from turbans to London bobby helmets, from deerstalker caps to "hangover hats" that had temperature-retaining liquid in them and were supposed to be kept in the freezer until needed. As the magazine hit the stands, Sarnoff sent a dark gray "demi-bowler" to the White House. Accompanying the bowler, a hat that "has dignity yet is youthful in concept," was a warm letter. Sarnoff wrote:

This is the letter of a happy man. Happy to see his choice as President, happy to see his judgement confirmed with each Washington news release, happy to know we're all moving forward again.

Yet, personally, there is a small cloud just lurking over

the horizon. A small cloud with the label, 'President Kennedy doesn't wear a hat, why should I.'

You, Mr. President, have set a new pattern for youth, but youth can be slavish. What may be a personal attitude for you is becoming a must for these young hatless people. Unfortunately, for the men's hat business, it is having a bad effect and is rapidly getting worse. We need help, just a bit!

The demi-bowler from Sarnoff joined a haberdashery's worth of hats pouring in from across the world. A plastic yachting cap. A fine Italian Borsalino. A knit stocking hat. A hat of Persian lamb. A variety of ethnic caps. Numerous cowboy hats. They were offered to the president for a spectrum of reasons, from concerns about his health to general goodwill to shameless attempts at self-promotion. And many more hats would have been sent but for the sticking point of the president's hat size. Letters offered everything from complete modern hat wardrobes to an elaborate feathered Indian war bonnet, all to be shipped immediately upon receiving permission and the proper measurements.

"Have just recently started an Indian Trading Post catering primarily to Indians that follow the show circuit," Edward Williams, proprietor of Little Wolf's Indian Trading Post in Roxbury, Massachusetts, wrote to Pierre Salinger. "I got the idea of sending the President one of my creations. I can assure you it will be beautiful, and truly an exacting symbol of the American Indian."

These gift hats should be put in perspective. Hats were just one current—among the largest, to be sure, second perhaps only to gifts for his children—of a river of presents that flowed into the White House every day Kennedy was in office. Chairs for the president, dolls for Caroline, ships for John Jr., dresses for Jackie. Some gifts—the nicer ones—were from foreign dignitaries, and there was never any question about keeping those. But about a hundred a week came over the transom from various groups and individuals. Gifts of every imaginable type: A hand-painted pillow cover. A brass planter. An E-Z-X Home Exercise Machine. A plastic table cloth. Hand-knitted socks. A nuclear attack survival kit. Pineapples from Hawaii. A Chatty Cathy doll, sent directly by Elliot Handler, the president of Mattel.

The handling of such gifts was a delicate matter that required thought and tact on the part of the president's staff. The White House had made public its "stated policy of not accepting gifts of any appreciable monetary value," but that broad standard was more of a convenient pretext to turn down tailors eager to come to Washington to fit Kennedy for a suit or businessmen hoping to get a free endorsement from the president of the United States for the price of a hat.

The actual policy was to weigh the gift against the giver. Articles of considerable value could be accepted if they came from foreign organizations or major social service groups, since rejecting gifts might insult a valued friend. Accepting them, however, also posed risks, such as being seized upon by the president's enemies and portrayed as graft.

Shortly after his inauguration, Kennedy received a two-hundred-year-old sterling silver christening cup from the citizens of County Wexford, Ireland, and a model of a Danish sailing ship from a resident of Denmark. He kept the gifts, the acceptance of which made the papers, prompting a tart upbraiding from a Texas real estate agent named Margaret Blackistone.

"Before you were inaugurated, our papers here carried a story that you were going to insist upon a policy within your organization that no one would be allowed to accept gifts," she wrote in a letter she copied to James Reston at the *New York Times*. "I would like to know what explanation there is for such a sudden change in policy just one short month after your inauguration."

The obvious solution for this sort of unpleasantness and its attendant risks of bad publicity would have been to reject all gifts, no matter the giver or the value. But with presents arriving from overseas, that wasn't practical—both for the cost of returning the items and for the possible insult that doing so could convey. Hats came to Kennedy from all over. Jorge H. Saenz, of Bolivia, sent a *lluchu,* a cap worn by the peasants in the colder regions, such as La Paz. Athanase Mangala, of the Congo, sent *un chapeau que nos chefs countunders portent pendant les jours de grandes fetes*—"a hat which the leaders of my tribe wear on big holidays." Kurt Tarik Oz-Han, of Turkey, sent a *dobpu,* a silk embroidered cap he said was the national costume of the Turks of Turkistan.

The White House accepted the Bolivian and the Congolese hats with gratitude. But Kennedy's staff rejected the Turkish cap—actually it didn't even acknowledge receiving it, but merely shipped the cap back to the American embassy at Ankara for return, on the advice of the State Department.

"We do not believe that the White House should reply to the letter from Mr. Kurt Tarik Oz-Han," the officer in charge of Turkish affairs wrote in a memorandum. "The writer is evidently a member of the Pan Turanist group and seeks to identify President Kennedy with their views, i.e., all Turks, including about 40 million residents of the USSR, should be under one government. . . . The group publishes several magazines in Turkey and Europe. A reply would most likely be published in one of these, probably along with the letter addressed to the President by Mr. Oz-Han. We believe any reply, even a simple acknowledgement of the gift, could be used now or at a later date to the detriment of our foreign policy with Turkey and neighboring countries."

While most gifts did not carry the international implications of the hat from the leader of the Turkish Nationalists Working for the Freedom of the Enslaved Turks in Russia, each represented various constituencies, sometimes powerful ones, or, at the very least, when dealing with gifts from Americans, potential voters. Thus there were no form letters, but individual replies, typed by the tireless Evelyn Lincoln and her staff.

"Dear Mr. Fisher: I have been asked to acknowledge your letter of June 12 to the President concerning the health shoe heels you invented and which you offer for his use. Much as we appreciate . . ." "Dear Mr. Safir: This is to thank you, on behalf of the President, for the all wool 'Rabhor Robe' that you so kindly sent him. He, of course, appreciated your thoughtful gesture, but wanted me to explain that due to his stated policy . . ." "Dear Mr. Williams: Thank you very much for your kind offer to give the President one of your war bonnets. As you probably know, the President's present policy is not to accept gifts . . ."

The sincere offerings of individuals—handmade quilts and such—were generally accepted. Evelyn Lincoln kept the Green Bay Packers hat entrusted to her for delivery to the president by a seven-year-old boy named James Russler, of Two Rivers, Wisconsin, who visited the White House with the Punt, Pass and Kick Champions. Products from stores and companies, however, were invariably declined, unless the givers had the forethought to arrange a powerful intermediary.

For instance, the Lee Hat Company gave a pair of hats to probate judge Julius Bielizna, of Danbury, who delivered them to Connecticut congressman Frank Kowalski, who sent them to the White House. Wayne Gilley, the mayor of Lawton, Oklahoma, gave a Lawton-made bulldogger hat to J. Carlos McCormick, of the State Department's Bureau of Inter-American Affairs, along with a reminder that southwestern Oklahoma was the only part of the state to go Democratic in 1960. The White House accepted those hats but rejected the fur cap sent directly by James Elias, of E. D. Elias, manufacturers of fine furs.

The worry that acceptance could be twisted into an embarrassing commercial endorsement was a valid one, as can be seen in the rare instances when products slipped through. For instance, certain items were so inexpensive they couldn't politely be returned as too valuable to keep. Thus, just as the White House accepted the half-dozen pair of white socks sent by Rudin & Roth Hosiery, proud that the distinctive band denoting their product had been revealed in a photo of Kennedy, his pants leg hiked up, sitting on the beach with Caroline, so it also kept the colorful terry cloth beach hats sent by Leonard and Seymour Goodman, proprietors of Max

Goodman's Sons Headwear Corporation on West 23rd Street in New York City. "THIS IS OUR WAY OF THANKING YOU FOR THE WONDERFUL JOB THAT YOU ARE DOING," the brothers wrote. The White House couldn't very well reject a few terry cloth hats as being items of excessive value. So Evelyn Lincoln dispatched the standard letter of presidential gratitude and good wishes.

The Goodmans framed the letter in their office, and matters developed from there, as described in the brothers' next communication to Kennedy, mailed a few days later.

"The delegates from our union headquarters, after having seen the letter, have asked us to contact you to ask a favor," the Goodmans wrote, sidestepping responsibility for their request. "As you know, our industry is suffering from the competition of foreign imports. We have undertaken a major publicity campaign to make the public hat-conscious and to accept new styles.

"If in any way possible, we would like to obtain any pictures which are taken of the President's family in which they are wearing the hats we sent or any other headwear. We would like to feature these pictures in publications throughout the country.

"We realize that it is beneath the station of the Presidential family to actively participate in any advertising program, however, putting us in touch with anybody who might have pictures of this nature would be of such a help to our long suffering industry, that we feel this request is not of an insulting nature."

They asked the favor of a reply, and they got one, fast, along with their supposed gifts. "I am obliged to return herewith the beach hats that you previously sent to the President as a gift," wrote Lincoln. "Since we naturally assumed that there would be no publicity on the acceptance of these items, we were somewhat surprised to learn of the action you are planning. I must caution you that under no circumstances should the names of the President or members of his family be used in any way for advertising purposes."

Dodging such commercial snares had been a constant nuisance for Kennedy's staff from the moment he took office, when big city department stores put mannequins of the president and Jackie in their windows. Not only was the wildly popular Kennedy name borrowed by manufacturers trying to sell products from rocking chairs to fish stew to shorts of the "same type worn by the President," but their image was seized for the creation of the products themselves, such as commemorative coins and key chains.

"I must have written dozens of letters and had dozens of phone conversations with merchants during my tenure as Press Secretary, telling them to desist in the sale of certain items," Pierre Salinger wrote in his memoirs, specifically mentioning the profusion of dolls modeled on the president's daughter and wife. "In a way, it was a compliment to the Kennedys that so many people were interested in putting out products revolving around them. But the White House has had a policy against commercialization of the presidential families for some time and has enforced this policy over the years."

More or less. History is studded with rare occasions where presidents or their wives lent their names to advertising, either for a product or for a cause they particularly liked.

In 1900, for example, President William McKinley, locked

in a tight reelection campaign against the fiery William Jennings Bryan gave Waterman pens his endorsement to be used in magazine ads ("I have been using one of your fountain pens for several months, and take pleasure in saying that I find it an invaluable pocket companion."). Nor was the formality of presidential permission always seen as necessary. It is hard to imagine William Howard Taft giving the Postal Life Insurance Company approval to run a 1912 ad with his photograph superimposed over a locked mail bag, printed in a row next to that of Teddy Roosevelt and Woodrow Wilson, under the headline "Three Distinguished Advocates." But there he is, over some particularly disingenuous copy. "These three distinguished Americans all speak in highest terms of the benefits of insurance-protection. One of them has had four years of POSTAL protection."

Other ads were sanctioned, despite their improbability. During her husband's presidency, Eleanor Roosevelt appeared in ads promoting air travel and for the movie *Stella Dallas,* and had a radio show sponsored by Pond's Cold Cream. Harry Truman appeared in ads for fire safety. Eisenhower lent his name and face to a campaign promoting the magazine industry.

So did John F. Kennedy. In July 1961, the White House announced that Kennedy had for the first time authorized his image to be used in an advertisement—following in Ike's footsteps in the magazine industry campaign.

It's easy to see why. The path for Kennedy's march to the presidency had been smoothed over by years of adoring magazine stories. Magazines had learned that putting the photogenic Kennedy and his wife or family on their covers—alone or in combination—boosted sales, so those issues tended to be promoted. Publications considered themselves a little more free than other products to use the Kennedy image in advertisements, since doing so both offered allure and described content. Permission wasn't seen as necessary. The ad for the March 1962 issue of *GQ* that William Agnew held up at the Hat Corporation of America stockholder meeting had run without White House knowledge or consent. "Our permission was not sought for the ad referred to in your letter," Pierre Salinger wrote to a woman complaining about the president posing for fashion spreads. "We agree that it is not in the best of taste."

* * *

Kennedy's magazine industry endorsement did not please the hatters. They did not understand why Kennedy would appear in ads for magazines but not even deign to wear their product. Like all clothiers, hatmakers craved association with the famous to both create business and lend themselves an aura of exclusivity, and always had. Hatting the famous wasn't a luxury; it was essential. In his 1865 book on hats, Henry Melton, identified on the title page as "Hatter to His Royal Highness the Prince of Wales," describes his entry into the profession this way: "I commenced business, as I may say, comparatively a youth, and my first impulse of pride in my calling was, to obtain the honour of making a hat for the Beau Brummell of my time, the Count d'Orsay. With the dash of youth I at once threw my bread upon the water, and wrote to the County in as delicate a manner as I well could, stating my ambition as desirous of making even my calling associated with art and taste."

In America, one early hatter, Charles Knox, who opened on Fulton Street in New York City in 1838, prided—and promoted—himself for making the hats of Daniel Webster, Henry Clay, and Abraham Lincoln. Knox had a miniature portrait painted of Horace Greeley wearing one of his hats, to show off to acquaintances, and his son, Colonel Edward Knox, in his official company history claimed that Teddy Roosevelt was in the habit of hanging around their store's doorway.

"Sometimes he would stand there for an hour at a time, holding on to one of the awning rods, staring out over the Square, and Knox repeatedly suggested to one of his clerks that he go out and 'tell young Roosevelt that door post will stay up all right without him supporting it.' "

Roosevelt, despite loitering around hat shops, became the twentieth-century president most comparable to Kennedy— youthful, dynamic, beloved, and with a photogenic family. And like Kennedy, he generally refused to be in ads, which forced advertisers to be circumspect when seizing his endorsement. For instance, in 1903 an ad for the Henderson Lawn Grass Seed company displayed a photograph, not of Roosevelt, but of his lush Oyster Bay estate, boldly labeled.

That was the year Roosevelt gave what is probably the most famous presidential product endorsement of all time, when he supposedly allowed his name to be affixed to a line of stuffed bears that a Brooklyn shopkeeper had made in honor of an incident in November 1902. Roosevelt, on a hunting trip in Mississippi, had refused to shoot a bear his hosts had tethered to a tree, and a *Washington Post* cartoonist drew a memorable cartoon about it. The creation of the Teddy bear actually buoyed two major toy companies: Ideal Toys, founded by the Brooklyn shopkeeper based on the success of his bears, and Steiff in Germany, which was a small European toy maker before 1903, when an American company imported three thousand of its bears to capitalize on the Teddy bear craze, a reminder of just how powerful the presidential name on a certain product—and at the right time—can be.

It was natural that Knox Hats would dragoon Roosevelt into an ad. Knox tried to dance around Roosevelt's desire not to be featured in advertisements with the help of a newspaper photograph that happened to show the Knox label in the lining of a hat Roosevelt was holding.[2] The resulting 1909 magazine ad features a close-up photo of Roosevelt's hand holding his hat. Under it is a panorama of American battleships, the headline "Highest Type of Hat and Man," and this copy:

The above is an exact reproduction of President Roosevelt's hand with his **Knox Hat** in it as he waved Godspeed from the deck of the yacht Algonquin on Dec. 16, 1907, to the American battleship fleet as it started on its wonderful trip around the world under the command of Admiral Evans, in the presence of fifty thousand cheering Americans. This remarkable photograph of Mr. Roosevelt now hangs over the desk of Col. E. M. Knox in the Knox Building, Fifth Avenue and 40th Street, New York City.

---

[2] Not all hatters were so fortunate. British hatter Henry Melton spends two pages in his memoirs decrying various paintings—one of the prince, another of one of the prince's dogs—showing Melton's handiwork but not the Melton label within. "Had the hat but luckily been placed just an inch more horizontally, the crown would have displayed my name," he agonizes. "Verily, these gentlemen of the brush would appear to have a design against me."

An exact reproduction would appear but for the wish expressed by the ex-President that his picture be kept out of advertisements.

Col. Roosevelt always had the best of everything.

Roosevelt being out of office made it far more tempting for advertisers to seize his image, since, like most former presidents, he retained affection and name recognition but had lost the intimidating aura of power. After death, presidents become fair game, such as the 1927 travelers checks ad that showed a full-faced photo of Roosevelt and the headline "When Roosevelt went to SOUTH AMERICA He Carried A.B.A. Certified Cheques." This is particularly true with the passing of the centuries, and the images of presidents such as George Washington and Abraham Lincoln—sometimes dandied up in sunglasses or comic expressions—are seized so often to promote new checking accounts and February white sales that it is easy to forget they were once revered icons. For all the grief associated with the Kennedy assassination, certain companies were not deterred from immediately offering up advertisements disguised as "tributes," such as John Hancock Life Insurance's salute to Kennedy that ran in magazines in 1964, not to mention the avalanche of kitsch Kennedy "memorial" products.

While he was alive, Kennedy's popularity was such that he didn't have to endorse products to excite interest in them—merely his use was enough to cast an aura over them, create news, and boost demand.

"Kennedy sets the style, taste and temper of Washington,"

wrote *Time.* "Cigar sales have soared (Jack smokes them). Hat sales have fallen (Jack does not wear them). Dark suits, well-shined shoes, avoid button down shirts (Jack says they are out of style)."

The small North Carolina factory that made his straight-back rockers couldn't handle the volume of orders when Kennedy was photographed rocking in the Oval Office. For other manufacturers, the temptation to make their pitch was overwhelming. In their letters to Kennedy, they grasped for any advantage they could to try to touch Kennedy's heart, avoid the rejecting hand of Mrs. Lincoln, and get their products in the charmed circle.

Harold Freed, of the Rainbow Girl Coat Co., appealed to native Massachusetts pride when shipping a coat for Caroline Kennedy—"The coat is made from cloth woven in Uxbridge, the lining dyed in Worcester, canvas knitted in Lowell, buttons made in Boston and coat manufactured in our Springfield factory"—and also let drop that Ted had visited the factory and received a warm welcome.

One clothier requested that Kennedy start wearing double-breasted suits. Emile Joseph, a Crowley, Louisiana, clothier, pointed out that he was giving his "Jack Kennedy neckties" not only to the president, but to Democrats in all fifty states. His letter is so warm it is almost possible to read it and not wonder if he is selling them as well.

Most of these entreaties never came close to reaching the president, of course. Usually they were dealt with either by Lincoln and her staff or someone from the press office or an employee in another area of the White House.

Though on rare occasions, a gift would find its way to his presence—a letter accompanying a pair of neckties from a Massachusetts supporter was marked "sent to president's bedroom."

No single group of manufacturers was as persistent and varied in their appeals as the hatters and their associates. At times, they surrendered completely to their desperation.

"Fifty inches is all we ask," implored John J. Lambert, president of the Traveling Hat Salesmen's Association, who wanted not to give Kennedy a hat, but to encourage him to actually wear the hats he already had. "Taking your hat from your hand to your head will do it. Fifty inches, Mr. President, will help an industry and the thousands of people in it to a better living standard and solve some of our unemployment. . . ."

Some were less concerned whether Kennedy wore a hat or carried at hat, so long as the hat he wore or carried was one of theirs. "We would very much like the pleasure of making a hat for you," wrote J. Calem, president of the Trans-American Panama Hat Corp. "We can assure you that we will make up a hat that will be smart and good-looking for either wearing or carrying."[3]

Other offers were surprisingly casual. "Dear Mr. Presi-

---

[3] The idea of carrying a hat for propriety's sake was not invented by Kennedy, but was done by many men trying to balance society's demand that they wear a hat with their own desire not to. At least according to a letter printed in the *New York Times* in the mid-1920s. "One may see any day a million New Yorkers going about hatless on the street, but, for appearances sake, carry their hats around wherever they go," wrote Samuel Bernard, of New Brunswick, New Jersey. "Why not leave the hat home and avoid unnecessary baggage?"

dent," someone at Cortley Custom Hatters scrawled on its catalog, featuring such models as the Summer Rex, the Casual Rogue, and the Continental Slim, "Please send us a note with your choice of hats and we will be most happy to send them to you with our compliments."

Kennedy's hatter friends also stopped by. On Thursday afternoon, April 13, 1961—two days before American bombers began hitting Cuban airfields, signaling the start of the Bay of Pigs fiasco—Alex Rose was the first labor leader invited to the Oval Office since the inauguration. He found Kennedy in an exuberant mood, smoking a cigar and complimenting the Liberal Party's A. A. Berle, who was chairman of Kennedy's Task Force on Latin America.

"Your man is doing an excellent job here," Kennedy said. Rose praised Jackie Kennedy's impact on the millinery industry, which was enjoying a temporary surge due to her pillbox hats.

Rose took the opportunity to remind Kennedy that he wasn't doing as well when it came to the men's hat industry. Kennedy, laughing, said in his defense that he always carried a hat, even if he didn't often put it on.

"Our people say that a hat on the head is worth two in the hand," Rose quipped. Kennedy, according to *New York Mirror* labor columnist Victor Riesel, "roared and swiftly let it out that he had just gotten a new hat and would wear it because he was growing to like it."

As Rose left, he passed through the usual crowd of newsmen, who asked him what he talked about with the president.

"Oh, we talked about hats," Rose said, repeating his line about a hat on the head being worth two in the hand.

Perhaps the personal lobbying worked. Less than two

weeks after Rose's visit, when Indonesian president Sukarno arrived in Washington to discuss the tense situation in West New Guinea, Kennedy met him at the airport and they drove to the White House in an open car. Upon arrival, they strolled into the White House together, Sukarno wearing his distinctive brimless hat, and Kennedy in a gray fedora with a wide black band. It was one of the rare moments when Kennedy was photographed, not grinning uneasily as he momentarily set some gift hat someone had pressed upon him onto his head, but merely wearing a hat and going about his business. The news photographers clicked away.

The AP Wirephoto ended up on the front pages of newspapers nationwide. But this gesture—if it was that—on Kennedy's part still did not satisfy the hatters. Perhaps they were jealous of the more dramatic efforts he made to shore up other struggling American industries. Not only did he willingly give his name to the magazine industry, but he came out swinging for milk.

Fear of contamination from the radioactive fallout of atomic tests had depressed milk and dairy product sales in the early 1960s: they dropped a couple percentage points in 1961 despite a rise in population, and even a small stumble sends shock waves when dealing with a basic American industry. The Department of Agriculture pulled out its secret weapon. On January 23, 1962, Kennedy appeared before the National Conference on Milk and Nutrition and said that milk not only "offers no hazards," but was so delicious that he had ordered it served at all White House meals. He revealed the stunning news that at a recent luncheon with newspaper editors there was actually one journalist who ordered milk instead of wine.

Kennedy concluded his speech by raising a toast to milk with a glass of milk. He was willing to perform the stunt because he knew it would have an impact.

"The President is keenly aware of the influence the first family has on the nation's buying habits," Jack Anderson wrote.

In contrast to the milk effort, Kennedy's carrying around a hat and occasionally putting it on seemed anemic, and by early 1962 the tone of some hatters shifted from the polite, beseeching appeals that followed the inauguration to something decidedly testier. A year after his friendly letter accompanying the gift of a demi-bowler, New York hatter Arthur Sarnoff was lashing out at Kennedy in public.

"Somewhere under all that hair there must be a hat," Sarnoff sneered, explaining that he was not mad, not angry, but "just bitter, bitter, bitter."

Sarnoff announced that he had designed a hat specifically for Kennedy: a clear plastic hat with a handle for carrying. The credulous press conveyed this obvious bit of sarcasm as if it were a potential new style.

The White House, too, grew snippish on the subject. The microscopic attention paid to Kennedy's personal habits grew to be a strain on the president. After *Time* magazine printed an innocuous report about Kennedy doing the twist at a patio party toward the end of 1961, a "furious" Kennedy exploded at *Time* writer Hugh Sidey.

"These little personal items began to eat away at him," Sidey said. "They bothered him more than discussions of the Bay of Pigs or what he was going to do in Berlin."

When the British tailors upbraided Kennedy for not

wearing a hat, there was no official response, but the unofficial comment from Hyannis Port was, "What, again?"

The economy was souring in the spring of 1962. Stocks had fallen at the end of May. Big industries were worried, and little ones were practically apoplectic. Hatters, remember, were just one of many marginal American industries desperate to be boosted by the Kennedy glamour. There were also, for instance, the baby-shoe makers. When John F. Kennedy Jr. was photographed toddling along barefoot, another small industry stirred in protest.

"Pictures of the Kennedy toddler without shoes, the manufacturers wail, may depress the shoe market," Jack Anderson wrote in his column in April 1962. "They can envision parents from coast to coast saying: 'The President's baby goes barefoot, why should we buy new shoes for our kids?'"

It seemed at times that Kennedy couldn't bump into a private citizen without an attempt being made to use him for commercial benefit. Trying to escape a crowd that had gathered during a shopping trip to Palm Beach, Kennedy and his entourage cut through a women's clothing store.

"Would it be all right if we pass through your store?" the president asked the owner.

"It is perfectly all right if you walk slowly going out the front door," she said. "I want everybody on Worth Avenue to see you coming out of my store."

Kennedy's popularity was such that whatever he did was certain to upset some and please others. When he showed up at a Washington Senators baseball game without a suit jacket—another milestone in the steady march toward casual living—the leather belt folks were "overjoyed" and predicted a 10 percent gain in volume the next year, based, in part, on the fact that Kennedy showed off his belt. Men's clothiers, on the other hand, complained. This was a common pattern.

"Whenever I say anything that upsets them, businessmen just die," Kennedy said. "I have to spend time and energy trying to prop them up."

In the summer of 1962, Robert Kennedy agreed to address the triannual hatter's convention that his brother had spoken to three years before. But he backed out, and the administration instead sent the secretary of labor, Arthur Goldberg. Goldberg's first words recognized his boss's continuing hat problem.

"I come to you as a member of the New Frontier who wears a hat," he said, to laughter and applause.

* * *

The hatters lobbied Kennedy, but they were too sophisticated to try to physically slap a hat on the president's head. Not all his guests were that savvy. The most routine White House ceremonies were a cause of concern for Kennedy.

"Kennedy had a horror of hats," Sidey wrote. "He had an even greater horror of being forced to don the unorthodox headdresses of visiting delegations."

Kennedy's military aide, Major General Chester Clifton, recalled a worried Kennedy taking him aside and seeking reassurance before the visit of a group of Native Americans in the Rose Garden.

"They're not going to give me a bunch of feathers to wear, are they?" Kennedy asked.

Whether Kennedy wore a proffered hat or not was definitely a function of who was making the attempt. While

Kennedy did not want to be crowned by just anybody, if the situation was right, he would permit it to happen. The president had enormous respect for Colonel John Glenn, the first American astronaut to orbit the earth. Kennedy had been worried about the flight, going so far as to invite Glenn to the White House beforehand to talk about safety. When *Friendship 7* later made its three and a half revolutions around the earth, there was indeed great concern that the heat shield had come loose, which would have doomed Glenn to a fiery death upon reentry.

But the shield held. Glenn survived his flight—for which he received an extra $245 in flight pay—to become the greatest American aviation hero since Charles Lindbergh. A relieved Kennedy hurried to Florida to congratulate Glenn in person and pin the Distinguished Service medal on him.

Kennedy, Glenn, the astronaut's family, and various NASA officials then toured the space facility, in a hectic scene, a "crush of reporters, photographers, Secret Service men, spectators and employees."

There was a small presentation at Launch Pad 14. Glenn produced a green hard hat that the base manager had given him. It was like those worn by the launch crew, except emblazoned "J. F. Kennedy, President, U.S.A." and "John Glenn, First Manned Orbital Flight, 2-20-62"[4] along with a painting of a globe surrounded by three orbits. He presented it to Kennedy.

"This will make him an honorary member of the launch

---

[4] The inscription conveniently forgets Soviet astronaut Yuri Gagarin, the first man—albeit a Russian—to orbit the Earth.

crew," said Glenn. Kennedy put the helmet on and then removed it. "Glad to have you aboard, sir," Glenn said.

The most interesting aspect of this particular encounter is that it reminds us of the power of image to corrupt impressions of history. Even though Kennedy undoubtedly wore the helmet—there are photographs of him wearing it—by the time the episode reached one memoir, it had been massaged so as to fit Kennedy's reputation.

"There was a bit of byplay as Glenn, knowing JFK's aversion to funny hats, tried and failed, as so many had failed before him, to put a hard hat on his head," wrote William Manchester in a book about his years with Kennedy.

Glenn, incidentally, denies knowing about Kennedy's dislike of hats or trying to put one on him mischievously. "I wasn't aware of his aversion to hats or anything," he said. "I didn't know anything of it. I just put it on, thinking it was okay."

Glenn said it was a spontaneous act on his part.

"We were out showing him the launch pad, and on the pad out there normally everyone is required to wear a hard hat," Glenn said. "So when we got out, standing there, I just put it on him. . . . He wore it for a little while. He didn't take it off immediately."

Kennedy valued his old friends, liked having them around, and happily doled out jobs and favors to them. He had joked for years about making his old Navy buddy Paul Fay the undersecretary of the Navy should he become president, and he surprised people by actually doing it, over the objections of the secretary of defense. When another Navy comrade, Al Webb, stopped by bearing gifts in September 1963, Kennedy called Fay into the Oval Office.

"Al Webb was in PT boats with us," remembers Fay. "He was in the hat business, and he knew that it would certainly move the sale of hats if the president wore hats."

All Kennedy's Navy buddies had nicknames for each other: Fay was "Red," Al Webb was "Nice Al," and Kennedy was "Shafty," though they didn't call him that to his face once he became president. Fay describes the encounter with Webb in detail in his memoirs:

> Nice Al Webb, who was the Eastern representative for one of the major hat manufacturers, was considered their only possible savior because of his friendship with the President.
>
> "We're dying in the business without you wearing a hat," Al told the President. "Can't you put one on now and then?"
>
> The President appreciated the serious effect his refusal to wear a hat had on the industry, as well as the great strain on Nice Al.
>
> "Al," he'd reply, "I've tried wearing hats, and I'm just not the type. When I get one on I feel like I'm wearing a tent. Look, I'll carry a hat for you. How would that be?"
>
> Poor Nice Al gave a weak smile of acceptance.
>
> I personally thought the President looked great in a hat. "To be completely honest, and not just to help good old Al, I think you look damn well in a hat," I told him.
>
> All these arguments were to no avail. But in a last attempt, Al said, "Mr. President, let me make up a hat for you. I know exactly the style you ought to wear. I'll bring it down next week."
>
> The week passed and Nice Al came down with two

hats, one for me and one for the President. I was seated in my office in the Pentagon when the phone buzzed.

"Red," the President said, "Nice Al is down with the hats. I told him he could bring them over at 5:30 p.m. Come over so we can satisfy Al once and for all."

At 5:30 we all gathered in the President's office for our hat-trying. Al was carrying the weight of the hat industry on his shoulders. If the President continued to refuse to wear a hat, the hat business would undoubtedly suffer.

Al took the hats out of their boxes as if he was handling a couple of Stradivariuses.[5] The President and I tried them on. Standing off like the master viewing his greatest work, Al said, "You both look great."

The President and I looked at each other and burst out laughing.

"Al," the President said, "are you willing to destroy the beloved image of our country's leader just to save the hat industry?"

The President called for a photographer to preserve a permanent record[6] of the hour the final decision was made that John F. Kennedy, thirty-fifth president of the U.S.A., would not wear a hat.

Kennedy "didn't want to let down his old pal," Fay said. "The only reason he ever put on the hat was because of Al Webb."

[5] Those observing skilled hat salesmen often commented on the elaborate care with which they handled the merchandise.

[6] "His photograph of the President and Red survives," wrote William Manchester, who boiled down the episode from Fay's book, complete with the line about the Stradivariuses, and then added, "In it they look like a couple of house detectives"—which they do.

Chapter 9

"We all felt the same way."

The central image that remains of John F. Kennedy's inauguration is that of his marvelous speech and its timeless phrasings, his breath steaming in the frigid air as his words rang out. How could it be otherwise?

That afterward he sat, watching a parade, wearing a top hat, occasionally lifting it in tribute or greeting to a passing float, is naturally forgotten. Though this, too, was on television and in the newspapers the next day, it did not register in the collective public memory. Even the most fastidious Kennedy historians overlook it.

"Kennedy stood bareheaded and without his overcoat while taking the oath, giving his address, and watching the three-and-a-half hour inaugural parade along Pennsylvania Avenue," wrote Robert Dallek in his acclaimed biography *An Unfinished Life,* despite, one assumes, having seen the photographs of Kennedy reviewing the parade, his overcoat on, his top hat firmly in place.

Why shouldn't the public and historians miss this? It

barely registered at the time. "Hatless Kennedy Reviews Parade in Bitter Cold," read a headline in the next day's *Chicago Sun-Times*. Kennedy watching the parade was neither as memorable or as dramatic as the inauguration, and most people doubtlessly tuned in their TVs for the ceremony and the speech, then drifted away as the hours wore on. Even for those who saw it, the incongruous, antique image—a gentleman tipping his top hat—would not wed itself easily to Space Age leader John F. Kennedy. A great deal of the public understanding of history is achieved by screening out the parts that don't fit.

Though Kennedy wore a top hat, it was against his nature—or at least was seen as against his nature—and so it was discounted, just the way that William Manchester didn't recognize that Kennedy actually wore the hat that John Glenn had given him. At his inauguration, Kennedy was driven from the White House to the Capitol and back in an open car—with Eisenhower, on his way to be sworn in, and with his wife, Jacqueline, on the way back. As newspaper photographers clicked away, he would occasionally place his top hat on his head. Pictures appeared all over the world the next day showing Kennedy smiling, waving, wearing a hat. But seasoned political reporters and Kennedy aides focused on the grin of unease frozen on Kennedy's face, and noticed how he was constantly donning and removing his hat, and explained this to the world.

"Mr. Kennedy, who is usually hatless, seemed self-consciously uncomfortable in his topper," wrote one reporter. "He wore it as briefly as possible in the trips back and forth from the White House to Capitol Hill."

Having made the decision to wear a top hat at his inaugural, Kennedy ended up not wearing it much during the most important moments. Those who tuned in to the television coverage of Kennedy arriving to give his speech, listening to the cardinal pray and Frost recite and Marian Anderson sing, then delivering his speech and departing, never once saw Kennedy put on his hat—no doubt an important factor in the creation of the myth that he didn't wear one at all that day. What is the cover of *Newsweek* compared to 50 million people watching television?

Which returns us to the still-unanswered question: Why didn't Kennedy want to wear a hat?

True, he was honing his image, and proving his toughness, and showing off his trademark hair. But there was another, even more basic, factor at work: he was an American man in his mid-forties. Kennedy was president of the United States, but he was also a member of his generation, and when it came to hats, he was not leading, as the public automatically assumed. He was following, in perfect step with his contemporaries.

"We all felt the same way," said Red Fay, born a year after Kennedy. "I don't know anybody of my contemporaries who wore hats. [Kennedy] felt better without hats—almost all of us did. I never wear a hat either. It just wasn't the style we were used to."

"I never liked wearing a hat," said Jim Reed, who also served on PT boats with Kennedy. "He and I had the same lack of interest in wearing a hat."

Kennedy only seemed to be ahead of the pack because he was among the first of his generation to be subjected to such intense public scrutiny. But he was not the first of his generation to express a preference regarding hats. With the election of Kennedy as president, the public began to perceive what those in the hat business had known for years.

In May 1947, the Grey Advertising Agency, working on behalf of the Hat Research Foundation, conducted a survey of 2,006 men nationwide. They found that 57 percent of men in Kennedy's age bracket at the time—twenty-five to thirty-four—preferred not to wear a hat. Even more ominous for the industry, they also learned that the desire to wear a hat was directly proportional to a man's age. The great majority of middle-aged men—78 percent of those over the age of forty-five—liked to wear a hat. But that number tumbled steadily among younger men. Only 15 percent of men age twenty and younger said they'd rather wear a hat than go hatless. The younger a man was, the less he cared for hats. Somehow, what once was a symbol of adulthood had become a sign of age.

This precipitous falloff came as a surprise to older generations, who assumed that hats were a permanent fixture in the male wardrobe. When Stetson bought Mallory hats in the early 1950s, it offered the account to New York advertising agency Kenyon and Eckhardt. The firm immediately dispatched a pair of experienced admen, Ed Cox and Draper Daniels, on a train to Philadelphia to get their "battle orders" from the hatters.

On their way, Cox, in his fifties, briefed Daniels, about thirty-five—roughly Kennedy's age at the time—on what Stetson was like:

"They're wonderful people, very easy to work with," Cox said. "As long as you remember to wear a hat, you'll never have any trouble."

Cox paused, struck by a sudden concern.

"You did bring your hat with you?" he asked.

"Hell, Ed," Daniels replied. "I haven't owned a hat for years."

Contrast Daniels's reaction with that of a previous businessman on a train, the fictional Mr. Hood in George Gissing's novel *A Life's Morning*. Three-quarters of a century is a long time, and fiction is not synonymous with real life. But a lot of social change had to take place to get from Gissing, who felt comfortable having a character steal from his employer rather than present himself to a client without a hat, to Daniels, who boarded a train to visit a client who *sold* hats without even considering that he should wear one himself.

What happened?

It couldn't be Kennedy: in 1947 he was just another freshman congressman, perhaps a little better known because of his father and PT-109, but certainly not a figure influencing the sartorial tastes of the nation.

The Grey Advertising Agency data, despite the promising title "What People Are Thinking About Men's Hats in 1947," provides no clear answer. Though interviewing thousands of men about a change they were at that moment involved in making, the report fails to pinpoint a specific cause. Of the dozen factors mentioned by respondents as the reasons they didn't wear a hat, only four were cited by more than 5 percent of the men, and those were broad categories: "Don't feel comfortable" (19 percent); "Hat is a nuisance" (17 percent); "Habit" (12 percent); and "Just don't like to wear one" (12 percent). The more specific reasons, from "Lots healthier" to "Cooler without" to "Causes headaches," each received a handful of percentage points.

The study never mentions the second reason popular cul-

ture often offers for the decline of hat-wearing: the burgeon-
ing popularity of the automobile, which had been influencing
more and more areas of American life since the 1920s.
Though it is possible that "hat is a nuisance" might include
those who found themselves driving more. In the late 1940s,
automobile manufacturers began to give their new models a
sleeker style,[1] which appealed to car buyers but made it more
difficult to wear a hat while driving than it had been in the
older, boxier models. The challenges of stowing a hat while
behind the wheel, however, were no greater than for a man on
a bus or subway, and no worse than the typical dilemma the
hat-wearing man faced while out on the town—there was
always the passenger seat, the backseat, the dashboard, the
rear ledge or, as a last resort, the trunk. Passengers could use
their laps. At least in a car nobody expected a quarter.

But the impact of automobiles on hats was not limited to
the ease or difficulty a man faced in wearing a hat—or putting
it somewhere—when he got behind the wheel. There was a
larger impact that cars had on society. The act of driving a car,
itself, as opposed to, say, taking a bus or subway, had to influence the increasing number of hatless men, though they may
not have even been aware of it at the time. A person going out
to the garage to start the car just does not bundle up as much
as a person walking to the corner to catch a bus, nor does he
interact with passersby in the same way. Cars not only under-

---

[1] This is true with the exception of Chrysler, whose president, K.T. Keller, felt
cars should neither be too stylish nor too low. "A car shouldn't knock a man's
eyes out or his hat off," said Keller—or someone working for him at Chrysler.
Chrysler sales suffered because of their boxy styling, and Keller was out by
1950.

cut the physical benefits of hats, but they eliminated much of the social pressure, and therefore must have had a role in their decline. Hatters back this up.

At Notre Dame in 1941, Bob Doran, of Doran Bros. Hats, did a study of outerwear sales versus car sales:

> I wrote to the Department of Commerce and I got production figures of what I informally classified as men's weather apparel. I started with felt hats, galoshes, woolen scarves, non-work mittens and gloves, heavy overcoats, woolen underwear—everything I could quickly classify as weather apparel for men. I took 1920 as a base figure and for the same period I got the production figures of the automotive industry. I graphed them out. The men's apparel lines started to decline in parallel lines to the inverse curve to the automotive curve. You didn't need that kind of clothing anymore.

But, as the statisticians like to say, correlation does not imply causation. And while we will return to automobiles as a factor in the death of hats, it can't be said that cars were responsible. Coats didn't fall from favor. And while the automobile was blamed for changes in everything from sexual mores to church attendance to the rise in the popularity of golf, few people—Bob Doran excepted—were connecting the growing popularity of cars to the decline of hats, at least not in 1947.

The Grey survey was mum on cars, but it was deeply concerned with the third popular explanation for the death of hats: World War II. According to the survey, the war, as a motivation, seemed paradoxically to inspire men to wear hats more *and* to wear hats less in about equal numbers. Of the men who said they were wearing hats less frequently in 1947 than they had before the war, 19 percent said they were not wearing hats because they "had to in the service."

But among the vets who said they wore hats more than before, "Got used to it during the war" was cited by 17 percent. Hat sales were strong immediately after the war, and the general consensus was it was due to returning vets, trained to wear hats in the military, now outfitting themselves for civilian life.

"Just when the men's hat industry was greatly concerned over a trend toward bareheadedness, the U.S. armed forces' uniform regulations make millions of males extremely conscious of headwear," *Business Week* wrote in April 1946. "Manufacturers are inclined to see some correlation between this and today's unprecedented order volume."

The Grey survey declared the matter a wash. "Hatlessness has not changed greatly since before the war," the study concluded, and explained while "the trend toward hatlessness appears to be greater among Veterans of World War II," it was not so much because that group were vets, but because they were young, and young men were abandoning hats whether they had served or not. Fewer men were wearing hats, and they knew it: 42 percent in the Grey survey said hatlessness was on the increase; only 10 percent held the opposite view. This was slightly more than before the war, when 39 percent in a 1940 survey said bareheadedness was on the rise.

This made the careful 1947 exploration of the war as a factor a little puzzling, since the study admitted that young men were abandoning hats *before* the war, as was clear if you picked up a pre-war etiquette book.

"Within recent years, a hat has become optional equipment for a young man in almost any situation," Dorothy Stratton and Helen Schlema wrote in *Your Best Foot Forward: Social Usage for Young Moderns,* a 1940 guide to polite behavior. "When he is dressed for the street, he wears a business suit, topcoat, and gloves if the weather requires them, and a hat if he chooses."

What made Stratton and Schlema's book more authoritative than most etiquette manuals was their technique: they drew their issues from the concerns of thousands of college students nationwide and found their answers by polling "leaders" on dozens of campuses. Whenever hats came up, they took pains to point out that the young men of the day weren't buying, in asides such as, "With the tuxedo, a derby or a soft hat in gray or black may be worn, but many college men refuse to wear any."

They never attempt to address *why* college men were so adamant, and their reluctance should not be surprising. This issue mystified some of the most analytical minds of the time. In his 1949 essay on Gissing and *A Life's Morning,* George Orwell, then 46, paused to muse how society had so utterly transformed:

This is an interesting example of the changes in outlook that can suddenly make an all-powerful taboo seem ridiculous. Today, if you had somehow contrived to lose your trousers, you would probably embezzle money rather than walk about in your underpants. In the eighties the necessity would have seemed equally strong in the case of a hat. Even thirty or forty years ago, indeed, bare-headed men were booed at in the street. Then, for no very clear reason, hat-lessness became respectable, and today the particular tragedy described by Gissing—entirely plausible in its context—would be quite impossible.

"For no very clear reason." Even Orwell, that daring social critic, author of both *1984* and *Animal Farm,* dismissed the possibility of understanding what had happened. Kennedy's surviving contemporaries express the same benign puzzlement. "I don't think any of us ever thought about it," said Fay.

Hatters certainly thought about it. Writing the same year as Orwell, E. A. Korchnoy, the president of the Hat Research Foundation, ignored political leaders, cars, and the war in his thirty-four-page report to the board of directors, "A Program to Sell More Hats in 1949–50." He placed the blame not on the customers and their inclinations, but on the hat industry itself. "Product improvement in our industry has been slow in design, in quality and in price," he wrote. "There are great areas of needed expansion."

He may have been onto something. The availability of many of the materials that go into a good dress hat—European rabbits, for instance, whose fur made superior felt—were greatly constricted by the war, and companies put their energies into the guaranteed sales and profits to be gained by supplying the military. Forty percent of men in the Grey survey felt the quality of hats had suffered since the war, from poor material and high prices. Hats were both shoddier and more expensive, a bad combination, and men didn't want them. "Styles not too good" was a reason cited by 10 percent of the men who found themselves wearing fewer hats in 1947 than before the war, and for a number of years young men had been complaining that the range of hat fashions offered nothing for them.

In 1944, Sydney J. Harris, a young newspaperman whose column had just begun in the *Chicago Daily News,* said that he and his friends "resented the bland uniformity of the dumb-looking hat," and as a result none of them "would be caught dead in a hat." Boldly predicting the death of men's hats as a fashion, Harris suggested that the "American male was seeking a new masculine image, and that the traditional hat foisted on him since Victorian times made him feel foolish, pompous and inept."[2]

Hatters were aware of this attitude, and the late 1940s were the high-water mark of efforts to promote hat-wearing. There were celebrations of hat history, such as the Hat Cavalcade in New York City that used store windows to focus on hat history and the hats of the famous, as if trying to shame the hatless by drawing attention to the rich history they were ignoring. There was also National Hat Week, Korchnoy's 1949 brainchild designed to raise awareness of hats nationwide with posters exhorting "HATS ON America!" and a national ad campaign in which adoring women encouraged their menfolk to wear hats while the men stared in goggle-eyed joy at their new fedoras.

These attempts were viewed with a high degree of bemused cynicism, as shown in the pages of *The New Yorker.*

[2]This prompted the president of Stetson to send Harris a "starchy" letter, sternly rebuking the young man. Thirty years later, when Stetson went bankrupt, Harris gleefully pulled the letter from his files and crowed about it.

Harold Ross had a fascination with the frantic drumming of the hatters, and his writing staff produced a series of deadpan reports on the latest efforts.

"National Hat Week rolled by last month and, by Jehoshaphat, caught us napping, but we've since made contact with Mr. E. A. Korchnoy, president of the Hat Research Foundation and father of the Week," began a 1949 "Talk of the Town."

"Asked one fellow about the notion that hats cause baldness, and he damn near exploded," wrote E. J. Kahn Jr., visiting Danbury in 1946 to have some fun with the hatters' affection for scientific study. " 'We made a survey and found that people who wear hats have fewer harmful bacteria on their heads than people who don't,' he said. 'We made another survey and found that only seven percent of adult Americans believe that old wives' tale about baldness anymore. That's as low a percentage as you can hope for, because a survey in 1943 showed that six percent of the people didn't know who the President was.' "

Highlighting your product's rich history and ordering customers to buy can't be expected to win over someone who doesn't want it in the first place, and the public didn't want hats. The young men at *The New Yorker* didn't wear hats; the hat industry pieces inevitably mention hatters pressing hats upon the authors. The Sydney Harris generation didn't wear hats. Not liking the styles available to men, styles worn without complaint for years and years, is not in itself an explanation. But one phrase of Harris's hints at something lurking behind the puzzling death of men's hats: "the bland uniformity of the dumb-looking hat."

For centuries, the standard way to criticize fashions, particularly the fashions of the young, was that they were extreme, outrageous, too big, too small, too tight, too showy, drawing attention to themselves with finery or with wild colors. Critics attacked fops and dandies for their bizarre ways. The fashions of those behind the times could be scorned as old, outdated, shabby, wrong.

But to view your fellow men, dressed in the approved style of the day, as exhibiting a "bland uniformity" is a clue that leads us back even further—to an almost identical phrase used by a Western observer to describe the Turks after they adopted hats in the 1920s: "dull gray uniformity." The mid-1920s were the high-water mark for hat fashion in this country, their zenith and thus, by definition, the beginning of the decline. The 1920s also marked the youth of the Alex Roses and the Bernard Saleskys of the 1960s, the union leaders and business owners who so vigorously struggled to force Kennedy to wear a hat. Understanding the era would also help explain what inspired these men. They had experienced a utopia, an ordered world where all men were expected—no, *compelled*—to wear the hats they sold, and those who broke out of the framework often met with rigid social disapproval, sometimes even violence. It was a lost Eden they would struggle to recover with all their strength. To understand where it went, we first need to understand what it was.

Chapter 10

"Beware! The fifteenth falls on Tuesday next."

When President Calvin Coolidge donned a straw hat and went for his usual afternoon stroll on a hot September 18, 1925, in Washington, D.C.—accompanied, *mirabile dictu*, by a lone Secret Service agent—the news was carried two days later on the front page of the *New York Times,* under the masthead, in a box. It was also on the front page of the *New York Herald and Tribune.* Not due to the walk, or the agent, or even the hat, necessarily, but because of the combination of the hat and the date. The president had decided to "ignore the unwritten law banning the wearing of straw hats after Sept. 15." The next day, this time with a larger security entourage, he wore the "taboo" hat again. The famously close-mouthed Coolidge explained his delinquency with a terse: "Summer isn't over yet."

With rare exceptions such as Coolidge, men in the 1920s knew that, no matter the weather, one just did not wear a straw hat after September 15. Past that date, almost any man who wasn't the president of the United States and wore his summer straw risked a stranger knocking the hat off his head and jumping on it. Or worse.

The tradition had been going on, across the nation, for more than twenty-five years. A British tourist in Philadelphia went to his hotel clerk on an unusually warm late-September day in 1899 and asked where he might buy a straw hat.

"In no uncertain terms, the clerk informed him that (a) nobody, but nobody in the City of Brotherly Love wore a straw hat at the end of September and (b) to venture outside with one so late in the season was to court danger." The man prudently chose to wear his derby.

Straw hats could only be worn in their proper season, which began in the spring on Straw Hat Day. Strict observance of this began around the turn of the century. Straw Hat Day came around in June then, a period when men seemed to spontaneously set aside their warm felt hats and pick up cooler summer straws. As it became formalized, Straw Hat Day began creeping into May, as hat stores tried to get a jump on their competition by pushing the new straws the moment warm weather took hold. One critic in 1910 saw the shift as part of the general muddling of the seasons. "We have asparagus in January and strawberries in March," he wrote. "And for the same reason we have straw hats before the time the straw hats of our fathers bloomed."

Straw Hat Day was seized by the hat trade and regimented, a public relations gimmick to prod men into the stores to buy their boaters and Panamas and leghorns. Hatters were used to working in lockstep—getting together to decide what the fashion would be this year, or when to discount the hats in midsummer as a way to draw men back into the stores. They also worked hand in hand with pliant politicians only too happy to help out the local businesses with an official proclamation:

"WHEREAS, the old felt hat has served its useful purpose during the past few months and has outlived its usefulness since warmer weather has arrived," began a typical decree, "AND WHEREAS, too much weight is not good for one's brow in warm weather, NOW THEREFORE, I, William T. Nobles, Mayor of the City of Wisconsin Rapids, do hereby proclaim and set aside Sunday, May 20, as Official Straw Hat Day in Wisconsin Rapids."

Thus Straw Hat Day rolled across the country, beginning around Easter in New Orleans and moving northward with the warm weather through May. Newspapers pitched in, with articles announcing the big switch running alongside hat shop advertisements. Gimmicks abounded. The *Tampa Times* sponsored a Straw Hat Day parade for the Washington Senators, who had spring training in Tampa, with advertising and editorial pulling together in the same direction.

"Off with the old lid!" announced an ad for Henry Giddens and Company. "On with the new Straw Hat!"

"Cast aside your weather beaten felt and put on one of the new straws!" an article echoed. "Step out with the new season with a new straw, knowing you have topped off your attire with the right sort of headwear."

The parade was just one of many promotional stunts used to catch men's attention—scantily clad women were, as always, popular. In Denver, a trio of bathing beauties were sent into the street wearing swimsuits and men's straw hats, and the newspapers there published joke photographs of them joshing with a downtown cop. In Long Beach, California, fifty waving "beach beautifiers" were posed in front of an enormous, seventy-foot-wide straw hat, some holding yard-high letters that spelled out "STRAW HAT WEEK." There were hat-throwing contests and airplanes dropping hats from the sky.

The ads and articles blossomed, store windows filled with straws, various publicity gimmicks of one kind or another were held, and men dutifully marched in and bought hats.

"Talk about regimentation? Those were the days!" *Men's Wear* reflected nostalgically in 1935, when the practice had already begun to wane. "The retailers let the calendar do their buying."

There were some who wouldn't play along. Howard W. Jackson, the mayor of Baltimore, was asked to officially determine when Straw Hat Day would take place in 1924.

"Nothing doing in that line," he told the *Baltimore Sun*. "Let people get out their straw hats now if they like or at any other time the straw hat will feel comfortable. I am going to get out my straw hat whenever I see fit."

As Jackson's comments indicate, when to hold Straw Hat Day was left to local discretion. But in mid-September came Felt Hat Day, and that was an entirely different matter. Here there was no flexibility. Felt Hat Day was nonnegotiable. It was enforced by mob rule and was so inviolable that it was only rarely referred to by name. The grim date was enough.

"Beware!" warned an article in the *New York Times* on September 13, 1925. "The fifteenth falls on Tuesday next and after that mystic notch in the calendar has been passed men may continue to wear straw hats at their peril." The message was the same, whether in articles or ads. "Today is the Day—September 15" was the headline in a large Truly Warner ad that ran in the *Times* on September 15, 1926. The date did not shift, no matter where you were, no matter the weather.

"Nobody seems to know, quite, why Sept. 15 should be the last day for straw hats. But it is," wrote the *New York Daily News* in 1923. "And if you don't believe it, wear one down the avenue (either Fifth or C) this morning. On any such adventure, however, be sure to have a card in your pocket bearing name, address—and the proper person to notify in case of accident. The boys just naturally don't like straw hats after the fifteenth."

Actually, the September 15 tradition was, at the time, barely fifteen years old. Before then, the dread date had been long established as September 1. "Under the usages following an ancient custom in Louisville, today was the last day on which a straw hat could be worn with personal safety on Main Street, the principal wholesale district of the city," the *Atlanta Constitution* wrote in 1908 in a story datelined "Louisville, Ky. September 1."

It was unusually warm that year, and merchants in Louisville—and elsewhere—appealed to their mayors to extend the straw hat season, for their own personal comfort and to continue selling straws. On August 31, 1908, the mayor of Chicago issued the following order: "In the absence of action by higher authorities, and owing to the continued hot weather, I, Fred A. Busse, mayor of the city of Chicago, do hereby extend the time for wearing straw hats from September 1, 1908, to and including September 15, 1908." One newspaper called it "the most drastic action in the administration of public affairs that has marked his term in office thus far."[1]

By the start of World War I, the tradition was set in mid-month. "Sept. 15 is hat day in nearly every city in the United States," the *Newark Advocate* wrote in 1914. "For many years it has been the practice to . . . smash straw hats that are worn by the unwitting on that day."

Who would wear a straw hat after the fifteenth? What kind of man might he be? A man who would "continue to appear in a tired and aged straw hat when all the town has changed its mode." A man who "may even be a Bolshevik, a communal enemy, a potential subverter of the social order. He is a backslider, a drone, careless of custom, a mocker of the herd gods—for, whether in malice or through sloth, he has defied them."

The writer might have been indulging in some exaggerated mockery, but the contempt was real, and men who wore straws were dealt with in a fashion befitting their standing aloof from society. In Philadelphia, the day before Coolidge's daring stroll, John Finn was arrested for seizing hats through the windows of streetcars, punching out the tops and hanging his trophies on a post. He had done this to twenty hats by the time he was taken into court and fined ten dollars. It "was worth it," Finn said, grinning.

[1] This serves as reminder that, despite the inclination to assume that all activities of our forebears were done in deadly earnest, a certain sense of irreverence was held regarding the setting of Felt Hat Day.

Those men on the streetcar were lucky; 1925 was actually a mild year. The year before, a man in New York was beaten to death when he objected to a gang leader knocking off his straw hat and stomping on it.

The greatest unrest came in 1922, when a "straw hat smashing orgy" broke out in New York City from the Bronx to the Battery and went on for the better part of three days, as gangs of "young hoodlums," jumping the gun early, roamed their neighborhoods, ripping straw hats off the heads of pedestrians and streetcar riders, trampling the hats and beating those who resisted.

It began about 5 PM the evening of the thirteenth, around Canal and Baxter, an area then known as Mulberry Bend. A street gang spent about an hour attacking passing garment workers—"the buttonhole makers and the cutters and the machine operators." The hat smashers "enjoyed prime sport" until they came upon a group of longshoremen, who did not passively accept their hats being smashed. The brawl poured into a street littered with injured men and discarded straw hats, and stopped traffic going onto the Manhattan Bridge. Local store owners, worried about their shop windows, called the police, who spent the rest of the evening dispersing—and eventually arresting—the rioters.

The next night was worse. Every police station in the city was affected. On the Lower West Side, teens armed with sticks, sometimes with nails driven through the ends, hid in doorways and then descended, a dozen at a time, on hapless, straw-hat-wearing men and forced them to run the gantlet. On Amsterdam Avenue, at 153rd Street, the mob of hat smashers was estimated at 1,000 strong. Gangs prowled Lexington Avenue. The East Side was the worst, police said, with unrest stretching from Chatham Square all the way up to Harlem. On the Lower East Side, boys used long sticks with wires on the end to unhat men, impaling the hats—sometimes twenty-five or thirty—on their poles and parading with their trophies held aloft in triumph. The rioters piled stolen straw hats in the street and made bonfires. Police estimated the doorway at 211 Grand Street was crammed with five hundred ruined straw hats.

The Oak Street station called out the reserves, but other precincts were slow to respond. This was, after all, a tradition. "The police of the East 104th Street station were inclined to regard their activities lightly in spite of numerous complaints at the police station," the *Herald and Tribune* noted, "until detectives and patrolmen in plain clothes began to fall victims to the hat smashers. Then sterner measures were adopted."

At the Men's Night Court, seven men were convicted of disorderly conduct for their role in a "hat-smashing saturnalia" at Bowery and East Houston Street, where the smashed hats were hung over the lampposts. They were offered the choice of a two-dollar fine or two days in jail. All chose the fine, and Magistrate Peter A. Hatting promised to jail the next man brought before him for smashing a hat.[2]

"It is against the law to smash a man's hat, and he has a right to wear it in a January snowstorm if he wishes," said

---

[2] Hat-smashing was not purely a male domain. In 1926, two young women—Rose Bellow, twenty-three, and Florence Mantro, twenty—appeared before a judge for having broken several men's hats during the end-of-season Mardi Gras at Coney Island. Each was fined one dollar.

Hatting. "To hit a man's hat is a simple assault, and in this court it will be treated as such."

The hat stores, kept open late, were crowded with customers who quite understandably deemed it an apt moment to purchase their new fall felts. Police observed that the hat smashers tended to operate in the neighborhoods around hat stores, and the *New York Times* couldn't help but see a connection, if not between the hatters and the rioters, then between the hatters and the iron law of September 15. "The origin of this law is obscure. Certainly it is not based on American meteorology, but reflection justifies at least the suspicion that it originated in the dark machinations of the only class that has an interest in its perpetuation.[3] Its enforcement is left to boys and others with undeveloped minds who delight in destruction for its own sake."

The editorial urged the straw hat wearing man to defend his right to wear whatever hat he pleased and "fight if he can and call the police if he can't."

That was bad advice. During the 1922 riots, Harry Gerbert was surrounded by a crowd at 115th Street and Park Avenue. He tried to put up a fight and was severely beaten, ending up in Harlem Hospital. A police detective giving chase to his hat after it was knocked into the street was tripped and left sprawling facedown in the gutter. Joseph Phalef was jabbed in the eye with a stick aimed at his hat on the East Side and nearly blinded.

Some victims managed to collar their attackers, particu-

---

[3] This was more than just a reference to hatters. Many hatters were Jews, and there must have been at least a whiff of anti-Semitism to this sentence at the time it was written.

larly if they were boys of twelve or thirteen, and haul them to justice. A dozen boys armed with sticks dashed out of a doorway on Third Avenue near 109th Street and attacked two plainclothes policemen. Officers King and Lamour caught eight and dragged them down to the station. Since they were all under fifteen, they were not charged, but they got a lecture, as did their parents. The lieutenant invited the boys' fathers to come down to the station and give "a good spanking to their offspring" and the fathers, to a man, complied.

Neither fines nor jail nor judicial speeches about straw hats in snowstorms stopped the practice. In 1929, the unrest began September 11 around Times Square and spread. An estimated one thousand smashed hats lay scattered around Mulberry and Broome streets.

To guard against becoming victims of random hat-smashing—or, more generally, particularly outside the cities, censorious looks, and comments—men would voluntarily toss away or wreck their own hats themselves. On the floor of the Pittsburgh Stock Exchange, tradition was for brokers to whoopingly destroy each other's hats on September 15. In small towns, the entire male population would turn out and toss their hats into a convenient river or lake. The Cubs baseball team would mark their first victory in September by destroying their straw hats, as would fans, raining their hats down upon the field—they not only did this in mid-September, but at Fourth of July games, when it was also traditional to replace summer straws, which wore out quickly (the cheapest kind of straw hats, made of a single layer of straw, were known as "throw-aways").

Nor was the practice confined to baseball. On September

14, 1923, when in a hotly anticipated contest, Jack Dempsey knocked out Luis Firpo in the second round of their scheduled fifteen-round battle with a left uppercut to the jaw followed by a right to the heart, many of the ninety thousand fans at the Polo Grounds vented their mingled enthusiasm for a great fight and displeasure at the quick finish by hurling their straw hats at the ring. So emboldened were men by the straw hat tradition that when Firpo, "the wild bull of the Pampas," walked out of the State Athletic Commission, a spectator grabbed his straw hat and smashed it. And while it was assumed that no man would be so bold as to knock the hat off the president of the United States, the *Herald and Tribune* did note, perhaps facetiously, after Coolidge paraded his straw hat past mid-September for a second time, "His guards were relieved when the stroll was over, with the hat still intact."

No wonder men wore their hats with a uniformity we marvel at today. They had to, goaded by business, government, the newspapers, and fellow pedestrians. The risk of being beaten by a mob, however remote, should not be underestimated as a force in fashion.

But we should not misconstrue uniformity for unanimity. Just as a photograph of hundreds of men wearing hats would not lead us to believe that everyone at the time was a man, so it shouldn't create the impression that everyone either wore or approved of this lockstep conformity. Saint Louis resident Cecil M. Baskett, visiting Decatur, Illinois, in a straw hat that was perfectly fine back home, found himself the recipient of "public comment and scorn" when walking the streets in mid-May 1924. He went back to his hotel, changed hats, and fired off a sarcastic letter to the local newspaper, which had mocked him, specifically, for his lapse.

"What about the 'undies'?" he wrote. "Why not an official day in regard to B.V.D.s?"

If we look back with a sense of wonder at the unbroken sea of identical hats at ballgames and train stations, so did certain men of the time. Here is Carl Sandburg, in a poem published in his collection *Smoke and Steel* in 1920:

> *On the rim of a skyscraper's forehead*
> *I looked down and saw: hats: fifty thousand hats*
> *Swarming with a noise of bees and sheep, cattle and*
> *waterfalls,*
> *Stopping with a silence of sea grass, a silence of prairie*
> *corn*
> *Hats, tell me your high hopes.*

Bees and sheep, cattle and grass—not exactly images reflecting the rugged individualism of the American ideal. In the shadow of the slaughter of World War I, conformity fell into particular disrepute. Hats, men began to realize, were the crowning symbol of that conformity.

Enter the American college student. Too young to have gone to the war that claimed their brothers and fathers, enjoying a level of wealth unprecedented in this country, "Flaming Youth" of the 1920s considered itself to be nobody's sheep, and it turned as a flock—as youth invariably does—away from the traditional pastures of their elders, seeking new places to graze. College students began breaking any taboo in sight. Aided by the mobility of automobiles, they unleashed a sexual revolution that was, at the time, every bit as shocking to society as the one in the 1960s would be. They danced lewdly and drank illegally, they coined strange slogans and shoved them in the faces of their elders by painting them on the backs of their raincoats and the sides of their cars.

And they stopped wearing hats. Given the negative example of their joyless, close-mouthed president—who, despite stepping over the straw hat boundary, was a religious hat wearer known to sometimes wear a hat while he shaved[4]— plus the edicts of advertisers and etiquette writers; and the absurd war going on in the streets between slavish convention and barefooted mischief, and the truly odd goings on abroad, it is hard to see how they wouldn't.

Sometime after the straw hat riots of 1922 and before Calvin Coolidge's stroll, on some college campus—nobody is sure when or where—American college men began going bareheaded. The change was noticed and imitated.

"The custom, conceded to have started with the college boy who found a hat a nuisance when crossing campus between classes, has spread to the young business man and even to his father," noted the *New York Times* in October 1925.

The unnamed author believed "the new fad" was a belated recognition that hats were utterly unnecessary but for the social pressure demanding them.

"Most men concede that hats are superfluous; that they would enjoy going without them, but confess an unreasonable slavishness to convention," he wrote, adding hats to the many items cast aside in a triumph of comfort over tradition.

---

[4] He explained that doing so kept his hair in place.

"Waistcoats and suspenders are no longer the necessary adjuncts they used to be. And now another insignia of masculine rank and dignity goes down before the modern cry for comfort. Will hats suffer the same eclipse as the corset?"

Though hatters had begun complaining that the fad was hurting business earlier in the year, the hatters cited in the article were unconcerned. But the unnamed writer—who had the swagger of a hatless young man himself—ended with a wink to the future.

"Fashion prophets predict that the first frost will see the last of the hatless man," he wrote, "but even fashion prophets are sometimes fallible."

The frost came and went, but hatlessness continued. College boys were joined by the publicity-prone. A self-promoting Broadway attorney named Abraham Vogel announced a "crusade" in 1925 against hats and the formation of an anti-hat group he called Hatless Manhattan.

"Whether he started the hatless idea among collegians in this country, or whether they gave the idea to him, is still a question," the *New York Times* noted in July 1928, the same year *Men's Wear* attended a house party at Princeton and found "few of the fashion leaders were wearing hats."

Vogel attacked hats as medically risky. The Victorian non-science about hats and baldness had grown into folk wisdom, and it created fans for the hatless students.

"More nerve to the young fellows who dare go without hats," wrote Joseph Ernest McAfee, whose letter to the *New York Times* was published on September 12, 1925, under the headline "DARE TO GO HATLESS!" His entire argument was based on the assumption that "we are becoming a bald-headed race" and that hats were to blame. Nor were women immune, due to their tight fitted cloches cutting off "the free air and the vivifying rays of the sun."

"Our women," wrote McAfee, an author of religious tracts, "will soon have no hair to bob."

At age fifty-four, McAfee mourned that he could not join the ranks of "these young fellows whose numbers are delightfully increasing."

"Here is one timid oldster who, though lacking the courage to follow the example, rejoices in the bravery and consequent huskiness of the young fellows who do dare," he wrote.

McAfee's ideas about health have more relevance to the decline of hats than their lack of validity would indicate. It wasn't that young men avoided hats to keep from going bald—though some must have been motivated by that. Rather, going hatless fed into a notion of robust outdoorsiness, of being exposed to the elements—the "consequent huskiness" McAfee refers to—that went straight back to Rousseau and the same foment of human rights and individual freedoms that spawned the American and French revolutions at the end of the eighteenth century. Those addressing hatlessness in the 1920s viewed it as something that emerged spontaneously from a college campus somewhere. Hatlessness didn't begin there, either, but owed its existence to roots that were far older.

Chapter 11

"I kept my hat off all the time."

John F. Kennedy loved convertibles. In Hyannis Port or Palm Beach, the first chance he'd get he would jump in one and roar off.

"He likes to drive," wrote Mary McGrory. "A recent sight in Florida was the windblown, sunburnt President-elect at the wheel pulling up to the airport with a triumphant grin while Secret Service men sat sheepishly in the back."

During the primary battles of 1960, Kennedy insisted on traveling in convertibles with the top down whenever he could. He wanted people to see him. The weather didn't matter. At one stop in the 1960 primaries, he arrived at an airport in his private plane, the *Caroline,* and was met by the usual convoy of convertibles. Driving into town it started to rain. Kennedy discovered he was riding in a convertible whose top was broken and wouldn't go down. So he ordered the driver to pull over and stop, had the photographers' car— also a convertible—pull over and switched vehicles with them, so when they drove into town, the public would see their candidate braving the elements in an open car.

Still, there was something more to this than just showing off to voters. Kennedy repeated his top down exercise with a Citroën convertible in a driving rain in Paris and there was hardly an American voter in sight, just a very unhappy Charles de Gaulle forced to ride along. Kennedy felt the people of Paris deserved a good show. Politics was theater, but so was life, and the actors had to look good at all times.

"He loved to ride with the top down, long before he was a congressman," remembered his friend Jim Reed. "I think it was to show the macho aspect."

Convertible automobiles might be a twentieth-century contrivance, but the idea of men braving the elements is very old. The practice of American leaders—whether deliberately or instinctively—subjecting their persons to the lash of the weather goes all the way back to George Washington traveling to his inauguration. He spurned the offer of a carriage when it began to rain in Philadelphia, insisting he would ride on horseback, like his escort, to the delight of onlookers.

"How different is power when derived from its own just source," marveled one witness. "Our beloved magistrate delights to show, upon all occasions, that he is a man."

Perhaps the most famous case of this was the ninth president, William Henry Harrison. At sixty-eight, the oldest man up to that point elected to the office, Harrison "was anxious to show people that he was the rugged 'Hero of Tippecanoe' his supporters had portrayed him to be during the recent campaign," according to historian Paul Boller. The first Whig elected president, as well as the first chief executive to arrive at Washington by train, "a committee of Whigs met him in the station, offered him an umbrella, which he declined, and walked him through the snow to city hall."

The day he was inaugurated—a cold March 4, 1841—he cast aside his hat and overcoat and gave one of the longest inaugural addresses on record, to show off his erudition. He caught a cold that led to the pneumonia that killed him, exactly thirty days after taking office.

Harrison's example carried little impact as a cautionary tale: facing the weather was practically a requirement of office. Franklin D. Roosevelt did the same thing at his 1937 inauguration, held in heavy rain and "penetrating cold." The congressional committee running the inauguration asked Roosevelt if he wanted to move the ceremony inside, despite the crowds that had already gathered.

"No," Roosevelt said. "If those people can take it, so can I." He delivered his address bareheaded, under an inadequate canopy that allowed the rain to pelt his face. He had been driven to the Capitol in a closed car, rolling down a window to wave to the people lining the streets. But for the return to the White House—over the Secret Service's objections—he had a convertible brought around, so he could ride the mile back while waving to the crowd, fully exposed to the downpour.

A leader wants his followers to see him. And those followers, too—more and more each year, seemingly in direct proportion to modern life's ability to insulate us from the weather—were moved to face the elements themselves, unprotected, as a demonstration of moral and physical excellence. A century ago, a man in shorts and a T-shirt running sweating up a mountainside would be considered insane, or in the midst of some personal calamity. Now he is automatically admired, his image used to sell everything from sports drinks to investment banks.

The universal appeal of this exposed individual can be directly traced to an idea that was popularized 250 years ago by French philosopher Jean-Jacques Rousseau, who argued that, uncorrupted by modern conveniences and contrivances, ancient man was both healthier and happier:

> Accustomed from their infancy to the inclemencies of the weather and the rigor of the seasons, inured to fatigue, and forced, naked and unarmed, to defend themselves and their prey from other ferocious animals, or to escape them by flight, men would acquire a robust and almost unalterable constitution. The children, bringing with them into the world the excellent constitution of their parents, and fortifying it by the very exercises which first produced it, would thus acquire all the vigor of which the human frame is capable.

Protection such as clothing and homes only sapped human vitality:

> It is plain in every state of the case, that the man who first made himself clothes or a dwelling was furnishing himself with things not at all necessary; for he had till then done without them, and there is no reason why he should not have been able to put up in manhood with the same kind of life as had been his in infancy.

From Rousseau, it is easy to draw a line straight to the general hatlessness of Kennedy and his generation. In Paris in 1792, the Assembly of the Revolution received a treatise, "*Sur un vetement libre, uniforme et national a l'usage des enfans ou reclamation solenelle des droits des enfants,*" written by a German doctor named Bernhard Christoph Faust. Quoting Rousseau, Montaigne, and Locke, he urged children to be liberated from their layers of petticoats, powdered wigs, and such. Faust argued children should go barefoot in the summer and bareheaded all year around because it was healthier.

Similarly, the tutor of the grandchildren of Louis XIV, the Duke of Beauville, wrote of his practice of freeing his charges from the hats that both adults and children wore at the time. "When out of doors, they never wear hats, they are nearly always bareheaded, and are so accustomed to it that they can scarcely be persuaded to go with their heads covered." The duke felt compelled to answer the obvious question by declaring, "This custom has never caused them the least illness."

People were of course concerned for the health of their children, particularly in centuries when medicine was still rudimentary, and did what they could to improve their constitutions, even if it meant leaving off their hats. It might seem odd to suggest that bareheadedness would then pass from children to adults. But if in the traditional world children were outfitted as small adults, in the modern world, adults increasingly took their fashion cues from the young, even children. Boys in England wore trousers, a fashion borrowed from the British navy, for forty years before adults emulated them and abandoned their knee breeches. And while the writings of men such as Faust and the Duke of Beauville were no doubt shelved and forgotten, the Rousseauian devotion to the idea of the morally and physically healthful quality of nature and the outdoors was not.

While monarchies toppled and new governments arose, in part based on Rousseau's notions of individual dignity, his attitudes toward clothing were also picked up and promoted. Andrew Combe's 1837 argument for looser dress standards, "Principles of Physiology" went through fifteen editions, and its influence on prominent men grew as the nineteenth century went on.

Coupled with a renewed appreciation of, if not actual nature, then a romantic notion of nature was a similar increase in the attractiveness of the idea of work. For most of human history, the highest ideal a man could aspire to was to be free of any taint of labor. The mark of a "gentleman" was spotless clothes of fine fabrics, free from the soil of earth or work, as well as pale skin and soft hands. Men who could in any way afford it wore elaborate high collars and silk hats, white gloves, tight jackets—the preferred clothing of the time that said the wearer did not work out of doors, or did not labor at all.

"Much of the charm that invests the patent leather shoe, the stainless linen, the lustrous cylindrical hat, and the walking stick, which so greatly enhance the native dignity of a gentleman, comes of their pointedly suggesting that the wearer can not when so attired bear a hand in any employment that is directly and immediately of any human use," Thorstein Veblen wrote in his groundbreaking *The Theory of the Leisure Class.*

Going back to Roman times, physical labor and the men

who did it had been scorned. But after the French Revolution and the rise of trade unionism and of labor-saving devices beginning with the steam engine, a new view of what was desirable in a man (and, later, a woman) gained popularity. Suddenly, the lazy leisure of the rich was not the unquestioned ideal it once had been.

"In a century perhaps nobody will want idlers any more," Stendhal's young hero is told in the 1839 *Charterhouse of Parma*. The romanticism of labor was just one element of the general rise in individualism that marked the nineteenth century. Kings and religious dogma had not been tottering in a vacuum, but were being swept away by individuals discovering their own sovereign power and venting their contempt for the established world and its traditions and demands, a contempt as always felt most acutely by the young.

"I have not loved the world, nor the world me," Lord Byron, twenty-eight years old,[1] wrote in Canto III of his wildly popular *Childe Harold's Pilgrimage*, published in 1816:

> *I have not flattered its rank breath nor bowed*
> *To its idolatries a patient knee*
> *Nor coined my cheek to smiles, nor cried aloud,*
> *In worship of an echo, in the crowd*
> *They could not deem me one of such, I stood*
> *Among them but not of them.*

---

[1] Of course being twenty-eight seems younger now, with the doubling of life expectancy and the delays of the onset of adulthood, than it did then.

A credo for the hatless young man if ever there was. Thirty years after Byron, Henry David Thoreau was sitting in his cabin at Walden Pond and, prompted by the memory of a seamstress brushing aside a request of his as something that just wasn't done, set to wondering why men bother with such silly matters as fashionable hats. "The head monkey at Paris puts on a traveller's cap, and all the monkeys in America do the same," he wrote.

These strands—belief in nature, appreciation of work, proud individualism—come together in Walt Whitman's manifesto of personal freedom, "Leaves of Grass." It begins with a bold declaration, "I celebrate myself," and goes on to revel in the sweat of work and the joy of nature: "You shall possess the good of the earth and sun."

Hats show up quickly in Whitman's masterwork and are just as quickly flung away, or worn, not as the crowd dictates, but as he himself fancies. Vowing never to "snivel that snivel the world over," Whitman announces: "Conformity goes to the fourth-removed. I wear my hat as I please indoors or out."[2]

Suddenly, to be outside, hatless, browned by the sun, was in some quarters an ideal to be envied.

"I kept my hat off all the time, and stayed where the wind and the sun could strike me, because I wanted to get the bronzed and weather-beaten look of an old traveler," Mark Twain wrote in *Life on the Mississippi.* "Before the second day was half gone I experienced a joy which filled me with the

---

[2]In the original 1855 edition the line is "I cocked my hat as I please," but in subsequent editions Whitman changed it.

purest gratitude; for I saw that the skin had begun to blister and peel off my face and neck. I wished that the boys and girls at home could see me now."

Yet for all their freedom and individuality, Whitman, Thoreau, and Twain still wore hats. Most men did. We must remember that society seldom moves en masse, but shifts in complex, sometimes opposite directions. While Whitman was making public his radical, sexually charged thoughts, others were recoiling in horror ("pure, unmitigated trash" sniffed one London critic, quoting what became the most famous lines of "Leaves of Grass" to give his readers an idea of how lousy he thought it was). Thus moments we think of as causing dramatic change—Kennedy's inauguration speech without a hat—are more typically just the moments that years-in-the-making changes were first widely recognized.

It usually takes a long time for the thoughts of poets and philosophers to be accepted and acted upon by working men and women. Despite the efforts of Rousseau et al., before 1890, being called "hatless" was bad. The word is found, invariably, as part of a description of someone suffering an extremity of debasement—either insane, drunk, impoverished, or some combination of all three, as was the "wild, haggard-looking man, hatless, coatless, bootless, with hair disheveled and eyes rolling in mad frenzy" who woke up marshal William Paxton early one morning in 1878, according to the *Idaho City World*.

Decent men wore hats, but there was some leeway as to what kind of hat they wore. In England, the wealthy, relaxing at their estates, began to feel foolish tramping through their gardens in tall hats and frock coats. They shifted to shorter, more comfortable jackets and less dramatic hats, and at the end of the nineteenth century comfort started to manifest itself. Top hats became shorter, bowlers were replaced by trilbys—a soft hat with a low crown—and fedoras.

The philosophical underpinnings were in place. All that was left now was for the spark, for someone to take the next logical step and stop wearing hats altogether.

In the summer of 1899, that spark struck.

"The habit of going about without a hat has been making inroads in the rising generation of both sexes," the *New York Times* wrote. "Beginning with college oarsmen, it has extended to those who inhabit canoes and yachts; now it is taken up by the cyclists; and in all the minor summer resorts young women may be seen riding and driving and playing golf 'in their own hair,' as our ancestors used to say in the days of wigs."

While a common speculation at the time was that the hatless fad was caused by college athletes tromping to practice across campus bareheaded, the historical evidence points to an element of society we would not expect to be recognized as influencing men's fashions in the Victorian era: women.

It was women, in the early 1890s, who first began removing their hats in situations where etiquette demanded that hats should have been worn, beginning in the theater. A woman was always supposed to wear a hat when in public. But the large hats at the end of the nineteenth century made this increasingly problematic at plays and the opera. People behind them couldn't see the stage.

Men could check or easily remove their hats and keep them in their laps. But women's hats were too large to check and too carefully affixed with hat pins to remove easily, and besides, modesty forbade it. But eventually the complaints of those behind them became too overwhelming and with great reluctance, and to the amazement of all, women started removing their hats in public.

"This really happened," begins a half-sarcastic, half-flabbergasted 1893 article in the *New York Sun*. "The reporter who witnessed the incident secured on the spot seven unassailable witnesses, all of whom pinched one another, took drafts of fresh air, water and other fluids, viewed the phenomena from all sides and points and generally took precautions against deception and delusion."

The wonder that had occurred at the Columbia Theater in Brooklyn was this: one lady, then others, removed their hats as the show began.

"All over the balcony first one and then another big hat came off until the balcony presented an array of beautiful, bareheaded women," the *Sun* wrote. "The stage disclosed itself as a ship coming out of a fog, and a wave of happy smiles swept over the house."

Eventually women going out to the theater—and soon just going out for the evening—left their hats at home, some wearing simple garlands of flowers in their hair. They even attended church hatless, leading some ministers to publicly bar hatless women, while others accepted them, such as the Rev. I. H. Albright, pastor of the Salem United Brethren in Christ Church in Lebanon, Pennsylvania, who not only invited men to come to his church in their shirtsleeves, but conducted the

service without a suit jacket, observing "it is no sin to pro-
pound the gospel while coatless."

For the first few years of the fad, women were in the fore-
front.

"Strange to say, it has attacked the young women more
vigorously than their brothers," the *North Adams Transcript*[3]
noted in 1899, one of many reports of the trend focusing on
women more than men.

"At Newport which sets summer fashions the bareheaded
girl is a familiar figure on trolley cars, on the streets and at roof
gardens, and stately dames are not behind in the procession of
fashion, but bare their white locks to the refreshing breezes,"
wrote the *Sandusky Daily Star* in late summer 1900. "While a
number of men are disciples of the hatless fad, with the conse-
quence of complexions rivaling the hue of mahogany."

In retrospect, this makes perfect sense. Men were famously
averse to changing their styles. Women were the gender with
the greatest motivation for dress reform. Men complained, but
women had been openly rebelling—in small numbers—against
the restrictive corset and their hobbling yards of ankle-length
dresses since the 1850s and the rise of Bloomerism. It was a
radical fringe, mostly, until athleticism hit in the 1890s, particularly the bicycle. We credit the car with reforming society in
the 1920s, but really it was the bicycle that thirty years earlier
transformed the culture, sending women out of the house with
men, unchaperoned, and casting off their protective layers of
clothing in the bargain. Women led the way and men followed.

"The fashion of going bareheaded has spread to the men in

[3] This was a Massachusetts newspaper.

Washington, and is particularly affected by horseback riders, and since equestrianism has become fashionable and popular, it is not unusual to see modern Absaloms galloping beneath the boughs of the Maryland woods, or cantering along the smooth, hard pavements of the asphalt avenues," wrote the Washington correspondent of the *Chicago Journal* in August 1902. "The uninitiated might suppose that they had accidentally lost their hats, but the fact is they have left them at home, purposely, at the command of Dame Grundy."[4]

You couldn't ride a horse or bicycle in a big hat covered with ostrich feathers, and women began leaving them at home, a move that, rather than being criticized, was celebrated.

"What's the use of a hat anyway?" wrote the *North Adams Transcript*. "Nobody wears them any more. Nobody, that is, except a few old fogies who imagine that they are in duty bound to wear hats just because they are provided with heads that they don't know how to use except as hat holders."

We think of the big Edwardian ladies hats, with their feathers and stuffed birds, as defining elegance, but at the time they were often loathed. Not only did they cause annoyance at the theater, but their long, exposed hat pins were a problem on crowded city streets and trolleys. Men were blinded by them, people were killed, and laws were passed. At best, the hats posed a constant challenge to wear and maintain, not to mention a tremendous expense, all prods toward hatlessness.

"One simply had to wear a monstrosity or go hatless," a fashion columnist pointed out in 1907.

---

[4] "Dame Grundy" was the personification of propriety.

The *Connecticut Western News* pinpointed a particular woman, "a wealthy Pittsfield young lady," who can be viewed as Patient Zero for the outbreak of hatlessness that followed and to whom "belongs the credit of making the bareheaded fad a perennial institution." The newspaper wrote: "After going without her hat through the summer of 1898 she made a wager that she would not wear any head covering until after August 1, 1899, and she won her wager, appearing in her carriage and cutter all winter long, wrapped in her robes and furs, but with no covering on her head except her beautiful hair."

By the summer of 1900, hatlessness had spread from the East Coast across the country. In Chicago, the style was said to take hold after a pillar of society, Mrs. Lydia Avery Coonley Ward, and three friends drove in a carriage down Lake Shore Drive one warm July evening with not a hat among them.

"There was a flutter of excitement among the promenaders," the *Chicago Chronicle* reported. "People looked admiringly after the party in the victoria and, nodding to one another, said laughingly, 'Yes, it has really come to pass.'"

Critics of the propriety of going hatless were silenced by one woman who said, "You don't suppose Mrs. Ward would go out without her hat if it wasn't the style, do you?"

As the fad continued, the cultural amnesia so common when it comes to men's hatlessness set in. The inspiration posed by hatless women was forgotten and the trend regarded as if it were something new. In 1903, the *New York Herald* wrote that at Yale "for several weeks students have been hatless in and about the campus. Who started the fad and why it would be difficult to trace. Perhaps it was the crew candidates, who threaded their way through the town to the boathouse

bareheaded." Another possible culprit, the newspaper specu-
lated, might be Theodore Roosevelt Jr. and his fashionable
Choate buddies.

It happened that 1903 was the peak of hat production in the
United States. But even then, experiencing the best year they
ever would, hatters were made edgy by bare heads. "Hat deal-
ers say that unless the fad stops soon they will be forced to hold
discount sales," the *Herald* wrote, finding the bad news for hatters was embraced by barbers. "It's great for the hair," said one.
"The wool grows thicker and healthier and we get the benefit."

As the new century unfolded, reaction set in. Educators
spoke out against hatlessness. Fashion columnist Julia Bot-
tomley warned her readers in 1911 that "mothers should discourage the fad for going hatless" because it led to coarse
skin, freckles, and bad hair.

"This fad is not likely to create much stir or disturb the
mandate of fashion very seriously, for the idea of a well-dressed
woman without a hat is somewhat incongruous," wrote a critic
in 1912. "A craze of this kind originates not so much from
hygienic motives, but from the desire for sensation."

Even after people had been going hatless for a dozen years,
doing so was still considered a "fad"—much in the same way
Mohawk haircuts have represented punk rebellion for the past
three decades. Despite the popularity of going hatless among
young people of both sexes, older people still saw it as an odd,
slightly ridiculous affectation, somewhat the way nudism is
viewed today. In a 1907 lecture entitled "Dexterity and the
Bend Sinister," Sir James Crichton-Browne, a prominent
nineteenth-century nerve doctor and the Lord Chancellor's
"Visitor in Lunacy," dismissed certain proponents of the

ambidexterity movement,[5] saying "some of those who promote it are addicted to vegetarianism, hatlessness, or anti-
vaccination and other aberrant forms of belief."

Sigmund Freud, in describing a patient's experience during
his summer holidays, mentions how the man decided he was
too fat and had to become slimmer. "So he began getting up
from table before the pudding came round and tearing along
the road without a hat in the blazing heat of an August sun."
Actions which, though universal today, Freud concluded were
disguised suicidal intentions comparable to the urge to jump
off a cliff.

In 1910, an article on William F. Hilleman, a Washington
University Law School student who never wore a hat, portrayed
him as an "eccentric" who "attracts attention" by his actions.

"Although he is often made the subject of gibes by his
fellow-students he takes the jokes good naturedly and persists
in going hatless," the *Decatur Review* noted.

World War I gave people something else to worry about,
and must have formed a kind of memory barrier, because
when hatlessness reemerged in the mid-1920s, few seemed to
recall that it had been hotly debated for the first decade of the
twentieth century.

While attention to hatlessness faded for a while, it might
be more accurate to view the first quarter of the century as one
long hatless fad, because men's hat sales continued to fall.
Between 1909 and 1929, the domestic production of fur felt

---

[5] The realization that the right and left halves of the brain controlled differing
functions led to the nineteenth-century notion that brain capacity was being
"wasted," and attempts were made to use brains more fully by mastering two
tasks at once, such as simultaneously playing the piano and writing a letter.

hats in the United States fell by 42 percent. A bit of that can be accounted for by cheap Eastern European imports. But the rest was a softening of demand, a change that the public continued to think would pass even as it was taking hold.

As the twentieth century progressed, other social factors piled on that tended to undermine hats. Tanning became popular, a dramatic shift in preference that broke with hundreds of years of tradition. Actually, more than a shift, it was a complete reversal. Once wealth could afford to protect itself from the elements, while toilers were browned by the sun. Now, because of industrialization, it was the inner-city drudge who was pale, while the socialites languorously browned themselves poolside.

In 1928, a Columbia University professor argued that suntans were a "youthful complexion fad" that defined modernity and set the young apart from the old. As with hatlessness, suntans were seen for a while as another peculiarity of the avant-garde. "Evelyn Waugh's Gilbert Pinfold hated suntans as much as he despised Picasso, plastic and jazz," notes critic Stephen Bayley in his book *Taste*. But tourists flocking to the Mediterranean—or wishing to create the impression they had flocked to the Mediterranean—spread the practice, as did further developments in the next decade.

"The heliophilia of the 1930s was based on cranky medical theories which gained popularity when colour film and cheap travel made explicit the link between suntans and stars," continued Bayley.

Suntans, jazz, rapid transportation, hatlessness—this was all very menacing to some. In 1936, bearded, pale, traditionalist King George V died and was replaced by the beardless, Riviera-loving, playboy Prince of Wales, the same prince who had showed up in America without his top hat in 1919 and, in general, made a stir by often going hatless. It might be difficult for the reader of today to realize how jarring the change was—think of a tattooed, pierced, computer-mesmerized youth of today becoming king. This new prince, whose reign as King Edward VIII would be cut short after just two years when he abdicated to marry Wallis Simpson—another triumph of private desire over public duty—was seen as the avatar of all who would be replacing the dull, stamp-collecting older generation: a new kind of vibrant young man, flying in airplanes, not wearing a hat. The shock is neatly encapsulated in Sir John Betjeman's brief, wry poem, "Death of King George V":

> *'New King arrives in his capital by air . . . '*
> *Daily Newspaper*

> *Spirits of well-shot woodcock, partridge, snipe*
>   *Flutter and bear him up the Norfolk sky:*
> *In that red house in a red mahogany book-case*
>   *The stamp collection waits with mounts long dry.*

> *The big blue eyes are shut which saw wrong clothing*
>   *And favourite fields and covers from a horse;*
> *Old men in country houses hear clocks ticking*
>   *Over thick carpets with a deadened force;*

> *Old men who never chatted, never doubted,*
>   *Communicated monthly, sit and stare*
> *At the new suburbs stretched beyond the run-way*
>   *Where a young man lands hatless from the air.*

* * *

"Going around without a hat is just a fad, one of those things that will die out," Alfred E. Carey, a Brooklyn salesman, told the *New York Daily News*'s "Inquiring Photographer" column in September 1933. "I've often observed these young fellows without hats. They don't look a bit more healthy than others, and certainly they do not appear as well-dressed as men with hats."

The other five Brooklyn pedestrians stopped along Eighth Avenue that day and asked by the *Daily News* if they considered a man well-dressed if he appeared on the street without a hat agreed with Carey, with the slight exception of Jens A. Jensen, of 69th Street, who allowed that while a man "looks ridiculous" if he is without a hat in winter, he could go hatless in summer, if his hair was "neatly arranged" and "not blowing in the wind in great disorder."

Around the mid-1930s, the hat industry began to realize it could no longer dismiss hatlessness. Looking back in horror from the perspective of November 1934, *Hat Life,* the journal of hat sellers, began an eight-page special report: "Hatlessness: What Shall We Do About It?" with the sort of remorse that would accompany recollection of a plague that had been met with inadequate alarm during its early stages:

It is just about ten years now since people began to notice a rather silly fad among some of the Eastern college boys, of going about with coat collar up and hat off. It was in 1925 that Elias Lustig, then a partner of Elias Lustig & Bro., wholesalers, and operating one small retail store under the name of Adam Hats,[6] asked us to drop in and have a talk about this new hatless fad. He felt that something ought to be done to discourage it right away, before it could have a chance to spread to serious proportions. No one else seemed to care much about it. 'Just a school-boy fad—a man will always wear a hat' was the usual comment.

Subsequent history need not be repeated—hat men know it too well.

Hatlessness was no fad, *Hat Life* admitted, but "one of the gravest threats ever aimed at the life of any business." The magazine quickly pinned the blame not on college boys, nor health concerns, but on the industry's failure to promote itself, cataloging a variety of slapdash efforts and lost chances, ending each with a Sid Caesar–like declaration of poverty: "This was also abandoned in the end—'NO MONEY.' " Thus Bud Roth's 1932 scheme to get college boys to wear straw hats by outfitting their hats with a hatband of their particular school's colors foundered for lack of funding. John Grossgebauer's educational placard designed to instruct banks, insurance companies, and other large white-collar businesses on the necessity of hats was never distributed.

"Scores of ideas, big and little, have been proposed and lie idle," the magazine complained. *Hat Life* had a point. No natural impetus demands that people put on deodorant, use mouthwash, or avoid dandruff. They have to be taught to care about these things. Men were shaved by their barbers until King Gillette, trying to sell safety razors, instructed them how

[6]This is an unspoken irony, as Adam Hats had become a large chain, known to all readers of *Hat Life* by 1934.

to shave themselves. Women used rags during their periods until Kimberly-Clark spent years training them to use Kotex and coaxing skittish druggists to stock it on their shelves.

People had to be taught by advertisers, and were, particularly in the 1920s and 1930s, when a number of our social ills, from athlete's foot to yellow teeth, were driven home to the public. The $50,000 that the Hat Institute spent on newspaper ads in 1929—the high-water mark of the hat effort for the decade, according to *Hat Life*—is a pittance compared to, say, the $2.3 million that Lambert Pharmacal spent in 1933 to warn the public of the dangers of halitosis and the appeal of its solution, Listerine. While hat companies naturally pushed their own particular brands and styles, no hat company stepped up to drum into men the importance of the hats themselves, at least to the satisfaction of *Hat Life*. That is why, the magazine believed, hats were falling out of favor.

Of course, that logic puts hats into the realm of superfluous consumer products like mouthwash. If you consider hats as a wardrobe staple spanning centuries, the argument isn't as persuasive. The shoe industry never had to urge men to continue to wear shoes, nor did the makers of socks remind customers of their necessity to the well-turned-out man, and the manufacturers of neckties—an entirely symbolic article of clothing with none of the practical applications of hats—have never had to mount extensive campaigns touting the various decorum-pleasing aspects of their product.[7]

---

[7]Maybe they should. Neckties are also falling from favor, as casual Fridays infect offices around the United States the rest of the week. Ties might be where top hats were in 1925—considered essential for presidents and diplomats, but waning elsewhere.

Hat Life noted the same impulse that moved young Mark Twain to cast off his hat in explaining why the salubrity of hats must be promoted.

"The effect of hats on health is *not* the principal story we have to tell, but it becomes an important one *because of the popular error that hatlessness is a healthful, he-man habit*. If a man honestly believes that it's good for the hair and the health to go hatless—as well as making him collegiate and saving him $5.00—he's smart to leave off his hat."[8]

No problem is beyond being blamed on the press, and despite the blizzard of possible reasons for hatlessness, *Hat Life* detected a journalistic bias toward spreading the anarchy represented by the hatless man.

"It is, and always will be, the characteristic of the newspaper man to sniff for trouble," wrote the journal. "Just as newspapers report divorces rather than happy marriages, so they will also report *hatlessness* rather than *enjoyable hat wearing*—unless the news is given them with the success angle that suggests that hatlessness is now dead or dying."

Hat companies did what they could, short of banding together to sponsor national campaigns. They designed hats in "extreme" styles specially intended for teenage boys. They gave their hats names like Fraternity House and Graduate ("a decidedly young-mannish hat"). Hat shops tried hiring "hat hostesses"—women salesclerks who were supposed to add a bit of feminine persuasion to the sales process.

If in Europe, hatlessness between the wars spread from the

[8]The hat industry came to counter the myth that hats cause baldness by boldly inventing its own myth: that hatlessness causes baldness, the inevitable result of dry, brittle, sun-baked, windblown, dust-laden hair.

aristocracy to the common people, in America, fittingly, bare-headedness went the other way, radiating from college campuses to businessmen to, finally, the haute monde. In the spring of 1931, *Men's Wear,* critiquing the Palm Beach hat season, felt compelled to note the trend, while dismissing it as a resort phenomenon: "It is claimed that a smart summer sports ensemble is not complete without a head covering of some kind. Yet, there are many men, who, being the possessors of many hats, did not wear any. These same men would never think of going about in town without a hat. Although there were sufficient numbers of hats seen to compile a survey of what is in fashion, it must be kept in mind that this is an analysis only of the hats observed."

The pinch was felt the world over. In Spain, the hatters union announced that the "bareheaded vogue" had thrown fifty thousand men out of work and began its own public campaign.

The hatless trend was reflected in the industry in subtle ways. Stetson, addressing the collegiate habit of beating up what hats they wore to affect a traveled, battered look, made a hat whose crown was blocked higher on one side than another—this unusual hat was said to have "nonchalance blocked in."

Nonchalance was the big adjective when it came to pitching hats at youth.

"Youthful, nonchalant—with just a bit of swagger," promised a 1920s ad for a new style from Knapp-Felt hats. "The spontaneity of youth is reflected in the rakish and smart lines of the popular Stylepark 'University,'" another company promised. "It represents the style trend of the modern college youth. Swagger and well built, it withstands abuse and meets the demand for nonchalance so characteristic of young men of today."

Flip open a dictionary to read that *nonchalance* is defined as "lack of enthusiasm or interest, indifference, unconcern," and it's easy to understand the difficulty hatters faced in trying to sell a product to young men who weren't interested in it. In some ads, you can practically feel the copywriters straining to bend lack of customer desire into a selling point. Another Stylepark hat, The Gipsy, was advertised both as being "weightless" and able to be folded flat: "It is the hat for striking that note of nonchalance . . . and the studied carelessness of modern dress."

Hat Life urged hatters to keep the big picture in mind, but couldn't resist going after those it felt were setting a bad example and encouraging the hatless menace. While thundering for a comprehensive, industry-wide assault, it still found time to hound prominent individuals who were caught bareheaded in the public eye. In the week prior to Thanksgiving 1933, the United Press moved a story on Secretary of Agriculture H. A. Wallace and his chief economic adviser, Mordecai Ezekiel, going about without their hats. It began, "Even in the subfreezing weather that lately has gripped Washington, two high administration officials cling to college days habits, going bareheaded."

Hat Life's editor E. F. Hubbard[9] printed his scolding letter

---

[9] As edited by Hubbard, *Hat Life* was sharply written and feisty, with a lot more humor than is typical of a trade journal. In a December 1933 article noting how boys no longer wore hats or caps, it wrote, "Nowadays, they pop from their swaddling clothes into leather jackets and bareheadedness. No wonder they turn into gun-men when they grow up."

to Wallace: "Your own hat won't make a dent in business, of course—but your *example*, due to your personal leadership and the prestige of your office, can quite conceivably make or break many a needed job." He also printed Wallace's unyielding reply: "If one is to remain sane isn't it necessary that he be permitted to go his own way on matters of this sort and concentrate on his job?"

Most efforts were local and sporadic, such as Hat Week, a United Hatters push that blanketed Philadelphia in 1938, complete with luncheons and speeches and four leggy models walking around under an enormous, six-foot-high fedora, only their lower halves visible, clad in French maid outfits. Trolley cars sported advertisements, an airplane towed a banner, and an illuminated sign across City Hall read: WEAR A HAT—THIS IS HAT WEEK.

With the Depression grinding on, and the U.S. government organizing businesses under the National Recovery Administration and appealing to consumers to help get the country going by spending what money they had, it was natural that the floundering hatters would try to hitch their cart to the NRA horse.

"PLAY FAIR WITH THE BLUE EAGLE," read one of the 250,000 cards, referring to the symbol of the NRA, handed out by the Truly Warner stores to hatless men in the streets of New York. "WEAR A FALL HAT AND PUT THOUSANDS OF HATTERS BACK TO WORK."

"If we are to abide by the teachings of the NRA, let us start at once by having National Recovery of Hats," a correspondent signing his name as "Sans-Culottes" wrote in the *New York Times* in September 1933.

As sincere as such appeals were, *Hat Life* cautioned its members against unseemly begging. Number one on its list of suggestions of "What NOT to Do" to improve hat sales was: "*Don't* appeal to men to wear hats to help a dying hat trade or to give work to unemployed hatters." The primary reason for this, the magazine said, is "*it always emphasizes the thought that hatlessness is the growing fashion.*"

The message didn't get through to hatters. On October 2, 1934, the American Federation of Labor held its convention in San Francisco. Looking to score some points in the press during their highly visible meeting, The Cloth Cap and Hat Makers Union sent a telegram to delegates asking them to please wear hats to the convention to help out the trade. That ended up in the *San Francisco Call-Bulletin* as a story headlined "Hat Makers Beg U.S. to Restore Chapeaux." The Associated Press picked up the story, and it appeared across the country in the next few weeks.

"Maybe a few charitable union delegates bought hats, instead of tossing their pennies to the blind man's cup," *Hat Life* noted. "But we think a great many more citizens were influenced *against* wearing hats by the news that the hat trade is slipping and that the big fashion is to go hatless."

During the summer of 1935, Edward J. Brooks, a writer for *Men's Wear* magazine, spent a few weeks with young men eighteen to twenty-four years old—the younger part of the scale being exactly the age of John F. Kennedy and his friends at the time. He "listened to their talk, studied their ideas, and tried to find what they are about."

They certainly weren't about dressing fancily. "In the matter of clothing, and of dress generally, they strive to get as near to the barbaric as possible," wrote Brooks. "Slacks, polo-shirt, or sweater-shirt, and a water-proof, are all they wear when fully dressed." From that description, which could be a summary of the preferences of most men today, he moved on to headgear. "On one floor seven men were able to muster three hats, and sorry specimens of headwear they were."

Brooks stressed that these weren't impoverished men unable to afford clothes; on the contrary, they were well-off college graduates. That, he said, might be the problem.

"Whether one likes it or not, the 'don't-give-a-damn' personality is one of the foremost products of our time, one that the clothing trade is well aware of but pretends to ignore," he wrote. "Men who have studied it tell me that it owes its origin to the sons of rich, self-made men and is an indication of the type of 'self' used in the making of those men."

Brooks doubted that theory: If lack of concern about clothing was inspired by the independently wealthy, how, he wondered, could it spread so widely to average men? Brooks underestimated the degree that men imitate the habits of the rich, forgetting the sumptuary laws that had to be enacted in the past to keep common folk from donning the velvets of the aristocracy. If the life of John F. Kennedy is any indication, the ideal of the impeccably dressed upper class was being undermined by a new image of wealth: the tousled, carelessly rich look that would later make Ralph Lauren a fortune. Millionaires who wore spats, waistcoats, and top hats produced a generation of sons who wore penny loafers, open shirts, and no hats at all.

In fact, Kennedy could have been one of those sloppy men

Brooks hung out with. As a young man, he was notorious for his personal disorder. His boarding school roommates complained of his messiness, particularly with clothes. He would show up with his shirt untucked, or without socks, or wearing a rag of a necktie. Or without a hat. Again, he was not alone.

"Today men seem to be making an effort to free themselves from the tyranny of the hat," wrote an etiquette writer in 1940. "These, however, are the extremists or perhaps the forerunners of a new order."

Hilaire Belloc was neither an extremist nor the forerunner of a new order in 1940; he was a seventy-year-old British journalist whose keen perceptions were only matched by his prodigious output. Yet in a *Sunday Times* essay that year on the rich history and deep importance of hats, he ends by nevertheless envisioning their passing:

> Since things are dying all around us at such a rate as never was before, I wonder whether hats will not also die? Many say they are not necessary, but mere ornaments, wherefore the Sphinx, addressing a traveler from Gaul who had no Greek, put her riddle thus:
>
> "Je suis un ornement qu'on porte sur la tete.
>
> Je m'appelle chapeau; devine gross bete."
>
> But I contest that view. A hat is necessary against the sun. It is even necessary against cold (except, for some reason I do not understand, in the city of London, where hats are not worn). Nevertheless, useful though it is, as well as decorative, the hat may well disappear. I, for one, should regret it, as I regret the passing of any custom or of any tradition, for these are the furniture of human life.

Belloc's claim of the necessity of hats might give us a hint as to why they could be abandoned. As we have noted previously, they are useful. But useful did not make them physically necessary—against the sun, or the cold, or for anything else—as proved by their abandonment.

Obviously it was social necessity that tipped the scales. Once the communal force requiring hats vanished, once that social necessity cracked, first among women in theaters and athletes on college campuses, and then everywhere else, it was only a matter of the cycling of the generations before the practice faded and then disappeared.

So why did the social necessity pass?

The abandonment of hats was only one marker in a world rapidly casting off rules of all kinds—sexual, social, intellectual. The taboo against obscenity crumbled. Words that were not hinted at in novels in 1900 were represented by dashes in the 1920s, sounded out in the 1940s ("fug" was the word Norman Mailer put in the mouths of his soldiers in *The Naked and the Dead*), but were, by the 1960s, printed for all to see, and by the 1980s printed without much controversy or discussion.

The system of people following certain preordained roles was pulled down, laboriously, over a century. Repressed minorities—first women, then blacks, then gays—stepped up and joined the society that had pigeonholed and shunned them.

Some of this change can be ascribed to the peculiar nature of the United States Constitution, which was something of a time bomb, enshrining all sorts of ideas about the rights and liberties of men that the average person didn't actually subscribe to in 1776. Black people weren't included, nor were women, but both groups were gradually able to use the laws of the United States to break out of the prison that society had built for them. Once people became adjusted to standing up for their individual beliefs and rights, the rule of the majority—the "herd" that 1920s writers complained of—began to crumble.

Some was technological. Speed, economy, and comfort act like water, eroding old social norms. When telephones were introduced, many people resisted them, aghast at the idea that the voices of strangers—of people to whom they had not been properly introduced—might suddenly pierce the cherished privacy of their homes. Whatever for? But the effective way that telephones conquered distance trumped those concerns and made them seem old-fashioned. A person objecting to a telephone on moral grounds very quickly went from being ordinary to being ridiculous. Coolidge could refuse to talk over the telephone, claiming it was undignified. Had Roosevelt also done so he would have been viewed as foolish. Who could stand up against such an efficient form of communication?

After the telephone, leading the technological change were those two society-shredding devices: automobiles and television. The impact of cars on hats were not on the individual—it wasn't that you couldn't drive in a hat—but on the culture. By 1960, 80 percent of American families had a car. We went from a society of pedestrians, looking at each other, noticing each other's hats, to a society flying past each other on the road. This is clear if we try to figure out how all those little boys could steal the hats from policemen in the 1920s, but would never dream of doing it after the 1950s. Because the police went from being the beat cops whom people knew or at least knew of, walking past their stoops, swinging their night-sticks, to a pair of strangers in mirrored sunglasses screeching up in a radio car. We also became an increasingly armed culture. Those cops in the squad car might very well shoot those who went for their hats; stealing police officers' hats lingered as a juvenile prank in Britain long after it became extinct in the United States, most likely because British policemen tended to be unarmed.

Factor in the sheer complexity of society: far more people moving at a far greater speed. In the days when one traveler a week passed by your door, you would stop, tip your hat, and visit and maybe offer a meal. When 100,000 people race by on the highway in front of your house, that is no longer possible.

And then there was TV. Television took people of all ages off the block and set them before a continuous show in their living rooms. The monitors of street life who would hoot at you for not wearing your hat were inside watching *Queen for a Day*. Houses were no longer built with front porches; you weren't sitting out front waiting to greet your neighbors because they weren't walking by. They got in their car in the driveway next door, backed out, and were driving thirty miles an hour and accelerating by the time they reached you.

Thus efficiency can be seen as inspiring societal change. It is inefficient—wasteful—to force people into particular roles where they may not be happy and thus will neither thrive nor work hard. Just as it is inefficient to insist people wear articles of clothing that they do not want or need. Closing stores on Sundays might have satisfied the desire for a Sabbath of rest, but you sold more stuff if you stayed open, thus blue laws forcing stores to close on Sundays fell away and then the corner grocery store turned into a mega-mart open twenty-four hours a day.

Economy drove the change. Think of our parents or grandparents recoiling at the thought of pumping their own gas, until they discovered that, to save a dime a gallon, they'd gladly do it.

Our electronic economy removed the need to evaluate people based on their appearance. Once, the state of your hat and your ability to deploy it respectfully was the only endorsement that you had as a person, and if you wanted to get a room for the night in a lodging house or cash a check at a store or gain the attention of a policeman, they were essential. Now your credit card is your fine homburg hat: it pays for your room in advance, it guarantees that your purchase will be paid for (the clerk hardly looks at you—in part because the card is the important actor in the transaction, in part because it isn't *his* store, and if you were a thief, the loss would be felt at headquarters one thousand miles away). And you summon the police by calling 911 and they come no matter who you are or what you look like.

People once "dressed" for dinner. In the 1930s, radio personalities wore evening clothes to broadcast to their unseen audiences. But gradually, people realized they would be more comfortable in their regular clothes, and dinner and radio would still continue. A dozen hats cost a lot of money. In a sense, it is the same lesson the French peasants learned in 1791. They bowed to the king because it was what society demanded. But, first gradually and then all at once, they realized that the king could be carted away in a tumbrel and they wouldn't have to bow to anybody.

Youth drove the change. Youth always "rebels"—the word used to describe rejection of the assumptions of the day and yearning toward their own set of assumptions. In 1963, the U.S. population was the youngest it had ever been: 41 percent of the population was under the age of twenty. They were going to rebel against something. In 1962, students at a New Jersey high school were disciplined for wearing their shirts buttoned to the neck, just because their school rules said they had to either wear a tie or keep their collar open. The Vietnam War was thought to galvanize youth—to give them a moral drama to rebel against—but they would have rebelled anyway, though perhaps not with the same ferocity.

The difficulty is finding a societal trend over the past century that *doesn't* act against men's hats. The growing taste for nostalgia, perhaps, and the acceptability of anachronistic styles and fashions.

The hatters tried to adapt. As customers continued to fall away from hats, you can see their complaints reflected in the efforts of the hatters trying to woo them back. It wasn't confined to the names of hats or how they were sold. The now-superfluous hat felt heavy on a man's head, so Knox offered the Fliteweight ("so soft and light it sets like a breeze on your brow") and Champ came back with the Featherweight ("Look! It weighs no more than 2 packs of cigarettes!" declared a 1951 ad, showing a man holding the hat and balancing the two packs on his head).

Some of the hatters' reactions could be particularly clever. One of their studies found that hats were rarely bought as gifts because it was almost impossible to get the size and the style right without the wearer being there. So they created little hat gift certificates in the form of miniature plastic hats, which came in fist-sized hatboxes intended to be hung on Christmas trees. The tiny hats would be brought into hat stores by their recipients and exchanged for the real thing, a promotion that hatters pushed for a number of years.[10]

They made appeals to Kennedy. What is most interesting is that Kennedy did try to satisfy them. He wore a hat at his inaugural. He posed for some pictures in hats. But Kennedy was not going to be seen as a hatted man, just as he is now not thought of as a man who wore glasses, though he certainly did wear them when out of public view.

* * *

It wasn't that the rules did not apply to Kennedy. He could not have displayed his vigor by going shoeless, not if he wanted to be elected to high public office. Rather—like other men his age—having processed the rituals and standards of the society he found himself in, he realized what rules applied and what rules could be discarded. As with all youth, he picked those rules that appealed to him when constructing his style and personality. First his mother and Joe Kane, later hatters and fashion leaders—all said that he needed to wear a hat, he *must* wear a hat. But he didn't need a hat. He knew that, instinctively. In fact, a hat would have been bad for him, would have tied him to the fusty 1950s image of Eisenhower that he was working so hard to escape. It can be argued that the reason Kennedy succeeded was that he understood America's grow-

---

[10] You may see dozens of these little hats at any time, incorrectly identified as "salesman's samples," offered for sale on eBay.

ing boredom and distaste with Eisenhower and his failing heart. The *National Review*'s David Frum writes:

> Kennedy's 1960 campaign was organized around one central theme—that Eisenhower's Republicans were too old and sick to cope with the Soviet threat. Eisenhower had suffered a heart attack in 1955 and then a mild stroke in 1957. After the stroke, Eisenhower sometimes had difficulty speaking, a disability that the White House press corps savagely mocked. When the mythical "missile gap" was discovered after the launch of the Soviet Sputnik satellite in 1957—and then when the economy slipped into recession in 1958—Eisenhower's illnesses became a handy metaphor for all that was supposedly feeble and out-of-date about the Republican administration.
>
> Unlike Franklin Roosevelt's concealment of his polio, Kennedy's pretended vigor was not a defensive maneuver. The pretense was the core of his message. When the leaders of the Western alliance gathered in 1959–60—Eisenhower, Macmillan, Adenauer, de Gaulle, Diefenbaker, they looked old. Kennedy offered the voters more than a new program and a new philosophy. He offered *vitality*—vitality that would "get the country moving again" after the supposed slough of the Eisenhower years. To sustain the pretense, Kennedy threw away his hat and played football for the cameras, kept up an artificial tan and ceaselessly promised "vigor."

Kennedy could throw away his hat because wearing it had become an unnecessary bit of conformity, something that men did to please their fellow men—an obligation. People no longer wanted to labor under strictures of obligations. They wanted to map their own independent courses. They had tired of rules, and what could be pared away was pared away.

"Interestingly enough, the disappearance of the conventional hat was accompanied and paralleled by a severe simplification of formal etiquette," wrote Alison Lurie. "On all but the most formal occasions, rules of precedence and seating were forgotten. Strangers were introduced by their first names alone, often without regard for rank, age and sex. . . . What seemed to be taking place both in terms of dress and in terms of manners was the abandonment of the formal public self symbolized by the hat. Men or women who had once been willing or even eager to assume a standardized role in public now wanted to operate at all times as spontaneous individuals. A 'gentleman' no longer tipped his symbolic hat to a 'lady' to show the conventional respect due her sex; he no longer had a hat to tip."

Kennedy's neglect of his hat needs to be viewed against generally dwindling duties to others, a change that can be clearly seen in the presidency, as the White House—like the people it represented—became insulated, and its need to respond to the demands of strangers across the board declined.

Consider how visitors to the White House were treated over the years. James Madison's wife, Dolly, felt compelled to return calls; that is, if a Washington, D.C., matron arrived and left her card, Madison would visit her at her home. She did this not because she wanted to: it was an enormous burden, but it was her social duty.

Half a century later, in Lincoln's time, Mary Lincoln did not return calls, though her husband answered his own mail, in longhand, and an unexpected visitor could, if his business was legitimate and he was willing to camp out long enough, be ushered into the president's presence for a meeting. Lincoln was plagued by these visitors—job hunters, mostly—but his being president did not mean he could simply ignore them.

The visitors "don't want much," Lincoln once said. "They get but little and I must see them." At the time, duty trumped personal preference.

Such accommodations became unworkable as the nation grew. In Lincoln's era, the White House was also thrown open to the public for New Year's Day receptions, when any and all could show up and be feted and meet the president. This practice began under Thomas Jefferson, and by Teddy Roosevelt's time, enormous crowds would arrive and the president would dutifully shake everyone's hand. On New Year's Day 1903, Roosevelt shook eight thousand hands. Even when it wasn't New Year's, Harding shook the hand of any citizen who stopped by the White House and asked. Coolidge would regularly greet tourists and Boy Scout groups, letting them watch him work if he was busy. "You have to stand every day three or four hours of visitors," he said, outlining the responsibilities of the job to his successor, Herbert Hoover.

During Hoover's administration, anyone leaving a calling card at the White House would be invited to one of the daily afternoon receptions, which typically drew one thousand people. He continued the New Year's Day receptions until 1933 when, bitter at his defeat to Roosevelt, Hoover decided to spend Christmas in Florida instead. They were never resumed—an example of how random breaks with precedent become custom if they flow in the direction of a societal trend.

Part of this was due to security concerns, which naturally increased during World War II, along with the size of the federal government. But after the war, Harry Truman would still go for his nearly solitary walks, just as Coolidge had; he would even step into the line at bus stops, to see people's reactions.

But year by year, there was a gradual withdrawing. Eisenhower had typically gone to the airport to greet visiting heads of state as they stepped off the plane; Kennedy decided it would be just as cordial, while saving himself time, if he greeted them at the front door of the White House, and so he did that, for most guests.

The sense of duty toward the public, in a direct, personal way, lingered on a bit with the first family, and we find traces here and there. In 1969, Richard Nixon's oldest daughter, Julie Nixon Eisenhower, then a twenty-year-old newlywed, spent the summer as a volunteer tour guide at the White House. She escorted the public through the building and, if her father was out, allowed children to sit in his chair in the Oval Office and make a wish. Today, the demands of security and a weakening sense of obligation make that fact seem as historically remote as Thomas Jefferson returning to his rooming house to lunch with his fellow boarders after being inaugurated president. By the time Chelsea Clinton was a young woman in the White House, her need for privacy was tantamount and no one talked about her having a duty toward the public, a dynamic that mirrored that of the majority of young Americans.

Of course the need for the president to present himself to the public wasn't eroding without something else assuming its place: the slack was being taken up by the mass media. The president didn't have to shake hands at gatherings of thousands of people because he could be encountered on the radio, first, and later on television. Thus a fleeting, though actual, intimacy was replaced by a more in-depth, illusionary one.

Kennedy was always onstage. In a sense, he was always having his picture taken, and this explains much about his setting aside his hat. Responding to one of the many letters Kennedy later received, asking him why he didn't wear a hat, Evelyn Lincoln wrote back with complete candor that Kennedy did indeed wear hats, sometimes, but he didn't like to be photographed in them.

This reflected a reluctance that goes back to ancient Greece. A hat was an enhancer of masculinity—they made men taller and more glorious—but, like all enhancers of masculinity, like elevator shoes or toupees, there is something effeminate about being caught wearing one. Thus while Julius Caesar certainly wore a hat, he wasn't carved into stone wearing it. Hats later appeared in portraits, during certain periods, because of their grandeur and expense—Louis XIV posed in his hat—but national leaders were generally reluctant about being immortalized in them. Hatters were always pointing this out, arguing that hats were worn more frequently than history indicated. "There is a statue of the great Sir Robert Peel, very black and grimy, standing on a stone post at the corner of Cheapside and Saint Martin's-le-Grand. He has no hat on," wrote George Augustus Sala in his 1880 treatise on hats. "Now I have seen Sir Robert many and many a time riding up

Constitution Hill, or walking down Whitehall towards the House; and I specially remember his hat."

Nor was this particular to leaders. Average men took off their hats to have their photos taken as well.

"The hat was evidently such an accustomed part of being dressed that a man was more comfortable with than without one," Joan Severa wrote in her study of old photographs. "When not actually worn in photographs, hats are often held, or seem to have been laid aside at the injunction of the photographer. A dent around the crown line of the hair, left by a hat recently removed, is frequently quite visible. The probable reason that photographers asked a male patron to remove his hat was to avoid having a shadow cast across the sitter's face."

Men set aside their hats to be immortalized, whether in bronze or in a photograph, a moment when their personal appearance trumped their duty to be adequately hatted. But as we approach the present, selfish concerns—to look good, to feel comfortable—begin to predominate, whether one was having one's picture taken or not.

We think of the social discord of the 1960s as somehow fracturing society and leading to our current day. But it is just as possible that these loosening bonds are what allowed the social discord to happen in the first place. Cause and effect have a way of dancing around each other: look at how the hairstyles of men influenced hats. Those who placed the death of men's hats around Kennedy's inauguration blame all the James Dean and Elvis Presley oiled, curled, and combed-back styles for helping to kill off hats. But once we understand that hats began their decline before Elvis Presley was born, it becomes clear—and, frankly, makes more sense—that young men found themselves hatless and were now free to express themselves by turning their hair into a dramatic showpiece, a point of pride that once would have been afforded by a nice hat.

In the Kennedy era, hats had already fallen from popularity and were about to become unimportant. All you had to do to see it was look around. In a photograph of Kennedy addressing a crowd of mostly college students outdoors in June 1963, not one man in twenty has a hat, and those who do invariably are older men. Despite this, the idea that the hat had died was difficult for the arbitrators of style to accept.

Esquire magazine, going through one of its periodic eras of irrelevance, thundered against bareheadedness in July 1963, sounding like a nineteenth-century manners chapbook.

"The admirably dressed man never goes hatless," it declared, introducing its annual summer tribute to straw hats. "There is a correct hat, no matter what the weather, what the occasion. Summer headwear offers scope and variety enough to afford a full wardrobe for the punctilious male."

Admirably. Correct. Punctilious. Could there be three words less in sync with where the young men of America were going as they headed into the mid-1960s?

Chapter 12

"Standing in the wind and the weather."

John F. Kennedy did not begin the morning of Friday, November 22, 1963, in Dallas. In the glare of the tragedy that followed, that fact is often overlooked. He awoke at the Texas Hotel in rainy Fort Worth, greeted the large crowd that had gathered outside to see him, and attended a breakfast with the Fort Worth Chamber of Commerce.

"This is a very dangerous and uncertain world," he told them. "No one expects our life will be easy."

Afterward, in the sprawling, low-ceilinged banquet room, with its wagon wheel chandeliers, there was a presentation. Ever since 1923, most visitors of note to Fort Worth—and every president of the United States—had been given a Shady Oak Western hat by the publisher of the *Fort Worth Star-Telegram*, which inevitably printed on its front page the resulting photo of the esteemed guest wearing his gift.

In Kennedy's case, the honors were done by chamber president Raymond Buck, a large, affable man who spoke in a charmingly halting fashion, a speech of pauses and touching emotion.

"Mr. President . . . your visit with us in Fort Worth today . . . the things you have said . . . have refreshed and renewed our appreciation of your great courage," said Buck. "You have brought . . . *rain* . . . to moisten our pastures and our fields. . . . You have brought sunshine to our hearts."

During the applause that followed, Buck reached into a box and removed a light-colored cowboy hat. Kennedy stood and looked at the hat.

"We know . . ." Buck said, "that you don't wear a *hat*." The room erupted into laughter. "We couldn't let you leave Fort Worth . . . without providing you with some protection . . . against the *rain*."

He handed the hat to Kennedy, who grinned sheepishly and looked inside the hat.

"Why don't you put it on?" someone yelled from the audience, and the cry was taken up, "Put it on! Put it on!"

"The television cameras were on the scene; still photographers down front trained their Rolleiflexes and their Nikons and got ready for the big moment," wrote Jim Bishop, in *The Day Kennedy Was Shot*. "Those who knew the President had heard him speak of such 'baloney pictures' with contempt. He thought that former Presidents sacrificed something when they adorned themselves with broadbrimmed hats or Indian feathers."

"I'll put it on in the White House on Monday," Kennedy said. "If you'll come up there you'll have a chance to see it then."

* * *

There was no Monday. Not for Kennedy, nor for his grief-wrapped nation, which experienced instead a day outside of time, beyond the ordinary routines of the work week, in a place of surreal sorrow. On the day that would have been Monday, the nation endured the solemn agony of his funeral. The shock of his death left Americans disconnected and uncertain—anything was possible, in the worst sense of the term. They felt cheated of the years to come with a president many admired, even loved. And the loss of President Kennedy cast a much starker light on the difficult events that followed in the 1960s. It is human nature to assume that the path not taken would have worked out far better than the trying way history inevitably transpires, and Americans were left with the unshakeable belief that if only Kennedy had survived, all the bad things to come might have somehow been avoided.

Underlining what had been lost with Kennedy's murder was the quality of the man who followed but did not replace him, Lyndon Baines Johnson. People yearned for LBJ to fit into the Kennedy mold—at times even Johnson himself seemed to want that—but he just wasn't suited. Tall in an ungainly way, jug-eared, unattractive, Johnson's drawl did not charm the way Kennedy's Boston accent had, nor did his rough physicality appeal the way Kennedy's feigned athleticism did. Even his wife and daughters were plain compared to Kennedy's attractive clan.

There was also something crude about Johnson. While Kennedy's aides reverently remembered the honor of consulting with him while he lounged in the bathtub, Johnson's aides cringingly described the humiliation of taking orders from him while he sat on the toilet. After his gall bladder operation,

Johnson lifted up his shirt to show off the scar on his stomach, a gesture that Kennedy would have found completely unimaginable. Nor did Johnson shed his mistakes the way Kennedy had. One editorial cartoonist quickly transformed the scar on his stomach into a map of Vietnam.

Of course "crude" is a judgment; it might be more fair to say that Johnson represented an older, more direct form of politics. If Kennedy shrank from touching people, then Johnson draped his arm around their shoulders and squeezed. In that sense, Kennedy and Johnson assumed the presidency in reverse order, with the newer version of politician coming first, to be replaced by his historical predecessor. If Kennedy was the man of detachment—cool, remote, who did not like kissing babies but who came off great on TV, Johnson was the opposite—a back-slapping, lapel-grabbing stump speaker who was at his best when talking one-on-one or working a crowd in front of him. After a 1960 speech, Johnson was described as "waving his arms, flapping his hands, pointing his finger, thrusting his head, pausing excessively, and lowering and raising his voice level, he appeared more like a preacher than a president." And while he eventually refined his style, his charm still did not transfer to TV, where he seemed stiff, uncomfortable, out of place—and old.

While Kennedy did not wear hats, Johnson's hat was his symbol. His headquarters during the 1960 Democratic Convention in Los Angeles featured a six-foot-wide hat. His campaign buttons showed a hat—shades of Horace Greeley's old white hat. Johnson wore a modified cowboy hat, a scaled-down version of the traditional ten-gallon Stetson. Byer-Rolnick made a line specially for Johnson: each hat had a map of Texas inside the crown with his ranch marked with a star. Johnson handed them out to nearly everyone of any importance who visited the ranch. Guests recalled that upon arriving they were escorted into a room that "resembled a hat store" to select their hats.

Johnson's hat was vastly important to him, as demonstrated by a jarring exchange that took place on the way back to Washington, D.C., the afternoon that Kennedy was assassinated. Johnson noticed something was missing.

"Rufus," he asked Secret Service agent Rufus Youngblood, "where's my hat?"

"Your hat, sir?" Youngblood replied.

"It was in the car during the motorcade." The agent said it was probably still there.

"Well, get the damn thing!" Johnson ordered. "Call Dallas and have one of your men get it!"

"I'll see to the hat, sir," said Youngblood.

Johnson had no reluctance to help the hatters. His press secretary announced the president "thinks every man ought to have and wear a cap," and in February he approved the industry's plan to create an "L.B.J. hat."

"Soon after President Johnson took office it dawned upon hat men that the new President, in sharp contrast to his predecessor, conveyed a strong hat image as one of his personal appearance traits," the house organ of the Pennsylvania-based Bollman Hat Company, the *Bollman cHatter,* wrote in the spring of 1964. "It was at this point that the idea of an L.B.J. hat was born. At least a half dozen companies or individuals have taken credit for themselves as the originator of the idea. That is of little importance now. The significant fact is that, with an election year coming up, the L.B.J. hat as a Johnson and party symbol could develop into a nation wide fad. Little imagination is needed to envision what this might do for the entire industry."

It was said that some aspiring officials adopted the hat as a way of currying favor, the way New Frontiersmen aped Kennedy's two-button suits. On a certain level, the nation was intrigued by Johnson's Texas roots—his ranch, his dignified wife, Lady Bird, who took to beautifying America's highways—though nothing compared to the affection and interest that had washed over Kennedy. No women screamed or fainted for Lyndon Johnson.

Any societal concern over the end of hats was eclipsed by the greater issue of long hair on men, which arrived with the Beatles in the winter of 1964.

The furor over long hair illustrates just how quietly hats went away at the end. What real public disapproval of hatlessness there was—outside the hatters—had spent itself half a century earlier. Long hair, on the other hand, was a crisis. In the mid-1960s, boys were suspended from school for arriving in Beatle cuts that, in retrospect, were not far removed from Jack Kennedy's haircut.[1] Football coaches forcibly cut the hair of players. Towns put up billboards denouncing long hair. There were lawsuits, though the issue was the same as it had been with hats: Who controls what a man displays atop his

---

[1] An argument can be made that the Beatles hairdo is a descendant of Kennedy's style, which in 1963 was just a little shorter than the hairstyle John Lennon was wearing. The chain of influence is definitely there: after Kennedy's election, barbers in the United Kingdom said that young men were imitating Kennedy's mop of hair.

head? "A central issue was exactly who had the authority to decide what was masculine appearance," wrote a sociologist. "Was it the school, the family, the courts or the boy? Fathers often disliked their sons' new hair length but found they had little or no authority to enforce their viewpoint. Sons did not politely follow their fathers' advice."

After he was elected in his own right in 1964, a landslide victory over Republican troglodyte Barry Goldwater, Johnson was smart enough not to attempt to re-create Kennedy's already mythical 1961 inauguration. He decided he would wear a plain business suit to his inauguration and a dinner jacket, instead of tails, at the balls afterward. He would wear black tie to the gala, which was hosted by Alfred Hitchcock.

The news was broken by *The Daily News-Record* of New York, a trade publication run by the same company as *Men's Wear*, and caused consternation among officials who had already made arrangements for fancier dress. The White House confirmed the story, and the press, digging into the vice presidential angle, dug up Hubert Humphrey's tailor, Sam Scogna, who, in fine loose-lipped Sam Harris style, told them all about the morning coat and striped trousers the senator had purchased. This was news to the vice president–elect, a foretaste of the isolation that would characterize his term in office.[2]

---

[2]The song "Whatever became of Hubert?" by Tom Lehrer also foretold this isolation:
Whatever became of Hubert?
Has anyone heard a thing?
Once he shone on his own,
Now he sits home alone,
And waits for the phone to ring.

Humphrey was not only caught flat-footed and out of the loop, but felt stuck with a dress suit he hadn't bought. He unleashed a tirade that, while characteristic of the Minnesotan's short fuse, is almost shocking to recall in our era of carefully manicured and restrained politicians.

"Number one, it was a rental," Humphrey fumed. "Number two, Mr. Scogna—he just lost a good customer. Number three, I'll even quit renting from him if the man can't keep his mouth shut. I've rented from Sam Scogna five, eight years. So have my sons. So has my staff. I've sent him a lot of business over the years and he's just lost all of it."

Humphrey notwithstanding, the general reaction to the change was one of acceptance, even joy.

"Can anyone upstage the President on his own big night?" the *Daily-News Record* asked. "Who would dare wear white tie in the face of the Johnson decision?"

The answer of course was nobody.

"Why would they?" asked a man described as "a Washington official who is the soul of punctilio on questions of dress and etiquette but who would not be named." "One would want to conform to . . . the democratically elected leader of the nation.' "

"Times change," he added.

The rest of officialdom "heaved a sigh of relief at being rid of what one elegant individual called 'those torture devices.' " Unlike at Eisenhower's first inaugural a dozen years earlier, not a voice was raised in defense of tradition, while a number took the opportunity of dancing on white tie's grave.

"Most men look like hell in rented full-dress suits," said a "man-about-town" who wouldn't lend his name to his daring opinion. "They've got to fit to perfection and they never do unless they're custom-made. And those hard-boiled shirts are rear-entry shirts—they fasten in the back and they break your arm. Most guys don't know how to sit down in tails and they wind up all wrinkled, with pleated tails."

The formalwear industry responded meekly, by doubting whether Johnson was an influence on fashion at all.

"Clothing stylists, who always seek to make the point that men should dress for the occasion, were critical," the *New York Times* wrote in December 1964. "Some went so far as to say that in their opinion the President does not influence dress, at least not the extent that President Kennedy did."

The hat issue also arose and the White House, in confirming news of LBJ's suit decision, would only say the president "is being pressed" on what hat he would wear, but that the answer would not be known "for some time." Rumors flew that he would wear a homburg or a fedora, or even his distinctive cowboy hat. It was noted that Johnson often wore casual, Western clothes. "They fear that other men may be prone to follow his example and that the business suit itself may eventually disappear."

Johnson was sworn in on a near-freezing day wearing a gray business suit, without topcoat or hat, a fact that was buried in the forty-fifth paragraph of the main story the next day in the *New York Times,* in sharp contrast to the prominent attention given Kennedy's hatlessness. The lack of a hat just didn't have the meaning for LBJ that it had for Kennedy, though the issue was brought up a few days later, when Johnson was hospitalized with bronchitis and the press wondered if it wasn't because he was underdressed at his inauguration.

The specter of William Henry Harrison was raised. But Johnson's doctor said the matters were unrelated—usually colds began twenty-four hours after exposure—and a coughing Johnson told the four reporters ushered into his room that he had been plenty warm during his inauguration, having worn "electric long underwear" under his clothes.

Fashion did not follow LBJ, who himself hesitated at being associated too closely with Western wear. Given the chance to appear on the March 1965 cover of GQ, arranged by staffers seeking to impart a little cache to their man, he decided to pose on his Texas ranch wearing a distinctly Kennedyesque suit, resulting in a photo that was "contrived and comical."

By the 1969 inaugural of Richard M. Nixon, concerns about presidential fashion were quaint relics of a gentler age. Not since Lincoln snuck into Washington in his cloth cap—if then—did a president take the oath under such a pall of hostility. Protesters waved signs and hurled stones, bottles, cans, and obscenities. They chanted, "Four more years of death! Four more years of death!" while other onlookers registered their displeasure with the protests by matching their obscenities and screaming epithets such as "Communist swine!" Elements of the Army's 82nd Airborne Division and the District of Columbia National Guard lined sections of the parade route, ready to quell riots.

The protesters were only a small portion of the crowd, of course, but the inauguration nevertheless had a somber quality. Much of the press had viewed Nixon with anywhere from unease to open loathing for the past twenty years, and while they had found fairyland romance to the blizzard that crippled Kennedy's inauguration, for Nixon the natural elements, though milder, were seen as symbolizing something far more malign. Reporters uncapped their pens and let rip. This is how Russell Baker began his report:

> Poets may note that nature scowled today as the United States gracefully put Lyndon Johnson aside and handed the power of the state to Richard M. Nixon.
>
> Physically, it was a day out of Edgar Allan Poe, dun and drear, with a chilling northeast wind that cut to the marrow, and a gray ugly overcast that turned the city the color of wet cement. No graves yawned and no lions roared in the streets in the Shakespearean manner, but the gloom of the elements seemed to have infected most of the proceedings.

Few cared what Nixon wore. His personal awkwardness was matched with a clumsy fashion sense. Henry Kissinger, sitting on the platform, saw Nixon arrive and noted—on the first page of his White House memoir—"He was dressed in a morning coat, his pant legs as always a trifle short."

Just as Johnson had failed to present himself as a sartorial model, so Nixon's attempts to show himself as some kind of stylish ideal backfired, badly. In 1970, Nixon tried to re-create those wonderful Jacques Lowe photos of Kennedy on the beach. The news media were summoned. And Nixon walked along the oceanfront. In black Oxford wingtips.

Hatters tried to survive. Some clung to the old ways. While "fashion has turned to youth for inspiration," *Men's Wear* wrote in 1967, "hatters still follow the father-to-son road." Others lunged to adapt to the changes, offering bizarre versions of the classic fedora—in fake fur, or op art patterns. Stetson introduced styles with faux-hip names like "Now" and "Skylark." It didn't help.

What was left of the hat industry finally collapsed. The Hat Corporation of America saw its sales fall 40 percent, and Charles Salesky liquidated its various divisions and sold the corporation itself to a company that made carpeting yarn. That offer his brother had made at the stockholder's meeting in 1962 to provide "hats for life" to anyone getting Kennedy to start or Khrushchev to stop wearing hats would only have been good for about seven years.

During Nixon's administration, fashion gave way to antifashion. Army surplus became hugely popular. Young men who only a few years before would have been wearing suits and ties were now buying used Navy bell-bottoms and pea coats. One new fashion magazine called itself "Rags."

Nixon's successor, Gerald Ford, was never elected and did not have an inaugural. Ford is a good marker to note how quickly the prestige of the presidency crumbled. It had been thirty years since Franklin D. Roosevelt, who could not walk unaided, held office, his polio artfully hidden by the press—*hidden* might be the wrong word, since there seemed to be no consideration given to publicizing it. Ford, on the other hand, a former athlete, stumbled on several occasions and was ruthlessly mocked for it, so much so that, to many, clumsiness is the distinguishing characteristic of his presidency.

Jimmy Carter fared only a little better. His inauguration reflected a nation mired in an energy crisis, shell-shocked by the recent humiliating end of the Vietnam War and generally skittish and uncertain. Carter wore a three-piece pinstriped suit he had purchased the week before in Americus, Georgia, for $175. The highlight of the inauguration was the Carter family's decision to walk the mile and half back to the White House, pausing so that nine-year-old Amy Carter could tie her shoe. That night, the president's twenty-two-year-old son, Chip, wore a denim tuxedo to the balls.

It is significant that, while in the late 1960s, long-haired, scruffy youth were considered the exception—"hippies"—ten years later it was well-dressed, career-oriented youth who were singled out and given a name—"preppies." A college student who went to class in a coat and tie—de rigueur for a century—was an oddity during Carter's administration, and stayed that way in the administrations that followed, as the nation became more and more casual, and men's clothing stores began to feel the pinch that had taken haberdashers the decades before.

In the end, numbers won. Long-haired boys who were persecuted as solitary individuals were accepted en masse. Personal freedom won. The lessons of the Quakers, that in a supposedly free society individuals can cleave to their own whims of style and behavior so long as they have a strong will and some friends to support them, were learned by everyone, and previously unimaginable practices—young men and women with nose rings, pierced lips, or large, conspicuous tattoos—were adopted without societal upheaval or even significant discussion.

* * *

Alex Rose died at the end of December 1976. His last public appearance was at his Liberal Party's $125-a-plate campaign dinner for Jimmy Carter three weeks before election day. By then, the United Hatters, Cap and Millinery Workers International Union had shrunk to 16,000 members from a high near 100,000. His front-page obituary in the *New York Times* noted, without irony, that some within his own party regarded him as "old-hat."

The hatters union limped on for a few years without him, under his lieutenant, Nicholas Gyory. In 1982, it was absorbed by the Amalgamated Clothing and Textile Workers Union. By that point the hatters union had 8,000 members, compared to the textile union's roster of 442,000.

Ronald Reagan took office with a burst of charm—the older, Republican version of Jack Kennedy's youthful Democratic glamor. He, too, could speak well and was personally vivacious, and he brought white tie back to the inauguration. He could have probably pulled off a top hat, had he wanted to. But he didn't.

The dress of Reagan, while admired, was lent a certain detached quality: it was a choice, removed from any idea of its representing the one "proper" way. Now the media described what was being worn at the inaugurations, not as a bellwether of where the nation might go, but as the latest link in the historical chain of inaugural fashion, tied to the past but not the future. That past was not a guide to what was correct, but a dry rendition of what had happened. A person could wear white tie—or not—depending, not on decorum, but on what he wanted to do.

In 1990, George Bush sparked a swan-song replay of the panicked business owners closely monitoring Kennedy's personal whims when he banned broccoli from Air Force One. The broccoli growers complained. But it was a minor incident and not an ongoing concern. The nation wasn't really taking its dietary cues from George Herbert Walker Bush.

Casualness has reached its zenith—so far—with Bill Clinton, an effusive Southerner who had no qualms about being photographed in his T-shirt and nylon running shorts, stopping by McDonald's for a post-jog junk-food fill-up. While he was being interviewed by teens in 1994 on MTV, a seventeen-year-old girl, Laetitia Thompson, stood up. "Mr. President," she asked, "the world's dying to know: Is it boxers or briefs?"

Even Clinton was stunned. He paused, smiled, then said, "Usually, briefs," adding, "Can't believe she did that."

But if Clinton was shocked, he didn't have much company. His reply was seen as a sign of his nimbleness of speech, and there was a minimum of press grumbling and practically zero public outrage. It was almost as if, having floated away from the more accessible presidencies of the past, we had returned, through the omnipresent media, to the days of Lincoln, when the average person could walk up to the president and make the most outrageous request. Had Clinton bristled, objected to the question, or refused to answer, he would only have looked stodgy, and frankly such a response from him is almost inconceivable.

With George W. Bush, we arrive too close to the present to make confident assessments, except perhaps to note that the trend toward casualness continues. Bush often appeared without a suit coat or necktie, as did his opponent, John Kerry, a strong indication that we will look up one day and those bedrocks of fashion will be gone, the way tuxedos suddenly disappeared at the 2004 Academy Awards. If the prospect of suits and ties vanishing seems unlikely, remember how people clung to the notion that silk top hats would remain as long as there were weddings and funerals, because those events were inconceivable without them. Nowadays, it is possible to go to a funeral where the pallbearers don't wear ties at all. A tieless, suit-jacketless future is not only within imagination, it is likely.

* * *

Predictions invariably betray more about the tacit concerns of a certain time than they reveal actual future possibilities. We might say that all indications are that the bonds that caused men to monitor each other's hats will continue to weaken, but that would only reflect the painful contrast between the remembered uniformity of past times and the disorder of the present. Though it is true we often seem only dimly aware that a public sphere even exists, such as when cell phone users conduct boisterous conversations, oblivious to the people around them.

Uniformity does not require coercion. We might all gather again at some border of casualness. Blue jeans were adopted as the universal fashion of the young, and then of everybody, without help from a single hectoring etiquette writer. A decade or two from now, all men might report to work in the same style, the street an unbroken sea of khakis and golf shirts.

They might wear hats as well. A significant percentage of the world's citizens wear baseball caps, and it is not difficult to imagine the baseball cap turning into part of a standard wardrobe—a bit of protection from the sun and rain, a small social boost from association with a beloved sports team, fancy product, or wry public statement.

Baseball caps are already popular among sports fans, hip-hop fans, and a large segment of the general public, and the wide range of wearers—from young boys to fashion models to commuting executives—holds out the promise that they will somehow take hold as universal. Though it is hard to imagine baseball caps being required—hard to imagine a boss asking "Where is your baseball cap?"—the future, again, is always hard to imagine.

It might be argued that technology is our new fashion. No style arbitrator could put phones in people's hands or computers on their laps with the success that technology does. Perhaps technology will come to the rescue of hats; it's easy to imagine a cell phone hat, the electronics and microphone in the brim, the speaker in the hatband by the ear. Perhaps then hats will strain back toward universality. Squinting and conjuring up the average man twenty-five years from now, the only image that comes readily to mind is someone in a T-shirt, baggy shorts, and deck shoes, eyes focused on the middle distance, talking into his hat.

* * *

In some ways, John F. Kennedy seems the prototype for that new man—mobile, independent-thinking, athletic, outdoorsy, quick-witted, in touch with his New Frontiersmen racing around Los Angeles with the first beepers in their pockets.

In other ways, he does not. The popular mind traces the start of the 1960s to November 22, 1963, and the Kennedy administration seems set apart from the rest of the decade, a last black and white extension of the 1950s, in contrast to the multicolored social unrest and protest that followed. Or else as a period all its own, Camelot, when a bubble of optimism grew out of the personal charm, youth, and vitality of the president and his beautiful, sophisticated wife.

Men's dress hats belonged to that black and white world. They would linger on but be segregated into periods and types. Hats were worn by detectives, by salesmen, by disco dandies, by urban cowboys, by rappers. A young man in a wide-brimmed fedora is passing through his Humphrey Bogart stage; in a narrow-brimmed fedora he is paying homage to Dick van Dyke and the early 1960s; a man in a bowler might be a banker living in his private Edwardian phantasm.

A few other pools of hat-wearing exist. Hats still have a place in African American communities, where being perfectly turned out for church and recreation still carries the kind of meaning it once did for the population at large—as a sign of respectability and success. Black urban populations are usually responsible for the lone fine hatter able to survive in each big city, still making homburgs in the classic style, though those homburgs might be purple or emerald green and made on century-old machinery.

Orthodox and Hassidic Jews also continue to keep the market alive for Borsalino hats and are so closely identified with them that, in Jewish circles, they are sometimes referred to as "the black hats." These groups fit in with a more modern image of America, not as a melting pot, but as a stew, where unique elements do not blend, but coexist, each pursuing his own vision of America, his own dream, his own hat.

We might be tempted to lay this at the feet of our modern, mobile, ostensibly classless society. But really, it is nothing new. Alexis de Tocqueville noticed it 170 years ago, writing a description of the manners of the 1830s that—as with so much of his writing—seems current today:

> True dignity in manners consists in always taking one's proper station, neither too high nor too low, and this is as much within the reach of a peasant as of a prince. In democracies all stations appear doubtful; hence it is that the manners of democracies, though often full of arrogance, are commonly wanting in dignity, and, moreover, they are never either well trained or accomplished. The men who live in democracies are too fluctuating for a certain number of them ever to succeed in laying down a code of good breeding and in forcing people to follow it. Every man therefore behaves after his own fashion, and there is always a certain incoherence in the manners of such times, because they are molded upon the feelings and notions of each individual rather than upon an ideal model proposed for general imitation.
>
> This, however, is much more perceptible when an aristocracy has just been overthrown than after it has long been destroyed. New political institutions and new social elements then bring to the same places of resort, and frequently compel to live in common, men whose education and habits are still amazingly dissimilar, and this renders the motley composition of society peculiarly visible. The existence of a former strict code of good breeding is still remembered, but what it contained or where it is to be found is already forgotten. Men have lost the common law of manners and they have not yet made up their minds to

do without it, but everyone endeavors to make to himself some sort of arbitrary and variable rule from the remnant of former usages, so that manners have neither the regularity and the dignity which they often display among aristocratic nations, nor the simplicity and freedom which they sometimes assume in democracies; they are at once constrained and without constraint.

Maybe de Tocqueville's critique rings true because it is a universal. We always look back over the horizon at a remembered time of gentility and community as an antidote for the harsh commotion of the present. We remember the sea of boaters, but not the intimidation needed to maintain it. We admire the grace of Edwardian women's hats and forget that their long-exposed hat pins blinded people on streetcars. It seems possible that the concern for station that led a man to wear a hat stemmed from the same brutal class and race distinctions that have been softened in the beginning of the twenty-first century, when the United States strives to be a society that honors the virtues of differences, or at least ignores them. If you get in line at McDonald's, the clerk will serve you lunch whether you are black or white, whether you wear a hat or don't, whether your hair is long or short, whether you are a man in a suit or a man dressed like Little Bo Peep. Your money is still good.

The passions of the past seem flat to us. The idea of knocking off a person's hat and trampling it because it is out of season is about as removed as the idea of burning a witch. From the perspective of today, such concerns are mystifying. Who cares how long your hair is? How you are dressed? The Silicon Valley boom of the 1990s had an influence on fashion that a president could only dream of, as young men in shorts, sandals, and Hawaiian shirts not only made fortunes without ever wearing a tie, but worked in social settings where such dressing up was scorned as evidence of being a corporate drone. Boardrooms gave way to game rooms, and who could argue? Money and success are always in fashion. In the 1960s, people working at IBM not only had to wear dress shirts and ties, but their shirts had to be white and their ties had to be blue. While IBM was the avatar of technological advance, the wisdom of dressing this way met little debate. Indeed, it was admired. But by the 1990s, IBM was a mastodon in a tar pit, their blue ties a symbol of the narrow mind-set that caused the company to ignore changes in the world of computers and fall by the wayside.

In only ten years, the styles of cutting-edge computer firms had spread to banks. While the LaSalle Bank in Chicago felt the need to place a sign in its lobby on casual Fridays in 2004, explaining that its dressed-down employees had contributed money to a charity, and thus earned the right to be comfortable, the signs were short-lived. Soon they were gone and tellers were wearing sweatshirts on Fridays. There is every reason to believe that, rather than suits returning anytime soon, those Friday sweatshirts will instead spread to the rest of the week.

* * *

John F. Kennedy didn't wear a hat. And now none of us do. Oddly, the description still sticks with him, as an artifact, the way his Catholic faith is mentioned, even though now, of course, a Catholic candidate is not considered extraordinary— it was not considered extraordinary, for instance, that Senator

John Kerry was Catholic, had been an altar boy, and considered the priesthood.

For years the assassination dwarfed the rest of Kennedy's legacy. Gradually it was nudged aside as tales of misbehavior and ill health dribbled out, and eventually the assassination conspiracy fixation will come to be seen for what it is: an indication of the shock that his death brought, the fever the American body politic suffered while recovering from its injury. There are so many theories—blaming Castro, organized crime, the unions, the FBI, Lyndon Johnson—that they cancel each other out. The careful observer goes from realizing they can't all be true to realizing that none of them are true.

Kennedy is the object of endless fascination that will only deepen as the next generation, unencumbered by the bias of living under his considerable spell, takes up the legacy anew. Not so much because of his politics, or his decisions, or his death, but because of his image. Eisenhower served three times longer than Kennedy and was involved in far more historically significant events, from D-Day to the U-2 crisis. Yet it is a safe bet to say that, as time unfolds, Eisenhower will not fascinate future generations the way Kennedy will, because of his style, his attractiveness, his sense of grace and wit, and "the pleasure of his company," to quote the title of Red Fay's memoir. His hatlessness, such a small footnote while he was alive, might be part of what helps carry him forward to intrigue new generations of Americans.

That is only fitting, as hatlessness played a role in his death, or, more precisely, the desire to be seen, to not be covered, that led to his riding in convertibles and shunning hats. He was in a convertible in Dallas, despite the threats of hostile

Texas reactionaries, despite the warnings of the Secret Service. He waved off the bubble top; he wanted people to see him and Jackie. He was unafraid, or at least pretended to be unafraid, which is even more courageous.

And while the examination and reexamination of Kennedy will no doubt go on as long as people study history, every particular exploration of him must come to an end. E. B. White penned a moving tribute to Kennedy that ran, unsigned, in the November 30, 1963, issue of *The New Yorker,* a farewell eloquent enough to serve as our last word on a subject that defies last words. It begins, "The death of a President enters the house and becomes a death in the family," and ends:

> When we think of him, he is without a hat, standing in the wind and the weather. He was impatient of topcoats and hats, preferring to be exposed, and he was young enough and tough enough to confront and to enjoy the cold and the wind of these times, whether the winds of nature or the winds of political circumstance and national danger. He died of exposure, but in a way that he would have settled for: in the line of duty, and with his friends and enemies all around, supporting him and shooting at him. It can be said of him, as of few men in a like position, that he did not fear the weather, and did not trim his sails, but instead challenged the wind itself, to improve its direction and to cause it to blow more softly and more kindly over the world and its people.

Acknowledgments

This book would not exist without my extraordinary agent, Susan Raihofer. I owe her much gratitude for her decade of tireless work, crucial support, vital friendship, and keen professional insight. Thanks as well to David Black, that distant deity who enfolds us both in his care in ways too subtle and mysterious for me to fathom, but which I appreciate nevertheless.

My editor at Plume, Julie Saltman, was generous with her encouragement and enthusiasm, and gave me the gifts that writers cherish most: a careful eye and a little more time.

Research for this book was conducted primarily at the Northbrook, Evanston, and Chicago public libraries, the library at Northwestern University, and the Chicago Sun-Times Library. Work was also done at the Chicago Historical Society, the Newberry Library, the Lake Forest College Library, and the Rockford Public Library. It was a joy to spend time—always too brief—at the New York Public Library, the British Library, and the Library of Congress. Thanks to their patient staffs, and to those of the Robert F.

Wagner Labor Archives at New York University's Tamiment Library and the Lester S. Levy Collection of Sheet Music at the Milton S. Eisenhower Library at Johns Hopkins University.

The professionals at the John F. Kennedy Library and Museum in Boston were particularly helpful in guiding me through their magnificent collection. Maryrose Grossman was enthusiastic beyond the call of duty: she is the first librarian in my experience to send follow-up materials, unbidden. Stephen Plotkin and James Hill were also extraordinarily cooperative. They made my days at their library wonderful. Key materials were also provided by Jacqueline V. Reid at the John W. Hartman Center for Sales, Advertising, and Marketing History at Duke University in Durham, North Carolina. The archivists at Leo Burnett, DaimlerChrysler and the U.S. Army at Fort Bragg, North Carolina, gave assistance, as did Donald J. Rongione, president of Bollman Hats in Adamstown, Pennsylvania. The late presidential scholar Steve Neal was always supportive, and selflessly allowed me to poach from his private collection of rare and marvelous political books. This book was enriched because of his kindness, as was I.

Thanks to those who knew John F. Kennedy and shared memories with me: Senator Edward M. Kennedy, Paul "Red" Fay Jr., Jim Reed, and Senator John Glenn, and to Melody Miller in Senator Kennedy's office. Special thanks to E. A. Korchnoy, the former president of the Hat Research Foundation, who spent hours talking to me about the intricacies of his business. Jerry Rolnick, Herbert Rose, and Nicholas Gyory also took time to speak with me.

It may break some research taboo, but I have to mention the important role the Internet played in gathering material for this book. Since one can find the most credulous untruths online, I tried not to use any Web materials without confirming them elsewhere—with the exception of unimpeachable sources such as Lexis-Nexis—but the Web is a fabulous bird-dog. While I used too many online library catalogs and e-text databases to mention each, I want to specifically cite the Google search engine, Alibris, NewspaperArchive.com, and eBay, which was an unexpectedly bountiful source of hat literature and materials such as hat advertisements.

The *Chicago Sun-Times* has been home to me for nearly twenty years, and there are too many valued associates there to name them all. But I want to express admiration and gratitude to my friend, the newspaper's editor in chief, Michael Cooke, for his constant wisdom and support. Thanks as well to publisher John Cruickshank, editorial page editor Steve Huntley, executive managing editor John Barron, and managing editor for news Don Hayner. And a warm thanks to my pals at the *Sun-Times* who still say hello to me: Cathleen Falsani, Bob Herguth Jr., Rich Harris, Frank Main, Dan Haar, Nancy Moffett, Jennifer Hunter, Maureen O'Donnell, Tom McNamee, Abdon Pallasch, Polly Smith, Greg Couch, Scott Fornek, John H. White, Robert Feder, Jack Higgins, and my constant friends, Bill Zwecker and Rich Roeper. Special thanks to Roger Ebert and Medill School of Journalism Professor Abe Peck, for their generous assistance in this project.

I'd also like to thank a few people on the Chicago scene: Rich Melman, for the wonderful book parties at his peerless restaurants; Gale Gand, for her sweetness and light; Phyllis Smith, who *knows*; Grant DePorter; Bob Sirott; Steve Dahl; Phil Corboy; Mary Dempsey; Maria Pappas; that grand gentleman

Ed McElroy; Lee Bey; Bill Zehme; Lee Flaherty; and three individuals who manage the neat feat of both working at the *Tribune* and staying on speaking terms with me, Mark Jacob, Rick Kogan, and Mark Bazer.

My old friends need no thanks, but I'll thank them anyway: Jim and Laura Sayler; Robert Leighton and Val Green; Kier Strejcek and Cathleen Cregier; Larry and Ilene Lubell; Carol Weston and Robert Ackerman; Cate Plys and Ron Garzotto; Didier Thys; and Bob and Dawn Davis.

Special thanks to Eric Klinenberg and Cate Zaloom, who permitted me to camp out at their apartment while researching at New York University. And to David Wallis at my online syndicate, Featurewell.com: thanks for the interest, the advice, and the checks. And to Adam Gopnik, for the captivating hours shared *en table* in Chicago, New York, and Paris . . . okay, not the Paris part, but it sounded too good to leave out.

Love and appreciation to my in-laws, Irv and Dorothy Goldberg, as well as the extended and beloved Goldberg clan: Alan, Don, who helped with the hat check problem, Janice, Jay, Cookie, and all the girls, Julia, Rachel, Esther, Sarah, and Beth. And to my parents, Robert and June Steinberg—your relief at this not being another book about our family is surpassed only by my own—and to my brother, Sam, my sister, Debbie, and my cousin, Harry Roberts, for that fun evening at Harvard.

My boys, Ross and Kent, graciously yielded the irreplaceable time needed to write this book—Kent only occasionally bursting into the office with a cry of "What page are you on now?" and Ross manfully struggling to suppress his conviction that I would have done better picking a subject that people are interested in. And finally, bottomless love and gratitude to my wife, Edie, specifically for giving the book a meticulous edit and, in general, for handing me my entire life with a casual generosity, the way you would toss someone a book of matches and say, "Here."

Notes

Introduction

xi   "Can't you do something about this?" "Hat Corp. Chairman Calls Hatless Kennedy 'Business Handicap,'" *Wall Street Journal,* March 1, 1962, p. 8.

xii   "referred to as 'Mr. Hat . . . ,'" *New York Times,* April 1, 1963.

xiii   "he does not feel he is himself out of doors," Holliday, p. 301.

xiii   "as the human hair is of the human head," Sala, p. 5.

xv   "not one man in 10,000," *Reminder Service,* September 3, 1970.

xvi   "must own a dozen hats," "Set 20-Suit Minimum for Well-Dressed Man," *New York Times,* February 1, 1929. "sat on his silk hat," Wall, p. 115. "WASPs wore wonderful haberdashery," O'Rourke, p. 165.

xix   "John Adams used his hat to hold corn," McCullough, *John Adams,* p. 90. "fanned their soup with their hats," Thurber, p. 21. "My Lord told me," Pepys, p. 261.

xxi   "to take the hat," Petitpierre, p. 1278.

xxii   "obviously a gentleman," Harrison, p. 106.

xxiii   "Dress hat sales tank," "Style Debate Presidential Hopefuls Need to Address Sartorial Deficit," *Detroit Free Press,* October 21, 2000. "The peak year for men's hat manufacture," Henderson, *Hat Talk,* p. 33.

xxiv   "I'll wear hats," Whitcomb, p. 351.

xxv   "I am in the hat business," letter, June 28, 1963, John F. Kennedy Library. "Please, Mr. President," letter, March 9, 1962, PP 13-10, John F. Kennedy Library.

xxvii   "Somebodies wear hats; Nobodies don't," Hartman Center Collection. "The American male is both the busiest," *New York Times,* February 14, 1962, p. 48.

Chapter 1

2   "That young whippersnapper," Whitcomb, p. 22.

3   "nothing of an emergency nature." *Washington Post,* January 20, 1961.

5   "They liked him," John F. Kennedy Library, Albert J. Hackman oral history, p. 2.

6   "He now represents the State of Massachusetts," *United Hatters, Cap and Millinery Workers International Union Convention Report and Proceedings,* June 1–5, 1959, p. 252. "We have a guaranteed wage for six years," speech reading copy, John F. Kennedy Library.

7   "the son of a Polish dealer in raw hides," *New York Times,* December 29, 1976.

9   "He would make his little pushing gesture at the crowds," Wicker, p. 124.

10 "relatively aloof and enigmatic," "How to Be a Presidential Candidate," *New York Times,* July 13, 1958.

12 "Our people built this country," White, p. 105.

14 "a bareheaded, coatless man," White, p. 83.

16 "A humorous footnote to history," Salinger, p. 109. "He smiled when I told him," Lincoln, *My Twelve Years with John F. Kennedy,* p. 176.

17 "Jack Buys Hat," *Sunday Gazette-Mail,* May 8, 1960, p. 14A.

18 "ever present fedora pulled down over one eye," Dallek, p. 121.

20 "masterpiece of contrived casualness," Dallek, p. 230.

21 "It must have been a tough decision," *Mansfield News Journal,* January 25, 1960. "perhaps just a little over-done," Martin, *A Hero for Our Time,* p. 143.

22 "Jumpers, shriekers, huggers," *Life,* November 7, 1960. "Elvis Presley and Franklin D. Roosevelt," White, p. 331. "I convinced George Meany," New York University Tamiment Labor Library, United Hatters, Cap and Millinery Workers International Union minutes, Wagner file #189, Box 1, June 11, 1960, p. 28.

23 "Key Kennedy aides carried," Salinger, p. 39.

24 "Tears were literally rolling down his cheeks," Miller, p. 258.

28 "Brother Mendelowitz spoke briefly," New York University Tamiment Labor Library, United Hatters, Cap and Millinery Workers International Union millinery minutes, Wagner file #41, Box 2, Local 110 executive board, October 18, 1960, p. 2.

31 "Stacks of gleaming gold bars," "New Gold Rush: Out of U.S.," *Life,* December 12, 1960, p. 15.

33 "They could see you if you'd take that hat off," "A Wild Time for the Press," *Dallas Morning News,* November 19, 1960.

34 "a suit of gold thread," Goodwin, p. 813.

38 "I say, 'Tommyrot," "Hat Champ," *The New Yorker,* September 15, 1956, p. 34.

39 "looked so good," "Snow Blankets the Inaugural," *New York Daily News,* January 20, 1961. "This is for you, Alex," *Hat Worker,* February 15, 1961, p. 3.

Chapter 2

41 "Didn't you get the word?" Anthony, p. 17

43 "a certain retrospective reverence," Jepson, p. 66. "In proportion as society has been put into a bustle," Jepson, p. 61.

45 "Hell is paved with silk hats," "Low Tide for the High Hat," *New York Times Magazine,* December 26, 1954, p. 12.

47 "Not Collapsible . . . Do Not Attempt to Fold," "About New York," *New York Times,* August 3, 1953. "As a slight testimonial of my admiration," Abraham Lincoln Papers at the Library of Congress, September 30, 1864.

48 "a sea of silk hats," Sandburg, p. 122. "He caused a sensation," McDowell, p. 29.

49 "ratcatchers' hats," de Marly, p. 119.

51 "He was in the gentleman's furnishing line," Twain, *A Connecticut Yankee in King Arthur's Court,* p. 178.

56 "For then he knew another American," "The Battle of the Clothes," *New York Times,* April 11, 1909, p. 7.

59 "There were only a few speakeasies," "The High Hat Turns the Corner, Too," *New York Times Magazine,* December 17, 1936, p. 8.

62 "The Soviet Executive also decided," "Tchitcherin in a Silk Hat," *New York Times,* April 11, 1922. "the complete and shining symbol," "Pro-Topper Bolshevism," *New York Times,* April 12, 1922.

63 "Up the age-worn stone steps," "Happy Throng Greets Mayor," *New York Daily News,* January 2, 1926. "To Tammany the stovepipe hat," "Talking Through Silk Hats," *New York Times,* January 4, 1926.

64 "vicious, vile and ugly symbol," "Canon Scores Top Hat," *New York Times,* February 18, 1927.

65 "The hat remains to this day a symbol," "The High Hat Turns the Corner, Too," *New York Times Magazine,* December 27, 1936, p. 8.

67 "It is true that the silk hat," "Silk Hats Au Fait," *New York Times,* September 14, 1930.

68 "In the summer of 1933, a nice old gentleman," Freidel, p. 205.

72 "I hate to go," Neal, p. 39. "quickly and as quietly," McCullough, *Truman,* p. 341. "for the astonishing variety of his hats," Thomson, p. 101.

73 "plain and simple," "Eisenhower Wants Inaugural to Be 'Plain and Simple' Affair," *New York Herald Tribune,* November 9, 1952. "almost a sacred affair,"

"Inaugural 'Almost Sacred'; Ike Orders 'Utmost Dignity,'" *Washington Post,* November 21, 1952.

74 "he had put up with many things," "Eisenhower Lowers Boom on Top Hats," *New York Times,* January 15, 1953. "We got a bit of a blink," Donovan, p. 5.

75 "caused high consternation," "Homburgs and Club Coats at Premium in Capitol," *New York Times,* January 16, 1953.

77 "where *nobody* ever wore a homburg before," "Up from Plugs," *The New Yorker,* February 7, 1953.

78 "For the past 15 or 20 years," ibid. "Homburg hats were definitely the order of the day," "Picnic Lunches Help Crowd Wait for Inaugural Parade," *Washington Times Herald,* January 21, 1953.

81 "The other fellow didn't know what headgear to wear," "Kennedy's Top Hat O.K. for Inaugural Ride Says Truman," *Chicago Tribune,* December 27, 1960.

82 "By 1960, the country was parched for ceremony," Lowe, *Kennedy Legacy,* p. 85.

83 "A smile spread across his face," Lincoln, *My Twelve Years with John F. Kennedy,* p. 107.

84 "Now this hat fits," ibid., p. 221.

86 "Not only do I not have a tie," "Kennedy Ball Too High Hat for Bill," *Chicago Daily News,* January 10, 1961.

Chapter 3

87 "Concern flashed over the faces," "As It Happened: The Kennedy Inauguration," NBC program.

88 "occasional poetry," "Poetry, Politics Blend at Inaugural Tomorrow," *Boston Globe,* January 19, 1961.

89 "like a beaten man," Dallek, p. 413.

90 "diamonds, rubies, sapphires," "Smuggling Diamonds in His Hat," *Ohio Democrat,* October 11, 1883, p. 2. "Walt Whitman was observed using his as a bowl," McDowell, pp. 77–78.

92 "Years afterward, in melodrama," "Here and There," *New York Times,* June 21, 1931.

93 "were written on bar napkins," *Capital Times,* March 28, 2000, p. 2A.

94 "In the Peninsular war," Doran, p. 153.

96 "I said to myself, 'Spinach!' " Boller, *Presidential Inaugurations,* p. 96.

98 "General, you don't have to carry anyone's coat," Lieberson, p. 110. "He looked around, hesitated and peered," Sandburg, p. 122.

99 "If I can't be president," Boller, *Presidential Inaugurations,* p. 147.

100 "Men tore the meat off turkey skeletons," ibid., p. 205. "There was a general scramble for the wraps," ibid., p. 205.

101 "These adventurers often practice the hat game," Martin, p. 205.

102 "He noticed that the male patrons," Liebling, p. 68.

103 "genteel kind of banditry," "Hat-Check Queen," *Newsweek,* March 17, 1947.

104 "If they don't give me something," Scott, p. 53. "it would be but a few minutes," Segrave, p. 15. "democracy's deadly foe," Scott, p. 7.

105   "I object to having a man take my hat," ibid., pp. 40–41.

106   " 'Check your hat, sir?' " "Parking a Man's Hat Adds to Its First Cost," *New York Times,* April 15, 1928.

107   "When I accept a coat," Carroll, p. 53.

108   "If you give a hat check girl less than a quarter," *Mansfield News Journal,* September 9, 1942.

111   "The Visitors' Hatrack," Guptill, p. 94.

112   "Lee Hats introduced a hat," Segrave, p. 83.

Chapter 4

114   "It is done," "Kennedy Puts Hand to Destiny's Plow," *Boston Globe,* January 21, 1961, p. 1.

117   "more hats were lost on its 241 miles of highway," *Hat Worker,* February 15, 1960.

119   "All the pedestrians waiting at the corner," Hall, p. 167.

120   "The Hat That Sailed Away," and other hat songs: Levy Collection of Sheet Music. "Dozens of vaudeville teams use 'em," "Where Do Straw Hats Go To-day?" *New York Herald Tribune,* September 15, 1925.

123   "While sitting in the train," *Trenton Times,* August 4, 1900.

124   "a large hall with machines standing in it," Freud, Vol. IV, p. 236.

125   "If you give me a week, I might think of one," Nixon, p. 219.

127   "I don't need overshoes," Thurber, p. 47.

128   "PUT IT BACK YOU BASTARD," Reynolds and Rand, p. 75.

129 "You are certainly a large-sized prick," Dallek, p. 43.

Chapter 5

131 "It is sleek as a lapdog," Jepson, p. 59.

132 "A startling thought occurs to me," "Circumnavigating Hat Welcomed by DePew," *New York Times,* May 9, 1925. "I'm never going to be able to go," "Air-Minded Hat to Be Guest Here," *New York Times,* September 22, 1936.

133 "We follow where the White Hat leads," Levy Collection of Sheet Music, Box 7, Item 94.

135 "It may seem strange, perhaps," Freud, Vol. IV, p. 361.

137 "Your hat is YOU," Henderson, *Hat Talk,* p. 4.

138 "Frank O'Connor, the Irish writer," *Public Papers of the Presidents,* [473] John F. Kennedy, p. 882.

139 "This is James Michael Curley's hat!," "Where Did He Get That Hat?" *Boston Globe,* January 19, 1961.

Chapter 6

141 "During the drive to the White House, the new President," *New York Times*, January 21, 1961.

142 "I remember the moment when my brother," Written answers from Senator Edward M. Kennedy.

143 "Take off your lousy hat, you bum!" Mitchell, p. 106.

144 "In the view of the ancient Jews," Ausubel, p. 191.

145 "God's radiance is above my head," ibid., p. 191.

146 "How shall I know the king," Doran, p. 155.

148 "When the Lord sent me forth into the world," Fox, p. 36. "Oh, the blows," ibid., p. 37.

151 "to all in the most stately manner ever seen," Strong, p. 278. "Rules of Civility and Decent Behaviour," the Papers of George Washington Web site, University of Virginia, http://gwpapers.virginia.edu.

152 "I happened to stumble against a crust," Swift, p. 93.

153 "Washington seated and with their hats on," McDowell, p. 28.

154 "He passed without moving his hat," McCullough, *John Adams,* p. 95. "You & I have formerly seen warm debates," the Thomas Jefferson Papers at the Library of Congress, Series I, June 24, 1797.

156 "Young men as they passed looked at her anxiously," Proust, p. 688.

157 "I'll tell you just what took place" "HIS HAT ON BEFORE KING," *New York Times,* June 24, 1907.

158 "He was fined twenty-five dollars in Coney Island Court," "Refusal to Doff Hat to Flag Costs Alien Fine," *New York Herald Tribune,* September 16, 1925.

159 "The deft touch of a raised hat," "Kennedy Prodded Anew," *New York Times,* July 6, 1963.

160 "he has a four-year lease," "Parade Chilly?" *Boston Globe,* January 21, 1961.

Chapter 7

161 "a chalk-white face," *Veritas,* October 1970, p. 20. "Those are very nice," ibid.

165 "The knitted caps so ordered to be worn," Harrison, p. 101. "In 1662, the assembly of Virginia," *Census Reports—Manufactures*, p. 110.

166 "In 1731, Jeremiah Dunbar," ibid.

167 "The three main British efforts," Draper, p. 333.

168 "Mad hatters claimed that bicycling," Panati, p. 13.

169 "cult of the head," "Il Duce's Portraits," *The New Yorker*, January 6, 2003, p. 38.

170 "The men's styles will come first," "Men's Hats to Come Under Fascist Rule," *New York Times*, April 1, 1928. "apologized and started wearing hats more frequently," deMarly, p. 121.

171 "fortune-tellers, magicians, witch-doctors," Kinross, p. 412.

172 "Political changes," Volkan and Itzkowitz, p. 252.

173 "civilized headgear," Kinross, p. 413. "The impact would be equal," Volkan and Itzkowitz, p. 253. "His audience were horrified," Froembgen, p. 237. "A civilized, international dress is worthy," Kinross, p. 415. "The shock thus administered," Macfie, p. 140.

175 "men were seen strutting through the streets," Froembgen, p. 238. "Losses in the world's picturesqueness," "Picturesque Native Headgear Is Replaced by Modern Modes," *New York Times*, October 17, 1926. "The color has disappeared from urban places," "New Turkey Looks to American Aid," *New York Times*, May 23, 1926.

Chapter 8

All letters in this chapter are in the White House correspondence files of the Kennedy Library.

178 "LESS PROFILE, MORE COURAGE," Salinger, p. 250.

180 "I was sorry to read that you had a cold," John F. Kennedy Library White House correspondence.

181 "I didn't call off anything," Dallek, p. 554.

182 "True, Kennedy has announced he'll wear a silk topper," *Holland Michigan Evening Sentinel,* November 28, 1960.

184 "This is the letter of a happy man," John F. Kennedy Library.

191 "same type worn by the President," "Name Dropping," *New York Times,* July 21, 1961.

192 "I have been using one of your fountain pens," Atwan, p. 289.

195 "Highest Type of Hat and Man," *Country Life in America,* November 1909, p. 109. "Verily, these gentlemen of the brush," Melton, p. 77.

199 "Oh, we talked about hats," *Hat Worker,* April 15, 1961.

200 "offers no hazards," "President Toasts Milk with Milk," *New York Times,* January 24, 1962.

201 "just bitter, bitter, bitter," *Gettysburg Times,* March 23, 1962.

202 "Pictures of the Kennedy toddler without shoes," *Valley Independent,* April 28, 1962.

203 "Whenever I say anything that upsets them," Dallek, p. 509. "I come to you as a member of the New Frontier," *United Hatters, Cap and Millinery Workers International Union Eleventh Convention Report and Proceedings,* June 12–15, 1962, p. 148. "They're not going to give me a bunch of feathers," Sidey, p. 5.

205 "There was a bit of byplay as Glenn," Manchester, p. 232. "I wasn't aware of his aversion to hats or anything," John Glenn.

206 "Al Webb was in PT boats with us," author interview with Paul "Red" Fay.

Chapter 9

208 "Kennedy stood bareheaded," Dallek, p. 322.

210 "We all felt the same way," author interview with Paul "Red" Fay.

211 "They're wonderful people," Daniels, p. 146.

214 "I wrote to the Department of Commerce," Henderson, *Hat Talk,* p. 2.

216 "With the tuxedo, a derby or a soft hat," Stratton, p. 230.

Chapter 10

221 "ignore the unwritten law," "Discard Date for Straw Hats Ignored by President Coolidge," *New York Times,* September 20, 1925, p. 1. "Summer isn't over yet,"

"Coolidge Dons Straw," *New York Herald Tribune,* September 20, 1925.

223 "WHEREAS, the old felt hat has served," *Wisconsin Rapids Daily Tribune,* May 18, 1934.

224 "beach beautifiers," "Welcoming the Straw Hat Season in a Big Way," *The Coshocton Tribune,* May 13, 1938. "Talk about regimentation?" "Yeddos Are Touted for 1936," *Men's Wear,* August 21, 1935. "Nothing doing in that line," "Remember When," *Baltimore Sun,* June 15, 1997, p. 6J.

226 "may even be a Bolshevik," "Good-bye to the Straw Hat," *New York Times,* September 13, 1925.

227 "straw hat smashing orgy," "Straw Hat Smashing Orgy Bares Heads from Battery to Bronx," *New York Tribune,* September 16, 1922.

228 "the doorway at 211 Grand," "Lids On, Lids Off," *New York Daily News,* September 14, 1922.

229 "The origin of this law is obscure," "A Right Worth Defending," *New York Times,* September 15, 1922.

230 "The Cubs baseball team would mark their first victory," Cahan and Jacob, p. 112.

232 "What about the 'undies'?" *Decatur Daily Review,* May 16, 1924.

Chapter 11

236 "He likes to drive," *Boston Globe,* January 20, 1961. "So he ordered the driver to pull over," Lowe, p. 172.

237 "a very unhappy Charles DeGaulle," Strober, p. 62.

240   "barefoot in the summer," Varron, p. 1160. "When out of doors, they never wear hats," Varron, p. 1138.

241   "Much of the charm," Veblen, p. 126.

243   "I kept my hat off all the time," Twain, *Life on the Mississippi,* p. 39.

244   "wild, haggard-looking man, hatless, coatless," *Indiana Progress,* January 10, 1878.

245   "The habit of going about without a hat," "The Hatless Age," *North Adams Transcript,* September 8, 1899.

246   "This really happened," "The High Hats Came Off," *Bucks County Gazette,* March 2, 1893.

247   "it is no sin," "Summer Church Garb," *Newark Advocate,* July 25, 1904. "At Newport which sets summer fashions," "Free and Easy Fashions," *Sandusky Daily Star,* September 4, 1900.

248   "The fashion of going bareheaded has spread," "Hatless Fad Prevails," *New Oxford Item,* August 15, 1902. "What's the use of a hat anyway?" *North Adams Transcript,* August 5, 1899.

249   "There was a flutter of excitement," " 'Hats Off' Is the Fad," *Anaconda Standard,* October 7, 1900. "for several weeks students have been hatless," "New Haven's New Fad," *Newark Advocate,* June 30, 1903.

251   "are addicted to vegetarianism, hatlessness," Ornstein, p. 57. "Although he is often made the subject of gibes," "Wears No Hat for 15 Years," *Decatur Review,* March 23, 1910.

258   "Swagger and well built," *Hats of the World,* p. 17.

259   "the studied carelessness of modern dress," *Hats of the World,* p. 18.

265   "Coolidge could refuse to talk over the telephone," Whitcomb, p. 274.

272   "They get but little," Whitcomb, p. 138. "You have to stand every day," Whitcomb, p. 275. "Hoover decided to Christmas in Florida," Whitcomb, p. 293.

274   "There is a statue of the great Sir Robert Peel," Sala, p. 8.

Chapter 12

278   "Mr. President . . . your visit with us in Fort Worth today," John F. Kennedy Library videotape. "The television cameras were on the scene," Bishop, p. 78.

281   "Your hat, sir?" Whitcomb, p. 369.

284   "Number one, it was a rental," "Humphrey's Suit Is Out of Fashion," *New York Times,* December 11, 1964.

285   "the President does not influence dress," "The Merchant's View," *New York Times,* December 13, 1964. "for some time," "Johnson to Be Sworn in a Business Suit," *New York Times,* December 10, 1964, p. 1.

286   "contrived and comical," Henggeler, p. 141.

287   "He was dressed in a morning coat," Kissinger, p. 1. "hatters still follow the father-to-son road," Frank, p. 215.

288   " 'Now' and 'Skylark,' " ibid.

Bibliography

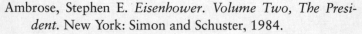

Ambrose, Stephen E. *Eisenhower. Volume Two, The President*. New York: Simon and Schuster, 1984.

Anonymous. *The Evolution of Hats*. Hat Corporation of America, 1947.

———. *Hats of the World: Interesting Styles in Hats in Many Lands*. Stylepark Hats, 1935.

Anthony, Carl Sferrazza. *The Kennedy White House: Family Life and Pictures, 1961–1963*. New York: Simon and Schuster, 2001.

Atwan, Robert, Donald McQuade, and John W. Wright. *Edsels, Luckies, & Frigidaires: Advertising the American Way*. Dell, 1979.

Ausubel, Nathan. *The Book of Jewish Knowledge*. New York: Crown, 1964.

Bayley, Stephen. *Taste: The Secret Meaning of Things*. New York: Pantheon, 1991.

Beebe, Lucious. *The Provocative Pen of Lucious Beebe, Esq.* San Francisco: Chronicle, 1966.

Belloc, Hilaire. *The Silence of the Sea, and Other Essays*. New York: Sheed & Ward, 1940.

Bishop, Jim. *The Day Kennedy Was Shot*. New York: Funk & Wagnalls, 1968.

Boller, Paul F., Jr. *Presidential Campaigns*. New York: Oxford University Press, 1984.

———. *Presidential Inaugurations*. New York: Harcourt, 2001.

Cahan, Richard, and Mark Jacob. *The Game That Was: The George Brace Baseball Photo Collection*. Chicago: Contemporary, 1996.

Carroll, Renee. *In Your Hat*. New York: Macaulay, 1932.

Dallek, Robert. *An Unfinished Life: John F. Kennedy, 1917–1963*. Boston: Little, Brown, 2003.

Daniels, Draper. *Giants, Pigmies, and Other Advertising People*. Chicago: Crain Communications, 1974.

De Marly, Diana. *Fashion for Men: An Illustrated History*. New York: Holmes & Meier, 1985.

Donovan, Robert J. *Eisenhower: The Inside Story*. New York: Harper, 1956.

Doran, John. *Habits and Men: With Remnants of Record Touching the Makers of Both*. London: Richard Bentley, 1854.

Draper, Theodore. *A Struggle for Power: The American Revolution*. New York: Times Books, 1996.

Dunsany, Lord. *The Lost Silk Hat*, in *Five Modern Plays*. Boston: International Pocket Library, 1936.

Eisenhower, Dwight D. *The White House Years. Mandate for Change, 1953–1956*. Garden City, N.Y.: Doubleday, 1963.

Fay, Paul B., Jr. *The Pleasure of His Company*. New York: Harper & Row, 1966.

Fox, George. *The Journal of George Fox*. Cambridge, UK: Cambridge University Press, 1952.

Frank, Thomas. *The Conquest of Cool: Business Culture, Counterculture, and the Rise of Hip Consumerism*. Chicago: University of Chicago Press, 1997.

Freidel, Frank. *Franklin D. Roosevelt: A Rendezvous with Destiny*. Boston: Little, Brown, 1990.

Freud, Sigmund. *The Standard Edition of the Complete Psychological Works of Sigmund Freud*, edited by James Strachey. Volumes IV, VI, X, XIV, and XV. London: Hogarth Press, 1968.

Froembgen, Hanns. *Kemal Ataturk: A Biography*. New York: Hillman Curl, 1937.

Gardiner, A. G. *Pebbles on the Shore*. London: J. M. Dent, 1917.

Genin, J. N. *An Illustrated History of the Hat: From the Earliest Ages to the Present Time*. New York: Simpkin, Marshall & Co., 1858.

Gissing, George. *A Life's Morning*. New York: AMS Press, 1969.

Goodwin, Doris Kearns. *The Fitzgeralds and the Kennedys*. New York: Simon and Schuster, 1987.

Guptill, Arthur L. *Norman Rockwell, Illustrator*. New York: Watson-Guptill, 1946.

Hall, James Norman. *Under a Thatched Roof*. Boston: Houghton Mifflin, 1942.

Harrison, Michael. *The History of the Hat*. London: H. Jenkins, 1960.

Henderson, Debbie. *Hat Talk: Conversations with Hat Makers About Their Hats—The Fedora, Homburg, Straw, and Cap.* Yellow Springs, Ohio: Wild Goose Press, 2002.

———. *The Top Hat: An Illustrated History of its Styling & Manufacture.* Yellow Springs, Ohio: Wild Goose Press, 2000.

Henggeler, Paul R. *In His Steps: Lyndon Johnson and the Kennedy Mystique.* Chicago: I. R. Dee, 1991.

Holliday, Robert Cortes. *Walking-Stick Papers.* New York: George H. Doran, 1918.

Jepson, R. W., ed. *New and Old Essays: 1820–1935.* New York: Longmans, Green, 1936.

Joselit, Jenna Weissman. *A Perfect Fit: Clothes, Character, and the Promise of America.* New York: Metropolitan, 2001.

Kidwell, Claudia Brush, and Valerie Steele, eds. *Men and Women: Dressing the Part.* Washington, D.C.: Smithsonian Institution Press, 1989.

Kin, David, ed. *Dictionary of American Maxims.* New York: Philosophical Library, 1955.

Kinross, Patrick Balfour. *Ataturk, the Rebirth of a Nation.* K. Rustem & Brother: 1981.

Kissinger, Henry. *White House Years.* Boston: Little Brown, 1979.

Kortum, Sarah. *The Hatless Man: An Anthology of Odd & Forgotten Manners.* New York: Viking, 1995.

Liebling, A. J. *Liebling at Home.* New York: PEI Books, 1982.

Lincoln, Evelyn. *My Twelve Years with John F. Kennedy.* New York: McKay, 1965.

———. *Kennedy and Johnson.* New York: Holt, Rinehart and Winston, 1968.

Loveday, R. S. "The Tall Hat and Its Ancestors," in *The English Literary Magazine* (15): 1896.

Lowe, Jacques. *Portrait: The Emergence of John F. Kennedy*. New York: McGraw-Hill, 1961.

Lowe, Jacques, and Wilfrid Sheed. *The Kennedy Legacy: A Generation Later*. New York: Viking Studio, 1988.

Lurie, Alison. *The Language of Clothes*. New York: Random House, 1981.

Manchester, William. *One Brief Shining Moment: Remembering Kennedy*. New York: Little, Brown, 1983.

Martin, Edward Winslow. *The Secrets of the Great City: A Work Descriptive of the Virtues and the Vices, the Mysteries and Crimes of New York City*. Philadelphia: Jones Bros., 1868.

Martin, Ralph G. *A Hero for Our Time: An Intimate Story of the Kennedy Years*. New York: Macmillan, 1983.

McCullough, David. *John Adams*. New York: Simon and Schuster, 2000.

———. *Truman*. New York: Simon and Schuster, 1992.

McDowell, Colin. *Hats: Status, Style and Glamour*. New York: Rizzoli, 1992.

McPherson, James M., ed. *"To the Best of My Ability": The American Presidents*. New York: Dorling Kindersley, 2000.

Melville, Herman. *Moby-Dick, or, The Whale*. New York: Random House, 1930.

Meyers, Joan, ed. *John Fitzgerald Kennedy . . . As We Remember Him*. New York: Atheneum, 1965.

Miller, Merle. *Lyndon: An Oral Biography*. New York: Putnam, 1980.

Mitchell, Joseph. *My Ears Are Bent*. Rev. ed. New York: Pantheon, 2001.

Neal, Steve. *Harry and Ike: The Partnership That Remade the Postwar World*. New York: Scribner, 2001.

Nixon, Richard. *RN: The Memoirs of Richard Nixon*. New York: Grosset & Dunlap, 1978.

O'Rourke, P. J. *Republican Party Reptile: Essays and Outrages*. New York: Atlantic Monthly Press, 1987.

Ornstein, Robert. *The Right Mind: Making Sense of the Hemispheres*. New York: Harcourt Brace, 1997.

Orwell, George. *The Collected Essays, Journalism, and Letters of George Orwell*. Edited by Sonia Orwell and Ian Angus. *Volume 4: In Front of Your Nose, 1945–1950*. New York: Harcourt, Brace & World, 1968.

Panati, Charles. *Panati's Parade of Fads, Follies, and Manias: The Origins of Our Most Cherished Obsessions*. New York: HarperPerennial, 1991.

Pepys, Samuel. *The Diary of Samuel Pepys. Volume I: 1660*. Berkeley: University of California Press, 1970.

Petitpierre, A. G. "The History of the Hat," in *Ciba Review*. September 1940.

Proust, Marcel. *Remembrance of Things Past, Volume 1*. Translated by C. K. Scott Moncrieff and Terence Kilmartin. New York: Random House, 1981.

Redman, Alvin. *The Epigrams of Oscar Wilde*. Bracken Books, 1995.

Reynolds, William, and Ritch Rand. *The Cowboy Hat Book*. Rev. ed. Salt Lake City, Utah: Gibbs-Smith, 2003.

Ross, Lillian, ed. *The Fun of It: Stories from "The Talk of the*

Town": *The New Yorker*. New York: Modern Library, 2001.

Rothman, Hal K. *LBJ's Texas White House: "Our Heart's Home."* College Station: Texas A&M University Press, 2001.

Rubinstein, Ruth P. *Dress Codes: Meanings and Messages in American Culture*. Boulder, Colo.: Westview Press, 1995.

Sala, George Augustus. *The Hats of Humanity: Historically, Humourously & Aesthetically Considered*. James Gee, 1880.

Salinger, Pierre. *With Kennedy*. Garden City, N.Y.: Doubleday, 1966.

Sandburg, Carl. *Abraham Lincoln: The War Years*. New York: Harcourt, Brace, 1939.

Schwarz, Urs. *John Fitzgerald Kennedy, 1917–1963*. London: Paul Hamlyn, 1964.

Scott, William R. *The Itching Palm: A Study of the Habit of Tipping in America*. Philadelphia: Penn Publishing Co., 1916.

Segrave, Kerry. *Tipping: An American Social History of Gratuities*. Jefferson, N.C.: McFarland, 1998.

Stoughton, Cecil, and Hugh Sidey. *The Memories: JFK 1961–1963*. New York: Norton, 1973.

Stratton, Dorothy C., and Helen B. Schleman. *Your Best Foot Forward: Social Usage for Young Moderns*. New York: Whittlesey House, 1940.

Strober, Gerald S. and Deborah H. *"Let Us Begin Anew": An Oral History of the Kennedy Presidency*. New York: HarperCollins, 1993.

Strong, Sir Roy. *The Story of Britain*. New York: Fromm International, 1996.

Swift, Jonathan. *Gulliver's Travels*. New York: Knopf, 1991.

Thomson, David S. *A Pictorial Biography: HST*. New York: Grosset & Dunlap, 1973.

Thurber, James. *A Thurber Carnival*. New York: Harper & Brothers, 1945.

Twain, Mark. *A Connecticut Yankee in King Arthur's Court*. The American Publishing Co., 1901.

———. *Life on the Mississippi*. New York: Collier & Sons, 1917.

United States Census Office. *Census Reports, Volume IX—Manufacturers, Part III: Special Reports on Selected Industries*. United States Census Office, 1902.

Updegraff, Robert R. *The Story of Two Famous Hatters*. New York: Knox Hat Company, 1926.

Varron, A. "Children in Adult Dress," in *Ciba Review*. April 1940.

Veblen, Thorstein. *The Theory of the Leisure Class: An Economic Study of Institutions*. Franklin Center, Penn.: The Franklin Library, 1979.

Volkan, Vamik D., and Norman Itzkowitz. *The Immortal Atatürk: A Psychobiography*. Chicago: University of Chicago Press, 1986.

Wall, E. Berry. *Neither Pest nor Puritan*. New York: Dial, 1940.

Webster, H. T. *The Best of H. T. Webster: A Memorial Collection*. New York: Simon and Schuster, 1953.

Whitcomb, John, and Claire Whitcomb. *Real Life at the White House: Two Hundred Years of Daily Life at*

America's Most Famous Residence. New York: Rout-
ledge, 2002.

White, Theodore H. *The Making of the President, 1960.* New
York: Antheneum, 1961.

Wicker, Tom. "Kennedy Without Tears," in *Esquire: The Best
of Forty Years.* New York: McKay, 1973.

Wilcox, R. Turner. *The Mode in Hats and Headdress, Including Hairstyles, Cosmetics, and Jewelry.* New York: Scribner, 1948.

Index